The Photographic History of The Civil War

In Ten Volumes

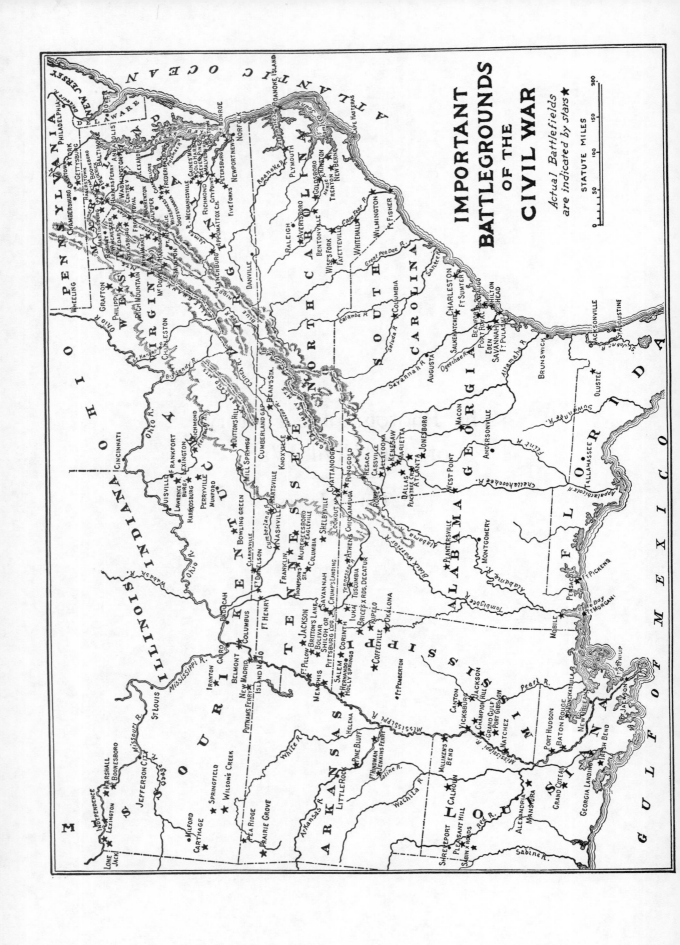

IMPORTANT
BATTLEGROUNDS
OF THE
CIVIL WAR

Actual Battlefields
are indicated by stars ★

PREPARING FOR WAR—A CONFEDERATE PHOTOGRAPH OF '61

Florida Opens the Grim Game of War. On a sandy point at the entrance to Pensacola Bay over two hundred years ago, the Spaniards who so long held possession of what is now the Gulf coast of the United States had built a fort. On its site the United States Government had erected a strong fortification called Fort Barrancas. Between this point and a low-lying sandy island directly opposite, any vessels going up to Pensacola must pass. On the western end of this island was the strongly built Fort Pickens. Early in 1861 both forts were practically ungarrisoned. This remarkable picture, taken by the New Orleans photographer Edwards, in February, 1861, belongs to a series hitherto unpublished. Out of the deep shadows of the sally port we look into the glaring sunlight upon one of the earliest warlike moves. Here we see one of the heavy pieces of ordnance that were intended to defend the harbor from foreign foes, being shifted preparatory to being mounted on the rampart at Fort Barrancas, which, since January 12th, had been in possession of State troops. Fort Pickens, held by a mere handful of men under Lieutenant Slemmer, still flew the Stars and Stripes. But the move of State troops under orders from Governor Perry of Florida, in seizing Fort Barrancas and raising the State flag even before the shot that aroused the nation at Fort Sumter, may well be said to have helped force the crisis that was impending.

The Photographic History
of The Civil War

The Opening Battles

Francis Trevelyan Miller
Editor in Chief

Contributors

WILLIAM H. TAFT
President of the United States

HENRY WYSHAM LANIER
Art Editor and Publisher

EBEN SWIFT
Lieutenant-Colonel, U. S. A.

FRENCH E. CHADWICK
Rear-Admiral, U. S. N.

GEORGE HAVEN PUTNAM
Major, U. S. V.

MARCUS J. WRIGHT
Brigadier-General, C. S. A.

HENRY W. ELSON
Professor of History, Ohio University

JAMES BARNES
Author of "David G. Farragut"

With a New Introduction by
HENRY STEELE COMMAGER

CASTLE BOOKS ★ NEW YORK

INTRODUCTION

Writing half a century after the attack on Fort Sumter, Francis Trevelyan Miller, editor of the *Photographic History of the Civil War,* discovered a general lack of interest in that war, and ascribed it, somewhat haphazardly, to the fact that "this is not a military nation." We are still not a military nation, not in the sense of Germany or France, for example, but no one now complains of any lack of interest in the Civil War. Indeed a passionate and pervasive preoccupation with the Civil War is one of the arresting intellectual phenomena of our time. Certainly no other war in which Americans have engaged, not the War of Independence, not even the titanic World Wars, has made a stronger or more lasting impression on the American mind and imagination. What explains this persistent and consuming interest; what explains the Civil War Round Tables, Civil War book clubs, Civil War magazines, the unearthing of scores of Civil War diaries and journals, the vast outpouring of biographies and monographs, the republication of such substantial works as *Battles and Leaders of the Civil War,* and, now, the massive *Photographic History?*

There is, to be sure, the circumstance of a Civil War centennial, but that is largely adventitious. There was no centennial when Douglas Freeman published his *R. E. Lee,* which, in a sense, started the whole thing, and in any case we have by now survived so many centenary celebrations that we are hardened to them. Other considerations are more persuasive. There is, for example, a livelier and more anxious interest in military history in general than there was half a century ago, and a realization that the Civil War was the first of the modern wars, and in many respects the most rewarding to study: the first war which involved the whole population, the first to depend on railroads and the telegraph, the first to use ironclads on a large scale, or entrenchments, or balloons, or the repeating rifle. There is the somewhat nostalgic realization that this was not only an all-American war, but the last of them, that it was a laboratory where we can analyze American conduct and character in more unadulterated form than we can in our twentieth-century laboratories. There is a growing appreciation of what the Civil War contributed to our emotional and sentimental heritage —our traditions, our songs and stories, above all our heroes: what other country has had the good fortune to have both a Lincoln and a Lee to stir its imagination and to solicit its sympathies in time of crisis? And there is, too, the very relevant consideration that the Civil War has left us a record that is abundant, and almost overwhelming, one that can occupy our attention for a long time to come.

The Civil War record is not only voluminous; it is authentic, it is intimate, it is universal, and it is, to a most remarkable degree, eloquent. "Through our great good fortune," wrote the thrice-wounded Oliver Wendell Holmes, "in our youth our hearts were touched with fire. . . . We have seen with our own eyes, beyond and above the gold fields, the snowy heights of honor, and it is for us to bear the report to those who come after us." And bear the report they did. Almost everyone, it seems, contributed to the record. The great captains wrote, Grant and Sherman, Longstreet and Gordon, and so, too, did the privates, by the hundred, for these were the most literate of armies. Surgeons wrote, and nurses, members of the Christian Commission and of the Sanitary Commission, engineers and telegraphers, scouts and spies, cabinet members and diplomats, all contributed their quota of recollection and criticism and, as the years passed, of celebration. Poets wrote as they fought— Buchanan Read and Stedman and Lanier and John Banister Tabb and Henry Timrod and, after a fashion, Walt Whitman; novelists caught the drama of the war even as they marched or fought or languished in prison; historians, like Thomas Livermore or John Ropes or

Introduction

Charles Francis Adams, did not await the end of the war before launching their interpretations. And there was one other group that contributed to the historical record as well, a group whose contributions are only now coming to be recognized and appreciated: the photographers.

For this was the first modern war in photography, as in other things. We have, to be sure, a few daguerreotypes from the Mexican War, and a handful of photographs from the Crimean, but it was with the American Civil War that photography came of age. Indeed, in his 1911 foreword to this collection, Francis Miller proclaimed the pious hope that "while the hand of the historian may falter, or his judgment may fail . . . the final record of the War is told in these time-dimmed negatives." That is saying a good deal; we are not so sure of finality, now, and we need not venture so sweeping a claim. It is enough that this collection of photographs provides us with a record of the Civil War more immediate, authentic, and comprehensive than that for any other chapter of history that is not contemporary.

Many things were new in the Civil War, but nothing was more dramatically new than the photograph. Louis Daguerre had introduced the process which bears his name some twenty years earlier, and at that time, too, the Englishmen William Henry Talbot and Sir John Herschel had made their first tentative gestures toward modern photography. Not until the fifties did the daguerreotype give way to the more manageable ambrotype, and then to paper photography; the tintype and the card photograph, so familiar to the last generation, made their appearance in 1860, and so, too, did aerial photography and the use of photographs by the Patent Office and other government departments. So, as with the ironclads and the repeating rifle, photography was ready for the war just in the nick of time.

"Photography" is an abstraction; if the war was to be recorded it was necessary to have photographers to record it. By great good fortune the photographers were there, too. Especially the greatest of them all: Mathew Brady.

What a remarkable man he was, this Brady, a technician, an administrator, an artist, a historian—and a patriot, too. He had learned the rudiments of photography from the great painter-inventor Samuel F. B. Morse who had visited Louis Daguerre in Paris and pronounced the daguerreotype "one of the most beautiful discoveries of the age" and hurried home to make his own. Brady had worked, too, with the English-born Professor John William Draper of the University of the City of New York, one of the scientific geniuses of his day, and a philosopher to boot. Draper had made the first photographic portraits ever recorded by sun, as he had made so many things, and like Brady he was to devote much of his talents to the interpretation of the American Civil War. In 1844 the youthful Brady opened his own studio in New York City, and within a year he had launched a project which, even by itself, would have insured him fame: a photographic gallery of distinguished Americans. It is to his pioneering enterprise that we owe those wonderful photographs of Presidents John Quincy Adams and Jackson and Polk, made just before they died, works of art, all of them. Happily, Brady's notion of distinction was eclectic, and he photographed not statesmen alone but artists and teachers, lawyers and engineers, actresses and clergymen, and foreign visitors as well. Our image of the fifties is largely a reflection on a Brady lens.

By 1860 Brady was successful and fashionable. His studios in New York and in Washington were crowded with eager patrons; he had won awards at the Crystal Palace Exhibition in 1851, and at a dozen others as well, and he was on the way to becoming an institution. To be photographed by Brady was a justification for a visit to New York or Washington, and almost a prerequisite to fame. From John Quincy Adams on, every ex-President, President, and Presidential candidate had been glad to pose for him, and with some prescience Lincoln sat for him when he came on to talk at Cooper Union. Brady was almost forty when the war broke out, and he might well have contented himself with the Washington political scene and left to younger and more vigorous photographers the record of the war itself. But he was the dean of them all, and looked on the war as his responsibility. "I felt that I had to go," he recalled later; "a spirit in my feet said 'go' and I went."

It was well that he did, for efforts by the American Photographical Society to persuade Secretary Cameron to organize a photographic record of the war had miscarried, and the whole thing was about to go by default. Others, to be sure, North and South, might have attempted the job, but it was Brady who really got the enterprise under way. It was Brady who went to see his old friend Winfield Scott about photographing the Army of the Potomac —Scott who was about to retire, and who could not help him; it was Brady who obtained the blessing of Lincoln; it was Brady who eventually wrested a grudging permission to go to the front from Secretary Stanton; it was Brady who organized a team of photographers and sent them to the battlefields; and it was Brady, too, who financed the whole thing, bankrupting himself in the process.

When the Blue and the Gray clashed at First Bull Run, Brady was there with his assistants and his equipment and his "what-is-it" wagon, and notwithstanding the confusion and the rout, he managed to come back with a pretty full album of photographs. "The public is indebted to Brady of Broadway for numerous excellent views of 'grim visaged' war," wrote a contemporary journalist. "He has been in Virginia with his camera, and many and spirited are the pictures he has taken. His are the only reliable records at Bull Run. The correspondents of the Rebel newspapers are sheer falsifiers; the correspondents of the Northern journals are not to be depended upon; and the correspondents of the English press are altogether worse than either; but Brady never misrepresents."

"Brady never misrepresents"! What better tribute than that, or what better historical epitaph! It might be supposed that photography, by its very nature, could not misrepresent, but the most superficial contemplation of much current journalistic photography should speedily dispel so naïve a notion. What is impressive about the work of Brady and Alexander Gardner and Timothy O'Sullivan and their associates is its integrity. There is no straining for effect; there is not even ostentatious partisanship. It was not their purpose to glorify war, or to whip up patriotism, or to exacerbate sectional animosities; it was their purpose to make a record of what they saw.

And what a record it was! The Brady collection alone ran to some seven thousand photographs, each one representing a small triumph of ingenuity and resourcefulness. We take photography for granted, now, and have forgotten (if we ever knew) the difficulties that characterized it in its infancy and the hazards that attended it in time of war. The lot of the Civil War photographer was not a happy one. He worked almost always under pressure, and often in danger. He had to carry all of his equipment with him, scores of bottles of chemicals, basins and sinks for washing, hundreds of glass plates—all of it breakable and vulnerable to the accidents of wretched roads and reckless handling, and all of it hard to replace. He had to make his pictures as best he could, when the situation permitted; develop them in his own dark wagon—the famous "what-is-it" wagon; and then preserve them from injury or destruction. Yet the result was, on the whole, wonderfully good, and we do not know now whether to be more astonished at the comprehensiveness of the record or at its clarity and finish and style.

It is to the fact that photography was still technically in its infancy that we are indebted for one of the virtues of that record: the concentration on the routine of war rather than on the drama. Photography was as yet unable to cope with motion, and photographers, even the best of them, had to catch their subjects in repose. Because Brady and his associates, North and South, were unable to photograph artillery bombardments or cavalry charges, they did not exhaust their energies getting to the scene of battle, but confined themselves rather to the housekeeping aspects of the war—what Carlton McCarthy called the "minutia of soldier life." This was just the sort of thing neglected by the journalists, the correspondents, and

Introduction

the historians. It was an age of romanticism, and, who would write home, or to the newspapers, about the dust, the sweat, and the tears, when he could describe the clash of arms? The clash of arms was precisely what the photographer could not catch, so he contented himself with the rest of the war—that is, most of it.

It is here that the *Photographic History of the Civil War* differs most arrestingly from that other great compilation, the *Battles and Leaders* series. The distinguished warriors and statesmen who contributed to that magnificent series addressed themselves, on the whole, to the battles themselves; after all, who would ask a Sherman or a Longstreet to write about the commissary? But the *Photographic History* devotes only three of its ten volumes to battles; the others are given over to the navies, artillery, cavalry, ordnance, fortifications, secret service, soldier life, the songs and poetry of the war, the men who fought in the ranks as well as the men who led them. The immense value of these volumes is that they do supply us with the housekeeping details. They tell us about weapons and give us hundreds of pictures of rifles and guns. They describe fortifications and take us into the very forts themselves, showing us the thickness of the walls and the development of earthworks and ramparts. They expose us to the prisons themselves, Andersonville and Libby, Camp Douglas and Elmira, and a dozen others, and enable us to understand something of the awful mortality rate of those dungeons. They show us field hospitals in action, the devoted workers of the Sanitary Commission, the nurses and the hospitals, and the wounded and diseased who died in them. They introduce us to Belle Boyd and Kate Greenough and Pauline Cushman, the only woman to be sentenced to death, and to the incredibly named Vespasian Chancellor of Jeb Stuart's staff, and to all the other spies and scouts who look so much less romantic than they were.

This does not mean that the great battles are neglected, or the great leaders, either. Here is General Sherman when he marched to the sea, and Thomas looking the "Rock" that he was, and the mighty Stonewall too modest to be photographed, and "Dutch" Longstreet with his generals all as hirsute as himself, and "Black Jack" Logan and O. O. Howard the Christian Soldier, and McClellan, posing, as always, and Grant, surrounded by his staff at Cold Harbor, but even in the photographs very much alone. Here, above all, is Lincoln, the weight of the world showing in his careworn features, and Lee, the only one to look as great as he was and to be as great as he looked.

When Mr. Miller and his staff first made this prodigious photographic archive available in 1911, it was as an exercise in nostalgia and in filial piety. How proud we are to be Americans, says Mr. Miller, as he contemplates the record, and how proud to be the heirs of Runnymede and the Armada! We cannot all claim that heritage now—was there ever a time when we could?—and our generation prefers to regard the Civil War in a less sentimental and less parochial fashion. It was not fought to provide the stuff of romance for hungry novelists, or of rhetoric for flag-waving patrioteers, nor even to prove the valor of the descendants of the Puritans and Cavaliers and Highlanders.

Perhaps ours is the first generation that is able to see clearly what was its significance, the first to appreciate to the full what Lincoln meant when he said that we should nobly save or meanly lose the last best hope of earth. For we can see now, as the generation of Theodore Roosevelt and Taft could not, the full historical meaning of Gettysburg and Vicksburg and Atlanta and the Wilderness and, in the end, Appomattox. Put most simply, an America which retained the institution of slavery could not have rallied to the defeat of twentieth-century tyranny; a divided America could not have stepped forth, in one of the great crises of history, to the rescue and liberation of the Old World. We can see now what Lincoln saw so clearly, that on the outcome of the struggle for union and freedom in America depended the fate of the Western world.

HENRY STEELE COMMAGER

Amherst, Massachusetts

CONTENTS

Contents

Part II

Part III

Part IV

PHOTOGRAPH DESCRIPTIONS THROUGHOUT THIS VOLUME
James Barnes

FOREWORDS

GREETING FROM PRESIDENT TAFT

DEDICATION

ACKNOWLEDGMENT

EDITORIAL INTRODUCTORY

We have reached a point in this country when we can look back, not without love, not without intense pride, but without partisan passion, to the events of the Civil War. We have reached a point, I am glad to say, when the North can admire to the full the heroes of the South, and the South admire to the full the heroes of the North. There is a monument in Quebec that always commended itself to me - a monument to commemorate the battle of the Plains of Abraham. On one face of that beautiful structure is the name of Montcalm, and on the opposite side the name of Wolfe. That always seemed to me to be the acme of what we ought to reach in this country; and I am glad to say that in my own alma mater, Yale, we have established an association for the purpose of erecting within her academic precincts a memorial not to the Northern Yale men who died, nor to the Southern Yale men who died; but to the Yale men who died in the Civil War.

Dedicated

FIFTY YEARS AFTER

FORT SUMTER

TO THE MEN IN BLUE AND GRAY

WHOSE VALOR AND DEVOTION

HAVE BECOME THE

PRICELESS HERITAGE

OF A UNITED

NATION

ACKNOWLEDGMENT

TO Mr. Francis Trevelyan Miller the publishers of these books must confess an obligation quite apart from the usual editorial services. Seldom indeed has it been possible to construct the text of such an extended history in accordance with a single broad idea. Yet it is true that the contributions throughout the entire ten volumes of the PHOTOGRAPHIC HISTORY are a direct outgrowth of the plan created years ago by Mr. Miller, and urged since by him with constant faith in its national importance—to emphasize in comprehensive form those deeds and words from the mighty struggle that strike universal, noble human chords. This was a conception so straightforward and so inspiring that the opportunity to give it the present embodiment has become a lasting privilege.

Readers as well as publishers are also indebted to the collectors, historical societies, and others who have furnished hundreds of long-treasured photographs, unwilling that the HISTORY should appear without presenting many important scenes of which no actual illustrations had ever before been available to the public. Hence the Civil War-time photographs in the present work are not only several times as numerous as those in any previous publication, but also include many hundreds of scenes that will come as a revelation even to historians and special scholars—photographs taken within the lines of the Confederate armies and of the hosts in the Mississippi Valley, whose fighting was no less momentous than the Eastern battles, but in the nature of things could not be as quickly or as fully heralded. With these additions to the "Brady-Gardner" collection—the loss and rediscovery of which Mr. Henry Wysham Lanier's introductory narrates—it is now possible for the first time to present comprehensively the men and scenes and types of the American epic, in photographs.

Deep acknowledgment is due the owners of indispensable pictures who have so generously contributed them for this purpose. Especial mention must be given to: Mrs. W. K. Bachman; Mr. William Beer; Mr. James Blair, C. S. A.; Mr. George A. Brackett; Mr. Edward Bromley; Mr. John C. Browne; Captain Joseph T. Burke, C. S. A.; Captain F. M. Colston, C. S. A.; Colonel E. J. Copp, U. S. V.; Colonel S. A. Cunningham, C. S. A.; The Daughters of the Confederacy; Mr. Charles Frankel; Mr. Edgar R. Harlan; Colonel Chas. R. E. Koch, U. S. V.; Miss Isabel Maury; Mr. F. H. Meserve; The Military Order of the Loyal Legion; Colonel John P. Nicholson, U. S. V.; General Harrison Gray Otis, U. S. V.; Captain F. A. Roziene, U. S. A.; General G. P. Thruston, U. S. V.; The University of South Carolina; The Washington Artillery, and the various State historical departments, state and government bureaus, military and patriotic organizations which courteously suspended their rules, in order that the photographic treasures in their archives should become available for the present record.

[14]

EDITORIAL INTRODUCTORY

ON this semi-centennial of the American Civil War—the war of the modern Roses in the Western World—these volumes are dedicated to the American people in tribute to the courage and the valor with which they met one of the greatest crises that a nation has ever known—a crisis that changed the course of civilization. We look back at Napoleon through the glamor of time, without fully realizing that here on our own continent are battle-grounds more noble in their purport than all the wars of the ancient regimes. The decades have shrouded the first American Revolution in romance, but the time has now come when this second American revolution, at the turning point of its first half century, is to become an American epic in which nearly three and a half million men gathered on the battle-line to offer their lives for principles that were dear to them.

It is as an American "Battle Abbey" that these pages are opened on this anniversary, so that the eyes of the generations may look upon the actual scenes—not upon the tarnished muskets, the silenced cannon, nor the battle-stained flag, but upon the warriors themselves standing on the firing-line in the heroic struggle when the hosts of the North and the legions of the South met on the battle-grounds of a nation's ideals, with the destiny of a continent hanging in the balance. And what a tribute it is to American character to be able to gather about these pages in peace and brotherhood, without malice and without dissension, within a generation from the greatest fratricidal tragedy in the annals of mankind. The vision is no longer blinded by heart wounds, but as Americans we can see only the heroic self-sacrifice of these men who battled for the decision of one of the world's greatest problems.

In this first volume, standing literally before the open door to the "Battle Abbey," in which the vision of war is to be revealed in all its reality, I take this privilege to refer briefly to a few of the intimate desires that have led to this revelation of THE PHOTOGRAPHIC HISTORY OF THE CIVIL WAR. As one stands in the library of the War Department at Washington, or before the archives of the American libraries, he feels that the last word of evidence must have been recorded. Nearly seven thousand treatises, containing varying viewpoints relating to this epoch in our national development, have been written —so Dr. Herbert Putnam, Librarian at the Congressional Library at Washington, tells me; while in my home city of Hartford, which is a typical American community, I find nearly two thousand works similar to those that are within the reach of all the American people in every part of the country.

With this great inheritance before us, military writers have informed me that they cannot understand why the American people have been so little interested in this remarkable war. Great generals have told how they led their magnificent armies in battle; military tacticians have mapped and recorded the movements of regiments and corps with technical accuracy, and historians have faithfully discussed the causes and the effects of this strange crisis in civilization—all of which is a permanent tribute to American scholarship. I have come to the conclusion that the lack of popular interest is because this is not a military nation. The great heart of American citizenship knows little of military maneuver, which is a science that requires either life-study or tradition to cultivate an interest in it.

The Americans are a peace-loving people, but when once aroused they are a mighty moral and physical fighting force. It is not their love for the art of war that has caused them to take up arms. It is the impulse of justice that permeates the Western World. The American people feel the pulse of life itself; they love the greater emotions that cause men to meet danger face to face. Their hearts beat to the martial strain of the national anthem "The Star Spangled Banner" and they feel the melody in that old Marseillaise of the Confederacy, "Dixie," for in them they catch mental visions of the sweeping lines under floating banners at the battle-front; they hear the roar of the guns and the clatter of cavalry; but more than that—they feel again the spirit that leads men to throw themselves into the cannon's flame.

THE PHOTOGRAPHIC HISTORY OF THE CIVIL WAR comes on this anniversary to witness a people's valor; to testify in photograph to the true story of how a devoted people whose fathers had stood shoulder to shoulder for the ideal of liberty in the American Revolution, who had issued to the world the declaration that all men are created politically free and equal, who had formulated the Constitution that dethroned mediæval monarchy and founded a new republic to bring new hope to the races of the earth—parted at the dividing line of a great economic problem and stood arrayed against each other in the greatest fratricidal tragedy that the world has ever witnessed, only to be reunited and to stand, fifty years later, hand in hand for the betterment of mankind, pledging themselves to universal peace and brotherhood.

This is the American epic that is told in these time-stained photographs—an epic which in romance and chivalry is more inspiring than that of the olden knighthood; brother against brother, father against son, men speaking the same language, living under the same flag, offering their lives for that which they believed to be right. No Grecian phalanx or Roman legion ever knew truer manhood than in those days on the American continent when the Anglo-Saxon met Anglo-Saxon in the decision of a constitutional principle that beset their beloved nation. It was more than Napoleonic, for its warriors battled for principle rather than conquest, for right rather than power.

This is the spirit of these volumes, and it seems to me that it must be the spirit of every true American. It is the sacred heritage of Anglo-Saxon freedom won at Runnymede. I recall General Gordon, an American who turned the defeat of war into the victory of citizenship in peace, once saying: "What else could be expected of a people in whose veins commingled the blood of the proud cavaliers of England, the blood of those devout and resolute men who protested against the grinding exactions of the Stuarts; the blood of the stalwart Dissenters and of the heroic Highlanders of Scotland, and of the sturdy Presbyterians of Ireland; the blood of those defenders of freedom who came from the mountain battlements of Switzerland, whose signal lights summoned her people to gather to their breasts the armfuls of spears to make way for liberty." It was a great battle-line of Puritan, of Huguenot, of Protestant, of Catholic, of Teuton, and Celt—every nation and every religion throwing its sacrifice on the altar of civilization.

The causes of the American Civil War will always be subject to academic controversy, each side arguing conscientiously from its own viewpoint. It is unnecessary to linger in these pages over the centuries of economic growth that came to a crisis in the American nation. In the light of modern historical understanding it was the inevitable result of a sociological system that had come down through the ages before there was a republic on the Western continent, and which finally came to a focus through the conflicting interests that developed in the upbuilding of American civilization. When Jefferson and Madison construed our constitution in one way, and Washington and Hamilton in another, surely it is not strange that their descendants should have differed. There is glory enough for all—for North, for South, for East, for West, on these battle-grounds of a people's traditions—a grander empire than Cæsar's legions won for Rome.

To feel the impulse of both the North and the South is the desire of these volumes. When, some years ago, I left the portals of Trinity College, in the old abolition town of Hartford, Conn., to enter the halls of Washington and Lee University in historic Lexington in the hills of Virginia, I felt for the first time as a Northerner, indigenous to the soil, what it means to be a Southerner. I, who had bowed my head from childhood to the greatness of Grant, looked upon my friends bowing their heads before the mausoleum of Lee. I stood with them as they laid the April flowers on the graves of their dead, and I felt the heart-beat of the Confederacy. When I returned to my New England home it was to lay the laurel and the May flowers on the graves of my dead, and I felt the heart-beat of the Republic—more than that, I felt the impulse of humanity and the greatness of all men.

When I now turn these pages I realize what a magnificent thing it is to have lived; how wonderful is man and his power to blaze the path for progress! I am proud that my heritage runs back through nearly three hundred years to the men who planted the seed of liberty in the New World into which is flowing the blood of the great races of the earth; a nation whose sinews are built from the strong men of the ages, and in whose hearts beat the impulses that have inspired the centuries—a composite of the courage, the perseverance, and the fortitude of the world's oldest races, commingled into one great throbbing body. It is a young race, but its exploits have equalled those of the heroic age in the Grecian legends and surpass Leonidas and his three hundred at Thermopylæ.

In full recognition of the masterly works of military authorities that now exist as invaluable historical evidence, these volumes present the American Civil War from an entirely original viewpoint. The collection of photographs is in itself a sufficient contribution to military and historical record, and the text is designed to present the mental pictures of the inspiring pageantry in the war between the Red and the White Roses in America, its human impulses, and the ideals that it represents in the heart of humanity.

[17]

Editorial Introductory

The military movements of the armies have been exhaustively studied properly to stage the great scenes that are herein enacted, but the routine that may burden the memory or detract from the broader, martial picture that lies before the reader has been purposely avoided. It is the desire to leave impressions rather than statistics; mental visions and human inspiration rather than military knowledge, especially as the latter is now so abundant in American literature. In every detail the contradictory evidence of the many authorities has been weighed carefully to present the narrative fairly and impartially. It is so conflicting regarding numbers in battle and killed and wounded that the Government records have been followed, as closely as possible.

The hand of the historian may falter, or his judgment may fail, but the final record of the American Civil War is told in these time-dimmed negatives. The reader may conscientiously disagree with the text, but we must all be of one and the same mind when we look upon the photographic evidence. It is in these photographs that all Americans can meet on the common ground of their beloved traditions. Here we are all united at the shrine where our fathers fought—Northerners or Southerners—and here the generations may look upon the undying record of the valor of those who fought to maintain the Union and those who fought for independence from it—each according to his own interpretation of the Constitution that bound them into a great republic of states.

These photographs are appeals to peace; they are the most convincing evidence of the tragedy of war. They bring it before the generations so impressively that one begins to understand the meaning of the great movement for universal brotherhood that is now passing through the civilized world. Mr. William Short, the secretary of the New York Peace Society, in speaking of them, truly says that they are the greatest arguments for peace that the world has ever seen. Their mission is more than to record history; it is to make history—to mould the thought of the generations as everlasting witnesses of the price of war.

As the founder of this memorial library, and its editor-in-chief, it is my pleasure to give historical record to Mr. Edward Bailey Eaton, Mr. Herbert Myrick, and Mr. J. Frank Drake, of the Patriot Publishing Company, of Springfield, Mass., owners of the largest private collection of original Brady-Gardner Civil War negatives in existence, by whom this work was inaugurated, and to Mr. Egbert Gilliss Handy, president of The Search-Light Library of New York, through whom it was organized for its present development by the Review of Reviews Company. These institutions have all co-operated to realize the national and impartial conception of this work. The result, we hope, is a more friendly, fair, and intimate picture of America's greatest sorrow and greatest glory than has perhaps been possible under the conditions that preceded this semi-centennial anniversary.

To President William Howard Taft, who has extended his autographed message to the North and the South, the editors take pleasure in recording their deep appreciation; also to Generals Sickles and Buckner, the oldest surviving generals in the Federal and Confederate armies, respectively, on this anniversary; to General Frederick Dent Grant and

General G. W. Custis Lee, the sons of the great warriors who led the armies through the American Crisis; to the Honorable Robert Todd Lincoln, former Secretary of War; to James W. Cheney, Librarian in the War Department at Washington; to Dr. Edward S. Holden, Librarian at the United States Military Academy at West Point, for their consideration and advice, and to the officers of the Grand Army of the Republic, the Military Order of the Loyal Legion, the United Confederate Veterans, the Daughters of the Confederacy, and the other memorial organizations that have shown an appreciation of the intent of this work. We are especially indebted to Mr. John McElroy, editor of the *National Tribune;* General Bennett H. Young, the historian of the United Confederate Veterans; General Grenville M. Dodge; Colonel S. A. Cunningham, founder and editor of the *Confederate Veteran,* General Irvine Walker, General William E. Mickle, and to the many others who, in their understanding and appreciation have rendered valuable assistance in the realization of its special mission to the American people on this semi-centennial.

This preface should not close without a final word as to the difficulty of the problems that confronted the military, historical, and other authorities whose contributions have made the text of THE PHOTOGRAPHIC HISTORY OF THE CIVIL WAR, whose names are signed to their historical contributions throughout these volumes, and the spirit in which, working with the editorial staff of the Review of Reviews, they have met these problems. The impossibility of deciding finally the difference of opinion in the movements of the Civil War has been generously recognized. With all personal and partisan arguments have been set aside in the universal and hearty effort of all concerned to fulfil the obligations of this work. I ask further privilege to extend my gratitude to my personal assistants, Mr. Walter R. Bickford, Mr. Arthur Forrest Burns, and Mr. Wallace H. Miller.

And now, as we stand to-day, fellowmen in the great republic that is carrying the torch in the foreranks of the world's civilization, let us clasp hands across the long-gone years as reunited Americans. I can close these introductory words with no nobler tribute than those of the mighty warriors who led the great armies to battle. It was General Robert E. Lee who, after the war, gave this advice to a Virginia mother, "Abandon all these animosities and make your sons Americans," and General Ulysses S. Grant, whose appeal to his countrymen must always be an admonition against war: "Let us have peace."

FRANCIS TREVELYAN MILLER,
Editor-in-Chief.

HARTFORD, CONNECTICUT,
Fiftieth Anniversary
Lincoln's Inauguration.

PHOTOGRAPHING
THE
CIVIL WAR

THE WAR PHOTOGRAPHER BRADY (WEARING STRAW HAT) WITH GENERAL BURNSIDE (READING NEWSPAPER)—TAKEN WHILE BURNSIDE WAS IN COMMAND OF THE ARMY OF THE POTOMAC, EARLY IN 1863, AFTER HIS ILL-FATED ATTACK ON FREDERICKSBURG

THE FLANKING GUN

This remarkably spirited photograph of Battery D, Second U. S. Artillery, was, according to the photographer's account, taken just as the battery was loading to engage with the Confederates. The order, "cannoneers to your posts," had just been given, and the men, running up, called to the photographer to hurry his wagon out of the way unless he wished to gain a place for his name in the list of casualties In June, 1863, the Sixth Corps had made its third successful crossing of the Rappahannock, as the advance of Hooker's movement against Lee. Battery D at once took position with other artillery out in the fields near the

"COOPER'S BATTERY" (SEE PAGE 32)

This is another photograph taken under fire and shows us Battery B, First Pennsylvania Light Artillery, in action before Petersburg, 1864. Brady, the veteran photographer, obtained permission to take a picture of "Cooper's Battery," in position for battle. The first attempt provoked the fire of the Confederates, who supposed that the running forward of the artillerists was with hostile intent. The Confederate guns frightened Brady s horse which ran off with his wagon and his assistant, upsetting and destroying his chemicals. In the picture to the left, Captain James H. Cooper himself is seen leaning on a sword at the

"LOAD!"

ruins of the Mansfield house. In the rear of the battery the veteran Vermont brigade was acting as support. To their rear was the bank of the river skirted by trees. The grove of white poplars to the right surrounded the Mansfield house. With characteristic coolness, some of the troops had already pitched their dog tents. Better protection was soon afforded by the strong line of earthworks which was thrown up and occupied by the Sixth Corps. Battery D was present at the first battle of Bull Run, where the Confederates there engaged got a taste of its metal on the Federal left

READY TO OPEN FIRE

extreme right. Lieutenant Miller is the second figure from the left. Lieutenant Alcorn is next, to the left from Captain Cooper. Lieutenant James A. Gardner, just behind the prominent figure with the haversack in the right section of the picture, identified these members almost forty-seven years after the picture was taken. This Pennsylvania battery suffered greater loss than any other volunteer Union battery; its record of casualties includes twenty-one killed and died of wounds, and fifty-two wounded—convincing testimony of the fact that throughout the war its men stood bravely to their guns.

THE

FIRST PHOTOGRAPH

OF IRONCLADS

IN ACTION

A

DARING

CAMERA–TRIUMPH

OF 1863

Copyright by Review of Reviews Co.

On the highest point of the battered dust heap that was the still untaken fortress of Sumter, the Confederate photographer, Cook, planted his camera on September 8, 1863, and took the first photograph of ironclads in action—the monitors *Weehawken, Montauk* and *Passaic*, as they were actually firing on the Confederate batteries at Fort Moultrie. The three low-freeboarded vessels, lying almost bows-on, at the distance of nearly two miles, look like great iron buoys in the channel, but the smoke from their heavy guns is drifting over the water, and the flames can almost be seen leaping from the turret ports. Although Fort Moultrie was the aim of their gunners, Cook, with his head under the dark cloth, saw on the ground glass a shell passing within a few feet of him. Another shell knocked one of his plate-holders off the parapet into the rain-water cistern. He gave a soldier five dollars to fish it out for him. He got his picture—and was ordered off the parapet, since he was drawing upon the fort the fire of all the Union batteries on Morris Island. It seems incredible that such a daring photographic feat, and one of such historic interest, could have remained unpublished for nearly half a century—until one recalls the absence of any satisfactory method for reproducing photographs direct during the generation succeeding the war. Before photo-engraving became perfected, thirty years or more had passed, and most of the few negatives taken by Confederates had vanished through fire, loss, and breakage. Fortunately, this has been preserved—one of the most vivid of any war.

A CONFEDERATE SECRET SERVICE PHOTOGRAPH OF THE FIRST INDIANA HEAVY ARTILLERY

This remarkable photograph is here published for the first time. It is but one of the many made by A. D. Lytle in Baton Rouge during its occupancy by the Federals. With a courage and skill as remarkable as that of Brady himself this Confederate photographer risked his life to obtain negatives of Federal batteries, cavalry regiments and camps, lookout towers, and the vessels of Farragut and Porter, in fact of everything that might be of the slightest use in informing the Confederate Secret Service of the strength of the Federal occupation of Baton Rouge. In Lytle's little shop on Main Street these negatives remained in oblivion for near half a century. War photographs were long regarded with extreme disfavor in the South and the North knew nothing of Lytle's collection, which has at last been unearthed by the editors of the "Photographic History." The value of Lytle's work to the Confederate Secret Service is apparent from this view, clear in every detail, of the Federal artillery drilling on the Parade Grounds of the Arsenal. The strength of the force, the number of the guns, the condition of the men, are all revealed at a glance. Many other "Lytle" photographs—gunboats, camps, infantry and cavalry—appear in the present work.

PERILOUS PHOTOGRAPHY AT THE FRONT

Here in imagination we may stand with Brady on the bank of the Rappahannock while he calmly focussed his cameras upon the town across the stream. The mighty Union army had arrived before Fredericksburg, and Brady, ever anxious to be in the thick of things, was early at his work. The only indication of war in the picture is the demolished railroad bridge, but behind the windows of the old mill at its farther end and in most of the houses of the town were Confederate sharpshooters, while along the river bank wooden barricades sheltered soldiers prepared to dispute the crossing of the river. No sooner had Brady placed his queer looking cameras in position than he and his assistants became the target for hundreds of rifles, but he calmly proceeded with his work and in accordance with his usual luck secured his pictures and returned uninjured. Almost a month of delay ensued before Burnside's futile crossing of the river furnished the photographers with a wealth of stirring scenes, many of which again had to be caught under fire.

CONFEDERATES BEFORE A UNION CAMERA

The single known instance in which the Union photographers succeeded in getting a near view of the Confederate troops. After Burnside's fatal attempt to carry the heights back of Fredericksburg he had retreated across the Rappahannock leaving more than 12,000 dead and wounded on the field. A burial truce was then agreed upon with Lee and afforded Brady and his men the sad opportunity to record many a gruesome spectacle. Near the end of the railroad bridge in Fredericksburg was secured a view of the living men of Lee's army which had inflicted such terrible punishment upon the Union forces but a short time before. They were evidently quite willing, during the suspension of hostilities, to group themselves before Brady's camera set up on the partially repaired end of the bridge. Here we get a nearer view of the old mill in the preceding picture. A cannon has been placed in one of its upper windows for defense. Although these houses had escaped injury from the Federal bombardment, other Brady photographs record the ruins of the little town.

A WASHINGTON BELLE IN CAMP

From Bull Run to Gettysburg the Federal capital was repeatedly threatened by the advances of the Confederates, and strong camps for the defense of Washington were maintained throughout the war. It was the smart thing for the ladies of the capital to invade these outlying camps, and they were always welcomed by the officers weary of continuous guard-duty. Here the camera has caught the willing subject in handsome Kate Chase Sprague, who became a belle of official society in Washington during the war. She was the daughter of Salmon P. Chase, Lincoln's Secretary of the Treasury. At this time she was the wife of Governor William Sprague, of Rhode Island, and was being entertained in camp by General J. J. Abercrombie, an officer of the regular army, well known in the capital.

A HORSE AND RIDER THAT WILL LIVE

Here is an extraordinary photograph of a spirited charger taken half a century ago. This noble beast is the mount of Lieut.-Col. C. B. Norton, and was photographed at General Fitz John Porter's headquarters. The rider is Colonel Norton himself. Such clear definition of every feature of man and horse might well be the envy of modern photography, which does not achieve such depth without fast lenses, focal-plane shutters, and instantaneous dry plates, which can be developed at leisure. Here the old-time wet-plate process has preserved every detail. To secure results like this it was necessary to sensitize the plate just before exposing it, uncap the lens by hand, and develop the negative within five minutes after the exposure.

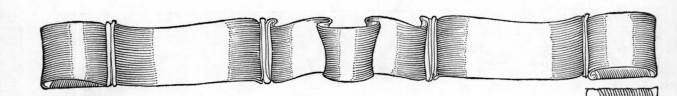

PHOTOGRAPHING THE CIVIL WAR

By Henry Wysham Lanier

EXTRAORDINARY as the fact seems, the American Civil War is the only great war of which we have an adequate history in photographs: that is to say, this is the only conflict of the first magnitude[1] in the world's history that can be really "illustrated," with a pictorial record which is indisputably authentic, vividly illuminating, and the final evidence in any question of detail.

Here is a much more important historical fact than the casual reader realizes. The earliest records we have of the human race are purely pictorial. History, even of the most shadowy and legendary sort, goes back hardly more than ten thousand years. But in recent years there have been recovered in certain caves of France scratched and carved bone weapons and rough wall-paintings which tell us some dramatic events in the lives of men who lived probably a hundred thousand years before the earliest of those seven strata of ancient Troy, which indefatigable archeologists have exposed to the wondering gaze of the modern world. The picture came long before the written record; nearly all our knowledge of ancient Babylonia and Assyria is gleaned from the details left by some picture-maker. And it is still infinitely more effective an appeal. How impossible it is for the average person to get any clear idea of the great struggles which altered the destinies of nations and which occupy so large a portion of world history! How can a man to-day really understand the siege of Troy, the battles of Thermopylæ or Salamis, Hannibal's crossing of the Alps, the famous fight at Tours when Charles "the Hammer" checked the Saracens, the Norman

[1] There have been, of course, only two wars of this description since 1865: the Franco-Prussian War was, for some reason, not followed by camera men; and the marvellously expert photographers who flocked to the struggles between Russia and Japan were not given any chance by the Japanese authorities to make anything like an adequate record.

The indomitable war photographer in the very costume which made him a familiar figure at the first battle of Bull Run, from which he returned precipitately to New York after his initial attempt to put into practice his scheme for picturing the war. Brady was a Cork Irishman by birth and possessed of all the active temperament which such an origin implies. At Bull Run he was in the thick of things. Later in the day, Brady himself was compelled to flee, and at nightfall of that fatal Sunday, alone and unarmed, he lost his way in the woods near the stream from which the battle takes its name. Here he was found by some of the famous company of New York Fire Department Zouaves, who gave him a sword for his defense. Buckling it on beneath his linen duster, Brady made his way to Washington and thence to New York. In the picture we see him still proudly wearing the weapon which he was prepared to use for the protection of himself and his precious negatives.

BRADY, AFTER BULL RUN

Below is the gallery of A. D. Lytle—a Confederate photographer—as it stood on Main Street, Baton Rouge, in 1864, when in the employ of the Confederate Secret Service Lytle trained his camera upon the Federal army which occupied Baton Rouge. It was indeed dangerous work, as discovery of his purpose would have visited upon the photographer the fate of a spy. Lytle would steal secretly up the Observation Tower, which had been built on the ruins of the capitol, and often exposed to rifle shots from the Federals, would with flag or lantern signal to the Confederates at Scott's Bluff, whence the news was relayed to New Orleans, and provision made for smuggling the precious prints through the lines. Like Brady, Lytle obtained his photographic supplies from Anthony & Company of New York; but unlike Cook of Charleston, he did not have to depend upon contraband traffic to secure them, but got them passed on the "orders to trade" issued quite freely in the West by the Federal Government.

THE GALLERY OF A CONFEDERATE SECRET-SERVICE PHOTOGRAPHER, BATON ROUGE, LOUISIANA, 1864

conquest of England, the Hundred Years' or Thirty Years' Wars, even our own seven-year struggle for liberty, without any first-hand picture-aids to start the imagination? Take the comparatively modern Napoleonic wars where, moreover, there is an exceptional wealth of paintings, drawings, prints, and lithographs by contemporary men: in most cases the effect is simply one of keen disappointment at the painfully evident fact that most of these worthy artists never saw a battle or a camp.

So the statement that there have been gathered together *thousands of photographs* of scenes on land and water during those momentous years of 1861 to 1865 means that for our generation and all succeeding ones, the Civil War is on a basis different from all others, is practically an open book to old and young. For when man achieved the photograph he took almost as important a step forward as when he discovered how to make fire: he made scenes and events and personalities immortal. The greatest literary genius might write a volume without giving you so intimate a comprehension of the struggle before Petersburg as do these exact records, made by adventurous camera-men under incredible difficulties, and holding calmly before your eyes the very Reality itself.

To apply this pictorial principle, let us look at one remarkable photograph, Cooper's Battery in front of the Avery house, during the siege of Petersburg, of which we have, by a lucky chance, an account from one of the men in the scene. The lifelikeness of the picture is beyond praise: one cannot help living through this tense moment with these men of long ago, and one's eyes instinctively follow their fixed gaze toward the lines of the foe. This picture was shown to Lieutenant James A. Gardner (of Battery B, First Pennsylvania Light Artillery), who immediately named half a dozen of the figures, adding details of the most intimate interest (see pages 22 and 23):

I am, even at this late day, able to pick out and recognize a very large number of the members of our battery, as shown in this photograph. Our battery (familiarly known as Cooper's Battery) belonged to the Fifth Corps, then commanded by Gen. G. K. Warren.

Our corps arrived in front of Petersburg on June 17, 1864, was put into position on the evening of that day, and engaged the Confederate batteries on their line near the Avery house. The enemy at that time

THE PHOTOGRAPHER WITH THE ARMY

Here are two excellent views in which we see the conditions under which the army photographer worked in the field. The larger picture is of Barnard, the Government photographer under Captain O. M. Poe, Chief Engineer of the Military Division of the Mississippi. Barnard was engaged to take photographs of the new Federal fortifications being constructed under Captain Poe's direction at Atlanta, September–October, 1864. Captain Poe found the old Confederate line of defense of too great extent to be held by such a force as Sherman intended to leave as garrison of the town. Consequently, he selected a new line of much shorter development which passed through the northern part of the town, making necessary the destruction of many buildings in that quarter. Barnard is here at work sensitizing his plates in a light-proof tent, making his exposures, and developing immediately within the tent. His chemicals and general supplies were carried in the wagon showing to the right. Thus, as the pioneer corps worked on the fortifications, the entire series of photographs showing their progress was made to be forwarded later to Washington by Captain

Poe, with his official report. In the background we see the battle-field where began the engagement of July 22, 1864, known as the battle of Atlanta, in which General McPherson lost his life. Thus Brady and all the war photographers worked right up to the trenches, lugging their cumbersome tents and apparatus, often running out of supplies or carrying hundreds of glass plates over rough roads or exposed to possible shells. To the many chances of failure was added that of being at any time picked off by some sharpshooter. In the smaller picture appears a duplicate of Brady's "What-Is-It," being the dark-room buggy of Photographer Wearn. In the background are the ruins of the State Armory at Columbia, South Carolina. This was burned as Sherman's troops passed through the city on their famous march through the Carolinas, February, 1865. The photographer, bringing up the rear, has preserved the result of Sherman's work, which is typical of that done by him all along the line of march to render useless to the Confederate armies in the field, the military resources of the South.

RUINS OF STATE ARMORY, COLUMBIA, 1865

was commanded by General Beauregard. That night the enemy fell back to their third line, which then occupied the ridge which you see to the right and front, along where you will notice the chimney (the houses had been burnt down). On the night of the 18th we threw up the lunettes in front of our guns. This position was occupied by us until possibly about the 23d or 24th of June, when we were taken further to the left. The position shown in the picture is about six hundred and fifty yards in front, and to the right of the Avery house, and at or near this point was built a permanent fort or battery, which was used continuously during the entire siege of Petersburg.

While occupying this position, Mr. Brady took the photographs, copies of which you have sent me. The photographs were taken in the forenoon of June 21, 1864. I know *myself*, merely from the position that I occupied at that time, as gunner. After that, I served as sergeant, first sergeant, and first lieutenant, holding the latter position at the close of the war. All the officers shown in this picture are dead.

The movement in which we were engaged was the advance of the Army of the Potomac upon Petersburg, being the beginning of operations in front of that city. On June 18th the division of the Confederates which was opposite us was that of Gen. Bushrod R. Johnson; but as the Army of Northern Virginia, under General Lee, began arriving on the evening of June 18th, it would be impossible for me to say who occupied the enemy's lines after that. The enemy's position, which was along on the ridge to the front, in the picture, where you see the chimney, afterward became the main line of the Union army. Our lines were advanced to that point, and at or about where you see the chimney standing, Fort Morton of the Union line was constructed, and a little farther to the right was Fort Stedman, on the same ridge; and about where the battery now stands, as shown in the picture, was a small fort or works erected, known as Battery Seventeen.

When engaged in action, our men exhibited the same coolness that is shown in the picture—that is, while loading our guns. If the enemy is engaging us, as soon as each gun is loaded the cannoneers drop to the ground and protect themselves as best they can, except the gunners and the officers, who are expected to be always on the lookout. The gunners are the corporals who sight and direct the firing of the guns.

In the photograph you will notice a person (in civilian's clothes). This is Mr. Brady or his assistant, but I think it is Mr. Brady himself.

It is now almost forty-seven years since the photographs were taken, yet I am able to designate at least fifteen persons of our battery, and point them out. I should have said that Mr. Brady took picture No. 1 from a point a little to the left, and front, of our battery; and the second one was taken a little to the rear, and left, of the battery. Petersburg lay immediately over the ridge in the front, right over past

THE FIELD DARK–ROOM

Here we get an excellent idea of how the business of army photography, invented by Brady and first exemplified by him at Bull Run, had become organized toward the close of the war. In the lower picture we see the outfit with which Samuel A. Cooley followed the fortunes of the campaigners, and recorded for all time the stirring events around Savannah at the completion of the March to the Sea. Cooley was attached to the Tenth Corps, United States Army, and secured photographs at Jacksonville, St. Augustine, Beaufort, and Charleston during the bombardment. Here he is in the act of making an exposure. The large camera and plate-holder seem to eyes of the present day far too cumbersome to make possible the wonderful definition and beautiful effects of light and shade which characterize the war-time negatives that have come down to us through the vicissitudes of half a century. Here are Cooley's two means of transportation. The wagon fitted to carry the supply of chemicals, glass plates, and the precious finished negatives includes a compartment for more leisurely developing. The little dark-room buggy to the left was used upon occasions when it was necessary for the army photographer to proceed in light marching order. In the smaller picture we see again the light-proof developing tent in action before the ramparts of Fort McAllister. The view is of the exterior of the fort fronting the Savannah River. A few days before the Confederate guns had frowned darkly from the parapet at Sherman's "bummers," who could see the smoke of the Federal gunboats waiting to welcome them just beyond. With Sherman looking proudly on, the footsore and hungry soldiers rushed forward to the attack, and the Stars and Stripes were soon floating over this vast barrier between them and the sea. The next morning, Christmas Day, 1864, the gunboats and transports steamed up the river and the joyful news was flashed northward.

THE CIVIL WAR PHOTOGRAPHERS' IMPEDIMENTA

the man whom you see sitting there so leisurely on the earthworks thrown up.

A notice in *Humphrey's Journal* in 1861 describes vividly the records of the flight after Bull Run secured by the indefatigable Brady. Unfortunately the unique one in which the reviewer identified " Bull Run " Russell in reverse action is lost to the world. But we have the portrait of Brady himself three days later in his famous linen duster, as he returned to Washington. His story comes from one who had it from his own lips:

He [Brady] had watched the ebb and flow of the battle on that Sunday morning in July, 1861, and seen now the success of the green Federal troops under General McDowell in the field, and now the stubborn defense of the green troops under that General Jackson who thereby earned the sobriquet of "Stonewall." At last Johnston, who with Beauregard and Jackson, was a Confederate commander, strengthened by reenforcements, descended upon the rear of the Union troops and drove them into a retreat which rapidly turned to a rout.

The plucky photographer was forced along with the rest; and as night fell he lost his way in the thick woods which were not far from the little stream that gave the battle its name. He was clad in the linen duster which was a familiar sight to those who saw him taking his pictures during that campaign, and was by no means prepared for a night in the open. He was unarmed as well, and had nothing with which to defend himself from any of the victorious Confederates who might happen his way, until one of the famous company of " Fire " zouaves, of the Union forces, gave him succor in the shape of a broadsword. This he strapped about his waist, and it was still there when he finally made his way to Washington three days later. He was a sight to behold after his wanderings, but he had come through unscathed as it was his fate to do so frequently afterwards.

Instances might be multiplied indefinitely, but here is one more evidence of the quality of this pictorial record. The same narrator had from Brady a tale of a picture made a year and a half later, at the battle of Fredericksburg. He says:

Burnside, then in command of the Army of the Potomac, was preparing to cross the Rappahannock, and Longstreet and Jackson, commanding the Confederate forces, were fortifying the hills back of the right bank of that river. Brady, desiring as usual to be in the thick of things, undertook to make some pictures from the left bank. He placed cameras in position and got his men to work, but suddenly found him-

THE CAMERA

WITH

THE ARMY

IN RETREAT

AND

ADVANCE

The plucky Brady-Gardner operatives stuck to the Union army in the East, whether good fortune or ill betided it. Above, two of them are busy with their primitive apparatus near Bull Run, while Pope's army was in retreat, just before the second battle on that fateful ground. Below is a photographer's portable dark-room, two years later, at Cobb's Hill on the Appomattox. Near here Grant's army had joined Butler's, and before them Lee's veterans were making their last stand within the entrenchments at Petersburg.

(ABOVE)

PHOTOGRAPHERS

AT BULL RUN

BEFORE THE

SECOND

FIGHT

(BELOW)

PHOTOGRAPHERS

AT BUTLER'S

SIGNALING

TOWER

1864

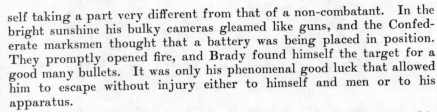

self taking a part very different from that of a non-combatant. In the bright sunshine his bulky cameras gleamed like guns, and the Confederate marksmen thought that a battery was being placed in position. They promptly opened fire, and Brady found himself the target for a good many bullets. It was only his phenomenal good luck that allowed him to escape without injury either to himself and men or to his apparatus.

It is clearly worth while to study for a few moments this man Brady, who was so ready to risk his life for the idea by which he was obsessed. While the war soon developed far beyond what he or any other one man could possibly have compassed, so that he is probably directly responsible for only a fraction of the whole vast collection of pictures in these volumes, he may fairly be said to have fathered the movement; and his daring and success undoubtedly stimulated and inspired the small army of men all over the war-region, whose unrelated work has been laboriously gathered together.

Matthew B. Brady was born at Cork, Ireland (not in New Hampshire, as is generally stated) about 1823. Arriving in New York as a boy, he got a job in the great establishment of A. T. Stewart, first of the merchant princes of that day. The youngster's good qualities were so conspicuous that his large-minded employer made it possible for him to take a trip abroad at the age of fifteen, under the charge of S. F. B. Morse, who was then laboring at his epoch-making development of the telegraph.

Naturally enough, this scientist took his young companion to the laboratory of the already famous Daguerre, whose arduous experiments in making pictures by sunlight were just approaching fruition; and the wonderful discovery which young Brady's receptive eyes then beheld was destined to determine his whole life-work.

For that very year (1839) Daguerre made his "daguerreotype" known to the world; and Brady's keen interest was intensified when, in 1840, on his own side of the ocean, Professor Draper produced the first photographic portrait the world had yet seen, a likeness of his sister, which required the amazingly short exposure of *only ninety seconds!*

Brady's natural business-sense and his mercantile training showed him the chance for a career which this new invention opened, and it was but a short time before he had a gallery

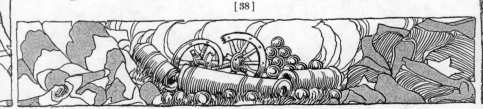

WASHING THE NEGATIVES

Photographers' Headquarters at Cold Harbor, Virginia.—In the lull before the fierce engagement which Grant was about to meet here in his persistent pushing forward upon Richmond, the cameraists were engaged in fixing, washing, and storing their negatives.

BEFORE SECOND BULL RUN

Brady's headquarters with his "What Is It?" preparing for the strenuous work involved in the oncoming battle.

AT WORK IN SUMTER, APRIL, 1865

At last thè besiegers were in Charleston, and the Union photographers for the first time were securing views of the position.

BRADY'S "WHAT IS IT?" AT CULPEPER, VIRGINIA

on Broadway and was well launched upon the new trade of furnishing daguerreotype portraits to all comers. He was successful from the start; in 1851 his work took a prize at the London World's Fair; about the same time he opened an office in Washington; in the fifties he brought over Alexander Gardner, an expert in the new revolutionary wet-plate process, which gave a negative furnishing many prints instead of one unduplicatable original; and in the twenty years between his start and the Civil War he became the fashionable photographer of his day—as is evidenced not only by the superb collection of notable people whose portraits he gathered together, but by Brete Harte's classic verse (from "Her Letter"):

> Well, yes—if you saw us out driving
> Each day in the Park, four-in-hand—
> If you saw poor dear mamma contriving
> To look supernaturally grand,—
> If you saw papa's picture, as taken
> By Brady, and tinted at that,—
> You'd never suspect he sold bacon
> And flour at Poverty Flat.

Upon this sunny period of prosperity the Civil War broke in 1861. Brady had made portraits of scores of the men who leaped into still greater prominence as leaders in the terrible struggle, and his vigorous enthusiasm saw in this fierce drama an opportunity to win ever brighter laurels. His energy and his acquaintance with men in authority overcame every obstacle, and he succeeded in interesting President Lincoln, Secretary Stanton, General Grant, and Allan Pinkerton to such an extent that he obtained the protection of the Secret Service, and permits to make photographs at the front. Everything had to be done at his own expense, but with entire confidence he equipped his men, and set out himself as well, giving instructions to guard against breakage by making two negatives of everything, and infusing into all his own ambition to astonish the world by this unheard-of feat.

The need for such permits appears in a "home letter" from E. T. Whitney, a war photographer whose negatives, unfortunately, have been destroyed. This letter, dated March 13, 1862, states that the day before "all photographing has

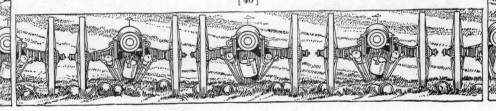

ESTABLISHING COMMUNICATION

Here the camera has caught the U. S. Military Telegraph Construction Corps in action, April, 1864. The 150-odd men composing it were active throughout the war in planting poles and stringing wires in order to keep the Central Telegraph Office in direct communication with the armies at all times. Lincoln spent many an evening in the War Department Building at the capital reading the despatches from the front handed to him by the operators. The photograph but faintly indicates the flexible insulated wire, which by this time had come into use, and in the picture is being strung along by the two men on the poles and the three in advance of them in the left foreground.

been stopped by general orders from headquarters." Owing to ignorance of this order on the part of the guard at the bridge, Whitney was allowed to reach the Army of the Potomac, where he made application to General McClellan for a special pass.

We shall get some more glimpses presently of these adventurous souls in action. But, as already hinted, extraordinary as were the results of Brady's impetuous vigor, he was but one of many in the great work of picturing the war. Three-fourths of the scenes with the Army of the Potomac were made by Gardner. Thomas G. Roche was an indefatigable worker in the armies' train. Captain A. J. Russell, detached as official camera-man for the War Department, obtained many invaluable pictures illustrating the military railroading and construction work of the Army of the Potomac, which were hurried straightway to Secretary Stanton at Washington. Sam A. Cooley was attached to the Tenth Army Corps, and recorded the happenings around Savannah, Fort McAllister, Jacksonville, St. Augustine, Beaufort, and Charleston during the bombardment; George M. Barnard, under the supervision of General O. M. Poe (then Captain in the Engineer Corps), did yeoman's service around Atlanta.

S. R. Siebert was very busy indeed at Charleston in 1865. Cook of Charleston, Edwards of New Orleans, and other unknown men on the Confederate side, working under even greater difficulties (Cook, for instance, had to secure his chemicals from Anthony in New York—who also supplied Brady—and smuggle them through), did their part in the vast labor; and many another unknown, including the makers of the little *cartes de visite,* contributed to the panorama which to-day unfolds itself before the reader.

One most interesting camera-man of unique kind was A. D. Lytle, of Baton Rouge, Louisiana, who made a series of views (covering three years and several campaigns—and consequently scattered through the present work) for the specific use of the Confederate Secret Service. That is to say, he was a " camera spy," and a good one, too. He secured his chemicals from the same great firm of Anthony & Co., in New York, but instead of running the blockade with them, they were supplied on " orders to trade." In many cases, for instance, the necessary iodides and bromides masqueraded as

[42]

A TRIUMPH OF THE WET-PLATE

It seems almost impossible that this photograph could have been taken before the advent of modern photographic apparatus, yet Mr. Gardner's negative, made almost fifty years ago, might well furnish a striking exhibit in a modern photographic salon. The view is of Quarles' Mill, on the North Anna River, Virginia. In grassy fields above the mill the tents of the headquarters of Grant and Meade were pitched for a day or two during the march which culminated in the siege of Petersburg. Among the prisoners brought in while the army was here in camp was a woman clad in Confederate gray, apparently performing the duties of a scout. She was captured astride of a bony steed and asserted that she belonged to a battery of artillery. This wild creature, with her tangled black locks hanging down her neck, became the center of interest to the idlers of the camp. At these she would occasionally throw stones with considerable accuracy, particularly at the negroes, who gave her a wide berth. As the faithful camera indicates, the river current at this point is strong and rapid. While General Thomas L. Crittenden's division of the Federal Ninth Corps was crossing the North Anna (June 24, 1864) by fording the mill-dam, many sturdy foot-soldiers as well as horsemen were swept over the falls. However, the division got across in good fighting shape and formed a line of battle around the ford on the southern bank just in time to head off a bold Confederate dash for the same coign of vantage. Crittenden's advance guard was hotly engaged in the woods beyond the mill and being roughly handled when the rear of the column reached the southern bank.

quinine.[1] Mr. Lytle's son relates that his father used to signal with flag and lantern from the observation tower on the top of the ruins of the Baton Rouge capitol to Scott's Bluff, whence the messages were relayed to the Confederates near New Orleans; but he found this provided such a tempting target for the Federal sharpshooters that he discontinued the practice.

There are contemporary comments on the first crop of war photographs—which confirm several points already made. *Humphrey's Journal* in October, 1861, contained the following:

PHOTOGRAPHS OF WAR SERIES

Among the portraits in Brady's selection, spoken of in our last number, are those of many leading generals and colonels—McClellan, McDowell, Heintzelman, Burnside, Wood, Corcoran, Slocum, and others. Of the larger groups, the most effective are those of the army passing through Fairfax village, the battery of the 1st Rhode Island regiment at Camp Sprague, the 71st Regiment [New York] formed in hollow square at the Navy Yard, the Engineer Corps of the New York Twelfth at Camp Anderson, Zouaves on the lookout from the belfry of Fairfax Court House, etc., etc.

Mr. Brady intends to take other photographic scenes of the localities of our army and of battle-scenes, and his collection will undoubtedly prove to be the most interesting ever yet exhibited. But why should he monopolize this department? We have plenty of other artists as good as he is. What a field would there be for Anthony's instantaneous views and for stereoscopic pictures. Let other artists exhibit a little of Mr. Brady's enterprise and furnish the public with more views. There are numerous photographers close by the stirring scenes which are being daily enacted, and now is the time for them to distinguish themselves.

We have seen how far Brady came from "monopolizing" the field. And surely the sum total of achievement is triumphant enough to share among all who had any hand in it.

And now let us try to get some idea of the problem which confronted these enthusiasts, and see how they tackled it.

[1] This statement is historically confirmed. Professor Walter L. Fleming, of the University of Louisiana, states he has seen many such orders-to-trade, signed by President Lincoln, but not countersigned by Secretary Stanton.

A SNAPSHOT IN THE WAR REGION

Another remarkable example of the results achieved by the old collodion process photographers quite indistinguishable from the instantaneous photographs of the present day. Although taken under the necessity of removing and replacing the lens cap, this negative has successfully caught the waterfall and the Federal cavalryman's horse which has been ridden to the stream for a drink. The picture was taken at Hazel Run, Virginia, above the pontoon bridge constructed for the crossing of the Federal troops. During the advances and retreats, while the Federal armies were maneuvering for position, the photographers were frequently at a loss for material. At such times, true to the professional instinct, they kept in practice by making such views as this. Less important from the strictly military viewpoint, these splendid specimens of landscape photography give us a clear conception of the character of the country over which the Federal and Confederate armies passed and repassed during the stirring period of the war.

Imagine what it must have meant even to get to the scene of action—with cumbersome tent and apparatus, and a couple of hundred glass plates whose breakage meant failure; over unspeakable back-country roads or no roads at all; with the continual chance of being picked off by some scouting sharp-shooter or captured through some shift of the armies.

The first sight of the queer-looking wagon caused amazement, speculation, derision. "What is it?" became so inevitable a greeting that to this day if one asks a group of soldiers about war-photographs, they will exclaim simultaneously, "Oh, yes, the 'what-is-it' wagon!" It became a familiar sight, yet the novelty of its awkward mystery never quite wore off.

Having arrived, and having faced the real perils generally attendant upon reaching the scenes of keenest interest, our camera adventurer was but through the overture of his troubles. The most advanced photography of that day was the wet-plate method, by which the plates had to be coated in the dark (which meant in this case carrying everywhere a smothery, light-proof tent), *exposed within five minutes*, and developed within five minutes more! For the benefit of amateur members of the craft here are some notes from the veteran photographer, Mr. George G. Rockwood:

First, all the plain glass plates in various sizes, usually 8 x 10, had to be carefully cleaned and carried in dust-proof boxes. When ready for action, the plate was carefully coated with "collodion," which carried in solution the "excitants"—bromide and iodide of potassium, or ammonia, or cadmium. Collodion is made by the solution of gun-cotton in about equal parts of sulphuric ether and 95° proof alcohol. The salts above mentioned are then added, making the collodion a *vehicle* for obtaining the sensitive surface on the glass plate. The coating of plates was a delicate operation even in the ordinary well-organized studio. After coating the plate with collodion and letting the ether and alcohol evaporate to just the right degree of "stickiness," it was lowered carefully into a deep "bath holder" which contained a solution of nitrate of silver about 60° for quick field-work. This operation created the sensitive condition of the plate, and had to be done in total darkness except a subdued yellow light. When properly coated (from three to five minutes) the plate was put into a "slide" or "holder" and exposed to the action of the light in the camera. When exposed, it was returned to the dark-room and developed.

[46]

AMENITIES OF THE CAMP IN 1864

This photograph, taken at Brandy Station, Virginia, is an excellent example of the skill of the war photographers. When we remember that orthochromatic plates were undreamed of in the days of the Civil War, the color values of this picture are marvelous. The collodion wet-plate has caught the sheen and texture of the silk dresses worn by the officers' wives, whom we see on a visit to a permanent camp. The entrance to the tent is a fine example of the rustic work with which the Engineer Corps of the various armies amused themselves during periods which would otherwise be spent in tedious inactivity. The officers' quarters received first attention. Thus an atmosphere of indescribable charm was thrown about the permanent camps to which the wives of the officers came in their brief visits to the front, and from which they reluctantly returned without seeing anything of the gruesome side of war. A review or a parade was usually held for their entertainment. In the weary waiting before Petersburg during the siege, the successful consumma- tion of which practically closed the war, the New York engineers, while not engaged in strengthening the Federal fortifications, amused themselves by constructing a number of rustic buildings of great beauty. One of these was the signal tower toward the left of the Federal line of investment. Near it a substantial and artistic hospital building was erected, and, to take the place of a demolished church, a new and better rustic structure sprang into being.

Mr. Rockwood also knew all about Brady's wagon, having had a similar contrivance made for himself before the war, for taking pictures in the country. He "used an ordinary delivery wagon of the period, much like the butcher's cart of to-day and had a strong step attached at the rear and below the level of the wagon floor. A door was put on at the back, carefully hung so as to be light-proof. The door, you understand, came down over the step which was boxed in at the sides, making it a sort of well within the body of the wagon rather than a true step.

"The work of coating or sensitizing the plates and that of developing them was done from this well, in which there was just room enough to work. As the operator stood there the collodion was within reach of his right hand, in a special receptacle. On his left also was the holder of one of the baths. The chief developing bath was in front, with the tanks of various liquids stored in front of it again, and the space between it and the floor filled with plates.

"With such a wagon on a larger scale, large enough for men to sleep in front of the dark-room part, the phenomenal pictures of Brady were made possible. Brady risked his life many a time in order not to separate from this cumbrous piece of impedimenta.

"On exceptional occasions in very cold weather the life of a wet plate might be extended to nearly an hour on either side of the exposure, the coating or the development side, but ordinarily the work had to be done within a very few minutes, and every minute of delay resulted in loss of brilliancy and depth in the negative."

Some vivid glimpses of the war-photographers' troubles come also from Mr. J. Pitcher Spencer, who knew the work intimately:

We worked long with one of the foremost of Brady's men, and here let me doff my hat to the name of M. B. Brady—few to-day are worthy to carry his camera case, even as far as ability from the photographic standpoint goes. I was, in common with the "Cape Codders," following the ocean from 1859 to 1864; I was only home a few months —1862–63—and even then from our boys who came home invalided we heard of that grand picture-maker Brady, as they called him.

When I made some views (with the only apparatus then known, the "wet plate"), there came a large realization of some of the immense

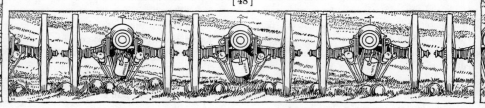

DIGGING UNDER FIRE AT DUTCH GAP—1864

Here for a moment the Engineering corps of General Benjamin F. Butler's army paused while the camera of the army photographer was focussed upon it. In August, 1864, Butler, with his army then bottled up in Bermuda Hundred, began to dig a canal at Dutch Gap to save a circuit of six miles in the bend of the James River and thus avoid the batteries, torpedoes, and obstructions which the Confederates had placed to prevent the passage of the Federal fleet up the river toward Richmond. The difficulties of this engineering feat are here seen plainly in the photograph. It took Butler's men all the rest of the year (1864) to cut through this canal, exposed as they were to the fire of the Confederate batteries above. One of the last acts of General Butler was an unsuccessful effort to blow up the dam at the mouth of this canal, and by thus admitting water to it, render it navigable.

difficulties surmounted by those who made war-pictures. When you realize that the most sensitive of all the list of chemicals are requisite to make collodion, which must coat every plate, and that the very slightest breath might carry enough "poison" across the plate being coated to make it produce a blank spot instead of some much desired effect, you may perhaps have a faint idea of the care requisite to produce a picture. Moreover, it took unceasing care to keep every bit of the apparatus, as well as each and every chemical, free from any possible contamination which might affect the picture. Often a breath of wind, no matter how gentle, spoiled the whole affair.

Often, just as some fine result looked certain, a hot streak of air would not only spoil the plate, but put the instrument out of commission, by curling some part of it out of shape. In face of these, and hundreds of minor discouragements, the men imbued with vim and forcefulness by the "Only Brady" kept right along and to-day the world can enjoy these wonderful views as a result.

Still further details come from an old soldier and photographic expert, Mr. F. M. Rood:

The plate "flowed" with collodion was dipped *at once* in a bath of nitrate of silver, in water also iodized, remained there *in darkness* three to five minutes; still in darkness, it was taken out, drained, put in the dark-holder, exposed, and developed in the dark-tent *at once*. The time between flowing the collodion and developing should not exceed eight or ten minutes. The developer was sulphate of iron solution and acetic acid, after which came a slight washing and fixing (to remove the surplus silver) with solution of cyanide of potassium; and then a final washing, drying, and varnishing. The surface (wet or dry), unlike a dry plate, could not be touched. I was all through the war from 1861–65, in the Ninety-third New York regiment, whose pictures you have given. I recognized quite a number of the old comrades. You have also in your collection a negative of each company of that regiment.

Fortunately the picture men occasionally immortalized each other as well as the combatants, so that we have a number of intimate glimpses of their life and methods. In one the wagon, chemicals and camera are in the very trenches at Atlanta, and they tell more than pages of description. But, naturally, they cannot show the arduous labor, the narrow escapes, the omnipresent obstacles which could be overcome only by the keenest ardor and determination. The epic of the war-photographer is still to be written. It would compare favorably with the story of many battles. And it does not

CAMP LIFE OF THE INVADING ARMY

This picture preserves for us the resplendent aspect of the camp of McClellan's Army of the Potomac in the spring of 1862. On his march from Yorktown toward Richmond, McClellan advanced his supply base from Cumberland Landing to White House on the Pamunkey. The barren fields on the bank of the river were converted as if by magic into an immense city of tents stretching away as far as the eye could see, while mirrored in the river lay the immense fleet of transports convoyed up by gunboats from Fortress Monroe. Here we see but a small section of this inspiring view. In the foreground, around the mud-spattered forge, the blankets and knapsacks of the farriers have been thrown carelessly on the ground. Farther on the patient army mules are tethered around the wagons. In the background, before the camp of the Fifth New York Volunteers (Duryée's Zouaves), a regiment of infantry is drawn up in columns of companies for inspection drill. From the 15th to the 19th of May the Army of the Potomac was concentrated between Cumberland Landing and White House. While in camp an important change was made in the organization of the army. The divisions of Porter and Sykes were united into the Fifth Corps under Porter, and those of Franklin and Smith into the Sixth Corps under Franklin. On May 19th the movement to Richmond was begun by the advance of Porter and Franklin to Tunstall's Station.

require much imagination, after viewing the results obtained in the face of such conditions, to get a fair measure of these indomitable workers.

The story of the way in which these pictures have been rescued from obscurity is almost as romantic a tale as that of their making. The net result of Brady's efforts was a collection of over seven thousand pictures (two negatives of each in most cases); and the expenditure involved, estimated at $100,000, ruined him. One set, after undergoing the most extraordinary vicissitudes, finally passed into the Government's possession, where it is now held with a prohibition against its use for commercial purposes. The $25,000 tardily voted to Mr. Brady by Congress did not retrieve his financial fortunes, and he died in the nineties, in a New York hospital, poor and forgotten, save by a few old-time friends.

Brady's own negatives passed in the seventies into the possession of Anthony, in default of payment of his bills for photographic supplies. They were kicked about from pillar to post for ten years, until John C. Taylor found them in an attic and bought them; from this they became the backbone of the Ordway-Rand collection; and in 1895 Brady himself had no idea what had become of them. Many were broken, lost, or destroyed by fire. After passing to various other owners, they were discovered and appreciated by Edward Bailey Eaton, of Hartford, Connecticut, who created the immediate train of events that led to their importance as the nucleus of a collection of many thousand pictures gathered from all over the country to furnish the material for this work.

From all sorts of sources, from the Atlantic to the Pacific, from Maine to the Gulf, these hidden treasures have been drawn. Historical societies, Government and State bureaus, librarians, private collectors, military and patriotic organizations, old soldiers and their families have recollected, upon earnest insistence, that they did have such things or once knew of them. Singly and in groups they have come from walls, out of archives, safes, old garrets, often seeing the light of day for the first time in a generation, to join together once more in a pictorial army which daily grew more irresistible as the new arrivals augmented, supplemented, and explained. The superb result is here spread forth and illuminated for posterity.

THE PASSING WAGON TRAIN

This historic bridge crossed Antietam Creek on the turnpike leading from Boonsboro to Sharpsburg. It is one of the memorable spots in the history of the war. The photograph was taken soon after the battle of Antietam; the overturned stone wall and shattered fences, together with the appearance of the adjacent ground, are mute witnesses of the conflict that raged about it on September 16–17, 1862, when the control of this bridge was important to both McClellan and Lee. The former held it during the battle; and the fire of his artillery from the ridges near the bridge enabled the disordered Union lines to recover in time to check the ferocious assaults of the Confederates.

Apart from all the above considerations, these invaluable pictures are well worth attention from the standpoint of pictorial art. We talk a great deal nowadays about the astonishing advances of modern art-photography; and it is quite true that patient investigators have immeasurably increased the range and flexibility of camera methods and results. We now manipulate negatives and print to produce any sort of effect; we print in tint or color, omitting or adding what we wish; numberless men of artistic capacity are daily showing how to transmit personal feeling through the intricacies of the mechanical process. But it is just as true as when the caveman scratched on a bone his recollections of mammoth and reindeer, that the artist will produce work that moves the beholder, no matter how crude may be his implements. Clearly there were artists among these Civil War photographers.

Probably this was caused by natural selection. It took ardor and zest for this particular thing above all others to keep a man at it in face of the hardships and disheartening handicaps. In any case, the work speaks for itself. Over and over one is thrilled by a sympathetic realization that the vanished man who pointed the camera at some particular scene, must have felt precisely the same pleasure in a telling composition of landscape, in a lifelike grouping, in a dramatic glimpse of a battery in action, in a genre study of a wounded soldier watched over by a comrade—that we feel to-day and that some seeing eye will respond to generations in the future. This is the true immortality of art. And when the emotions thus aroused center about a struggle which determined the destiny of a great nation, the picture that arouses them takes its proper place as an important factor in that heritage of the past which gives us to-day increased stature over all past ages, just because we add all their experience to our own.

SECOND PREFACE

THE PHOTOGRAPHIC
RECORD
AS HISTORY

WITH THE DEFENDERS OF WASHINGTON IN 1862;
THE SALLY-PORT AT FORT RICHARDSON

"HISTORY BROUGHT AGAIN INTO THE PRESENT TENSE"

The value of "The Photographic Record as History" is emphasized in the contribution from Mr. George Haven Putnam on page 60. This photograph of a dramatic scene was taken on a July day after the photographer's own heart—clear and sunny. The fort is at the end of Peach Tree Street, Atlanta, to the north of the city. Sherman had just taken possession, and the man at the left is a cavalryman of his forces. The mire-caked wheels of the guns show that they have been dragged through miles and miles of muddy

CONFEDERATE EARTHWORKS BEFORE ATLANTA, 1864

roads. The delays Sherman had met with in his advance on Atlanta resulting in constant and indecisive fighting without entrapping Johnston, had brought about a reaction at the North. A large party wished to end the war. Election Day was approaching. Lincoln was a presidential candidate for the second time. He had many enemies. But the news of Sherman's capture of Atlanta helped to restore confidence, and to insure the continuation of the administration pledged to a vigorous prosecution of the war.

A STRIKING WAR PHOTOGRAPH OF '63

The introduction on page 30, "Photographing the Civil War," remarks on the genius required to record such vivid action by camera in the days of '61. The use of the instrument had not then become pastime; it was a pioneer science, requiring absolute knowledge, training, and experience. Only experts like the men that Brady trained could do such work as this. There were no lightning shutters, no automatic or universal focus. In positions of danger and at times when speed and accuracy were required, there was the delicacy of the old-fashioned wet plate to consider, with all its drawbacks. No wonder people were surprised that pictures such as this exist; they had grown used to the old woodcut and the often mutilated attempts of pen and pencil to portray such scenes of action. There are many who never knew that photography was

ARTILLERY "REGULARS" BEFORE CHANCELLORSVILLE

possible in the Civil War. Yet look at this Union battery, taken by the shore of the Rappahannock, just before the battle of Chancellorsville. Action, movement, portraiture are shown. We can hear the officer standing in front giving his orders; his figure leaning slightly forward is tense with spoken words of command. The cannoneers, resting or ramming home the charges, are magnificent types of the men who made the Army of the Potomac—the army doomed to suffer, a few days after this picture was taken, its crushing repulse by the famous flanking charge of "Stonewall" Jackson; yet the army which kept faith and ultimately became invincible in the greatest civil war of history. Within sixty days after the Chancellorsville defeat the troops engaged won a signal triumph over the self-same opponents at Gettysburg.

THE PHOTOGRAPHIC RECORD
AS HISTORY

By George Haven Putnam

Adjutant and Brevet Major 176th New York Volunteer Infantry

'TIS fifty years since. The words recall the opening sentence of Scott's famous romance, "Waverley," and Scott's reference, like my own, had to do with the strenuous years of civil war.

To one examining the unique series of photographs which were secured, during the campaigns of our great war, by the pluck and persistence of Brady and Gardner, and the negatives of which have, almost miraculously, been preserved through the vicissitudes of half a century, comes, however, the feeling that these battles and marchings were the events not of fifty years back, but of yesterday, if not, indeed, things of to-day. These vivid pictures bring past history into the present tense; the observer sees our citizen soldiers as they camped, as they marched, and as they fought, and comes to know how they lived and how they died. There are revealed to the eye through these lifelike photographs, as if through a vitascope, the successive scenes of the great life-and-death drama of the nation's struggle for existence, a struggle which was fought out through four eventful years, and in which were sacrificed of the best of manhood of the country, North and South, eight hundred thousand lives.

In September, 1862, I landed in New York from the Bremen steamer *Hansa,* which was then making its first transatlantic trip. I had left my German university for the purpose of enlisting in the Union army, and, with the belief that the

"CITIZEN SOLDIERS"—THE 93D NEW YORK.

This informal photograph of the Ninety-Third New York Infantry was taken in 1862 just before Antietam. In it we see the quality of the men who dropped the pursuits of civil life and flocked to form the armies of the North. Thus, in camp and on the battlefield the camera did its work and now takes us back over the four terrible years, showing us to the minutest detail how our men marched and lived and fought. The youth of the troops is strikingly evident in this picture as they stand assembled here with their arms hastily stacked for the ever-pleasurable experience of having their pictures taken.

war could hardly be prolonged for many further months, I had secured leave of absence from my university only for the college year. I have to-day a vivid recollection of the impression made upon the young student by the war atmosphere in which he found his home city. In coming up from the steamship pier, I found myself on Broadway near the office of the *Herald,* at that time at the corner of Ann Street. The bulletin board was surrounded by a crowd of anxious citizens, whose excitement was so tense that it expressed itself not in utterance but in silence. With some difficulty, I made my way near enough to the building to get a glimpse of the announcement on the board. The heading was, " A battle is now going on in Maryland; it is hoped that General McClellan will drive Lee's army back into the Potomac."

I recall to-day the curious impressiveness of the present tense, of the report of a battle that was actually " going on." To one who reads such an announcement, all things seem to be possible, and as I stood surrounded by men whose pulses were throbbing with the keenest of emotions, I felt with them as if we could almost hear the sound of the cannon on the Potomac. The contrast was the stronger to one coming from the quiet lecture-rooms of a distant university to the streets of a great city excited with twelve months of war, and with the ever-present doubt as to what the hours of each day might bring forth. The fight that was then " going on " is known in history as the battle of Antietam. History tells us that Lee's army was not pushed into the Potomac. There were two causes that prevented this result—George B. McClellan and Robert E. Lee. McClellan was a skilled engineer and he knew how to organize troops, but he never pushed an enemy's army before him with the energy of a man who meant to win and who had faith that he could win. It was his habit to feel that he had made a brilliant success when, having come into touch with the foe, he had succeeded in withdrawing his own army without undue loss; and it is fair to say that when the enemy

THE PRESIDENT INVESTIGATES

Lincoln at McClellan's Headquarters, October 1, 1862.—The serious, impassive features of the President give no hint of the thoughts that were coursing through his mind as his calm eyes gazed upon the General and his staff. He knew that "Little Mac," as the soldiers fondly termed him, was the idol of the army and had the staunch support of his officers. Lincoln also knew that he and McClellan differed radically as to the conduct of the war. Politics had crept into the Army of the Potomac, the politics which during the campaign of 1864 opposed McClellan to Lincoln as a candidate for the presidency. As he stood there before the General's tent the Commander-in-chief could have summarily removed McClellan, but in accordance with his patient policy of leaving the future event to justify his course, Lincoln merely inspected the camp, talked with McClellan and his officers, and pondered all he saw and heard in an effort to find some military reason for the strange failure of the splendid army to end the war by a decisive campaign.

was Robert E. Lee, such a successful withdrawal might almost be considered as a triumph.

A fresh and vivid impression of the scene of the bloody struggle at Antietam Creek is given in one of the photographs in this great war series. The plucky photographer has succeeded in securing, from the very edge of the battle-field, a view of the movements of the troops that are on the charge; and when, on the further edge of the fields, we actually see the smoke of the long lines of rifles by which that charge is to be repulsed, we feel as if the battle were again " going on " before our eyes, and we find ourselves again infused with mingled dread and expectation as to the result.

In looking at the photographs, the Union veteran recalls the fierce charge of Burnside's men for the possession of the bridge and the sturdy resistance made by the regiments of Longstreet. He will grieve with the Army of the Potomac and with the country at the untimely death of the old hero, General Mansfield; he will recall the graphic description given by the poet Holmes of the weary week's search through the battle-field and the environs for the " body " of his son, the young captain, who lived to become one of the scholarly members of the national Supreme Court; and he may share the disappointment not only of the army, but of the citizens back of the army, that, notwithstanding his advantages of position, McClellan should have permitted the Confederate army to withdraw without molestation, carrying with it its trains, its artillery, and even its captured prisoners.

Another photograph in the series, which is an example of special enterprise on the part of Mr. Brady, presents Lincoln and McClellan in consultation some time after this bloody and indecisive battle. The pose and the features of the two men are admirably characteristic. Two weeks have elapsed since Lee's withdrawal across the river, but the Army of the Potomac, while rested and fully resupplied, has been held by its young commander in an inexplicable inaction. Lincoln's per-

THE BATTLE FOG AT ANTIETAM

The sulphur smoke of the guns, covering the field like a sea mist, tells us to-day as clearly as it told the photographer on September 17, 1862, that a battle is in progress off to the right. It was indeed the bloodiest single day's action of the war, and there probably exists no finer picture of an actual engagement than this remarkable photograph. At the moment of exposure the firing must have been terrific. Down in the meadow are seen the caissons of the artillery; the guns are engaged less than a quarter of a mile away.

The battle-field of Antietam was the first that remained in complete possession of the Union troops since the disasters that began to overtake them after Fair Oaks in June. On Antietam were staked the Confederate hopes for the conquest of Maryland. The battle proved, however, to be the turning-point in establishing the sovereignty of the Union. Lincoln had awaited a Union victory to justify a proclamation of emancipation. This he issued September 22, 1862, almost before the sound of the mighty battle had died away.

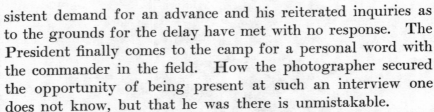

sistent demand for an advance and his reiterated inquiries as to the grounds for the delay have met with no response. The President finally comes to the camp for a personal word with the commander in the field. How the photographer secured the opportunity of being present at such an interview one does not know, but that he was there is unmistakable.

These vivid photographs which constitute the great historic series bring again into the present tense, for the memories of the veterans, all of the dramatic scenes of the years of war; and even to those who are not veterans, those who have grown up in years of peace and to whom the campaigns of half a century back are but historic pages or dim stories, even to them must come, in looking at these pictures of campaigns, these vivid episodes of life and death, a clearer realization than could be secured in any other way of what the four years' struggle meant for their fathers and their grandfathers.

The fine views of Fort Stevens and Fort Lincoln recall the several periods in which, to the continuing anxieties of the people's leader, was added immediate apprehension as to the safety of the national capital. On the 19th of April, 1861, the Massachusetts Sixth, on its way to the protection of Washington, had been attacked in Baltimore, and connections between Washington and the North were cut off. A few hundred troops represented all the forces that the nation had for the moment been able to place in position for the protection of the capital.

I have stood, as thousands of visitors have stood, in Lincoln's old study, the windows of which overlook the Potomac; and I have had recalled to mind the vision of his tall figure and sad face as he stood looking across the river where the picket lines of the Virginia troops could be traced by the smoke, and dreading from morning to morning the approach of these troops over the Long Bridge. There must have come to Lincoln during these anxious days the dread that he was to be the last President of the United States, and that the torch, representing the life of the nation, that had been transmitted

THE COMMANDER-IN-CHIEF

ere the gaunt figure of the Great Emancipator confronted General McClellan in his headquarters two weeks after Antietam had ecked Lee's invasion of Maryland and had enabled the President to issue the Emancipation Proclamation. Brady's camera has eserved this remarkable occasion, the last time that these two men met each other. "We spent some time on the battlefield and nversed fully on the state of affairs. He told me that he was satisfied with all that I had done, that he would stand by me. He rted from me with the utmost cordiality," said General McClellan. The plan to follow up the success of Antietam in the ort to bring the war to a speedy conclusion must have been the thought uppermost in the mind of the Commander-in-Chief of the my as he talked with his most popular General in the tent. A few days later came the order from Washington to "cross the Potomac d give battle to the enemy or drive him South." McClellan was relieved in the midst of a movement to carry out the order.

to him by the faltering hands of his predecessor was to expire while he was still responsible for the continuity of the flame.

And it was not only in 1861 that the capital was imperiled. The anxiety of the President (never for himself, but only for his country and his responsibilities) was to be renewed in June, 1863, when Lee was in Maryland, and in July, 1864, at the time of Early's raid. It was during Early's hurried attack that Lincoln, visiting Fort Stevens, came into direct sight of the fighting by which Early's men were finally repulsed. For the President, the war must indeed at this time have been something in the present tense, something which meant dread possibilities always impending.

The month of July, 1863, marked the turning point of the great contest. If the Federal lines had been broken at Gettysburg, Lee would have been able, in placing his army across the highways to Baltimore and to Philadelphia, to isolate Washington from the North. The Army of the Potomac would, of course, have been reconstituted, and Lee would finally have been driven across the Potomac as he was actually compelled to retire after the decision of the battle. But such a check to the efforts of the North, after two years of war for the maintenance of the nation, would in all probability have secured success for the efforts of the Confederate sympathizers in Europe and have brought about recognition and intervention on the part of France and of England. Such an intervention would have meant the triumph of the Confederacy and the breaking up of the great Republic. The value for the cause of the success of Meade in repelling, with heavy loss, the final assaults of Lee was further emphasized by a great triumph in the West. On the very day on which Lee's discomfited army was making its way back to the Potomac, the troops of General Grant were placing the Stars and Stripes over the well-defended works of Vicksburg.

A beautiful little picture recalls the sharp fight that was made, on July 2, 1863, for the possession of Little Round

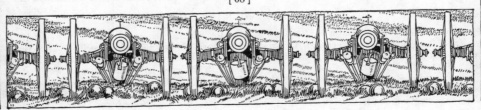

FORT RICHARDSON—DRILL AT THE BIG GUNS, 1862 *Copyright by Review of Reviews Co.*

OFFICERS OF THE FIFTY-FIFTH NEW YORK VOLUNTEERS

DEFENSES OF WASHINGTON—CAMP OF THE FIRST CONNECTICUT HEAVY ARTILLERY

Here we see some of the guardians of the city of Washington, which was threatened in the beginning of the war and subsequently on occasions when Lincoln, looking from the White House, could see in the distance the smoke from Confederate camp fires. Lincoln would not consent to the withdrawal of many of the garrisons about Washington to reinforce McClellan on the Peninsula. There was little to relieve the tedium of guard duty, and the men spent their time principally at drill and in keeping their arms and accouterments spick and span. The troops in the tents and barracks were always able to present a fine appearance on review. In sharp contrast was that of their battle-scarred comrades who passed before Lincoln when he visited the front. Foreign military attachés often visited the forts about Washington. In the center picture we see two of them inspecting a gun.

Top. It was the foresight of General Warren that recognized the essential importance of this position for the maintenance of the Union line. After the repulse of Sickles's Third Corps in the Peach Orchard, Longstreet's men were actually on their way to take possession of the rocky hill from which the left and rear of the Union line could have been enfiladed. No Union force was for the moment available for the defense, but Warren, with two or three aides, raised some flags over the rocks, and the leader of Longstreet's advance, getting an impression that the position was occupied, delayed a brief spell for reenforcements.

This momentary respite gave Warren time to bring to the defense of the hill troops from the nearest command that was available, a division of the Fifth Corps. A few minutes later, came the first attack, followed by a series of fierce onsets that continued through the long summer afternoon. With some advantages of position, and with the realization that the control of the hill was absolutely essential for the maintenance of the line, the Federals held their own; but when darkness fell, the rocks of Devil's Den and the slopes of the hill were thickly strewn with dead, the bodies of the Blue and the Gray lying closely intermingled. A beautiful statue of Warren now stands on Little Round Top at the point where, almost single-handed, he placed his flag when there were no guns behind it. The general is looking out gravely over the slope and toward the opposite crest, where have been placed, in grim contrast to the smiling fields of the quiet farm behind, the Confederate field-guns that mark the position of Longstreet's lines.

The editors have fortunately been able to include with the great Brady series of army photographs a private collection, probably unique, of more than four hundred views of the gunboats on the rivers of the West. Each of these vessels represents a history of its own. One wishes for the imagination of a Homer which could present with due effectiveness a new "catalogue of the ships."

LITTLE ROUND TOP—THE KEY TO GETTYSBURG.

A "slaughter pen" at Gettysburg. On this rocky slope of Little Round Top, Longstreet's men fought with the Federals in the second day's conflict, July 2, 1863. From boulder to boulder they wormed their way, to find behind each a soldier waiting for the hand-to-hand struggle which meant the death of one or the other. After the battle each rock and tree overshadowed a victim. The whole tangled and terrible field presented a far more appalling appearance than does the picture, which was taken after the wounded were removed. Little Round Top had been left unprotected by the advance of General Sickles' Third Corps. This break in the Federal line was discovered by General Warren just in time. Hastily procuring a flag, with but two or three other officers to help him he planted it on the hill, which led the Confederates to believe the position strongly occupied and delayed Longstreet's advance long enough for troops to be rushed forward to meet it. The picture tells all too plainly at what sacrifice the height was finally held.

Admiral Farragut, while accepting the armored vessels as possessing certain advantages and as apparently a necessity of " modern warfare," had the impatience of the old-fashioned sailor against any such attempt at protection. He preferred for himself the old type of wooden frigate of which his flag-ship, the famous *Hartford,* was the representative. " Why," said he, " if a shell strikes the side of the *Hartford* it goes clean through. Unless somebody happens to be directly in the path, there is no damage, excepting a couple of easily plugged holes. But when a shell makes its way into one of those ' damned tea-kettles,' it can't get out again. It sputters round inside doing all kinds of mischief." It must be borne in mind, apart from the natural exaggeration of such an utterance, that Farragut was speaking half a century ago, in the time of slow-velocity missiles. His phrase " damned tea-kettles " came, however, to be the general descriptive term for the ironclads, applied not only by the men in the ranks but by the naval men themselves.

There were assured advantages given by the armor in time of action against most of the fire that was possible with the weapons of the day, but for the midsummer climate of Louisiana, the " tea-kettles " were most abominable abiding places. During the day, the iron of the decks would get so hot that the hand could barely rest upon it. At night, sleep was impossible. The decks were kept wetted down, and the men lay on them, getting, toward the morning hours when the hulls had cooled down, such sleep as could be secured.

The progress of the armored transports making their way up the Red River under fire from the shore was an inter-esting feature of that campaign. The steepness of the banks on the Red River gave peculiar advantages for such fire, as it was frequently the case that the guns of the boats could not be elevated so as to reach the foe's position. It was difficult to protect the man at the wheel from such plunging fire, but bales of cotton were often placed around the upper

THE FATEFUL FIELD

No picture has ever been painted to equal this panorama of the very center of the ground over which surged the struggling troops 'mid shot and shell during the thickest of the fighting at Gettysburg. The camera was planted on Little Round Top, and through its eye we look northward over the valley toward and beyond the little town of Gettysburg. Across the plain in the middle distance, over the Federal breastworks near the crest, and up to the very muzzles of the guns on Cemetery Ridge which were belching forth grape and canister, swept the men in gray under General Pickett in the last brave but unsuccessful assault that left Meade in possession of the field on Independence Day, 1863. The daring gallantry, utter coolness, and grim determination with which that charge was made have rarely been paralleled in history. The spirit of complete devotion to the conviction which prompted Pickett and his men is one of the most precious heritages of a united nation.

works which were sufficient to keep off at least musketry fire. This improvised armor proved, however, not only insufficient but a peril when the enterprising Confederate gunners succeeded in discharging from their field-pieces red-hot shot. It happened more than once (I recall witnessing one such incident) that the cotton was brought into flames by such shot and it became necessary to run the vessel ashore.

A photograph in the series which presents a picturesque view of the famous Red River dam recalls some active spring days in Louisiana. The photograph gives an excellently accurate view of a portion of the dam, through the building of which Admiral Porter's river fleet of eleven " turtles " was brought safely over the rapids at Alexandria, and the army of General Banks, repulsed and disappointed but by no means demoralized, was able to make its way back to the Mississippi with a very much lessened opposition. Through a sudden fall of the river, the " turtles " had been held above the rapids at Alexandria. Without the aid of Porter's guns to protect the flank of the army retreating along the river road, it would have been necessary to overcome by frontal attacks a series of breastworks by which this road was blocked.

The energetic Confederate leader, General Taylor, had managed to cut off all connections with the Mississippi, and, while we were feeding in the town of Alexandria the women and children whose men folks were fighting us from outside, we had rations sufficient for only about three weeks. The problem was, within the time at our disposal and with the material available (in a country in which there was no stone), to increase the depth of water on the rapids by about twenty-two inches. The plan submitted by the clever engineer officer, Lieut.-Colonel Bailey, of the Fourth Wisconsin, was eagerly accepted by General Banks. Under Bailey's directions, five wing-dams were constructed, of which the shortest pair, with the widest aperture for the water, was up-stream, while the longest pair, with the narrowest passage for the water, was

WHERE REYNOLDS FELL AT GETTYSBURG.

At this spot Major-General John F. Reynolds met his death. During the first day's fighting this peaceful cornfield was trampled by the advancing Confederates. The cupola of the seminary on the ridge held at nightfall by Lee's forces is visible in the distance. The town of Gettysburg lies one mile beyond. General Reynolds' troops, advancing early in the day, had encountered the Confederates and had been compelled to fall back. Later, the Federal line by hard fighting had gained considerable advantage on the right. Impatient to retrieve the earlier retrograde movement at this point, General Reynolds again advanced his command, shoving back the enemy before it, and his line of skirmishers was thrown out to the cornfield in the picture. Riding out to it to reconnoiter, General Reynolds fell, pierced by a Confederate bullet, near the tree at the edge of the road.

placed at the point on the rapids where the increased depth was required. The water was thrown, as it were, into a funnel, and not only was the depth secured, but the rush downward helped to carry the vessels in safety across the rocks of the rapids. As I look at the photograph, I recall the fatiguing labor of "house-breaking," when the troops were put to work, in details on alternate days, in pulling down the sugar-mills and in breaking up the iron-work and the bricks.

On the further side of the river, a territory claimed by the sharpshooters of our opponents, men selected from the Western regiments, protected more or less by our skirmish line, are applying their axes to the shaping of the logs for the crates from which the dams were constructed. The wood-chopping is being done under a scattered but active fire, but while hastened somewhat in speed, it loses none of its precision.

I recall the tall form of the big six-footer, Colonel Bailey, leading the way into the water where the men had to work in the swift current at the adjustment of the crates, and calling out, "Come along, boys; it's only up to your waists."

As in duty bound, I marched after the colonel into the river, calling upon my command to follow; but the water which had not gone very much above the waist of the tall colonel, caught the small adjutant somewhere above the nostrils, with the result that he was taken down over the rapids. He came up, with no particular damage, in the pool beyond, but in reporting for the second time, wet but still ready for service, he took the liberty of saying to the Wisconsin six-footer, "Colonel, that was hardly fair for us little fellows."

After the hot work of tearing down the sugar-mills, the service in the cool water, although itself arduous enough, was refreshing. The dams were completed within the necessary time, and the vessels were brought safely through the rapids into the deep water below.

The saving of the fleet was one of the most dramatic incidents of the war, and the method of operation, as well as the

The army engineers laughed at this wide-browed, unassuming man when he suggested building a dam so as to release Admiral Porter's fleet imprisoned by low water above the Falls at Alexandria at the close of the futile Red River expedition in 1864. Bailey had been a lumberman in Wisconsin and had there gained the practical experience which taught him that the plan was feasible. He was Acting Chief Engineer of the Nineteenth Army Corps at this time, and obtained permission to go ahead and build his dam. In the undertaking he had the approval and earnest support of Admiral Porter, who refused to consider for a moment the abandonment of any of his vessels even though the Red River expedition had been ordered to return and General Banks was chafing at delay and sending messages to Porter that his troops must be got in motion at once.

COLONEL JOSEPH BAILEY IN 1864

THE MAN WHO SAVED THE FLEET

Bailey pushed on with his work and in eleven days he succeeded in so raising the water in the channel that all the Federal vessels were able to pass down below the Falls. "Words are inadequate," said Admiral Porter, in his report, "to express the admiration I feel for the ability of Lieut. Colonel Bailey. This is without doubt the best engineering feat ever performed. . . . The highest honors the Government can bestow on Colonel Bailey can never repay him for the service he has rendered the country." For this achievement Bailey was promoted to colonel, brevetted brigadier general, voted the thanks of Congress, and presented with a sword and a purse of $3,000 by the officers of Porter's fleet. He settled in Missouri after the war and was a formidable enemy of the "Bushwhackers" till he was shot by them on March 21, 1867. He was born at Salem, Ohio, April 28, 1827.

READY FOR HER BAPTISM

This powerful gunboat, the *Lafayette*, though accompanying Admiral Porter on the Red River expedition, was not one of those entrapped at Alexandria. Her heavy draft precluded her being taken above the Falls. Here we see her lying above Vicksburg in the spring of 1863. She and her sister ship, the *Choctaw*, were side-wheel steamers altered into casemate ironclads with rams. The *Lafayette* had the stronger armament, carrying two 11-inch Dahlgrens forward, four 9-inch guns in the broadside, and two 24-pound howitzers, with two 100-pound Parrott guns astern. She and the *Choctaw* were the most important acquisitions to Porter's fleet toward the end of 1862. The *Lafayette* was built and armed for heavy fighting. She got her first taste of it on the night of April 16, 1863, when Porter took part of his fleet past the Vicksburg batteries to support Grant's crossing of the river in an advance on Vicksburg from below. The *Lafayette*, with a barge and a transport lashed to her, held her course with difficulty through the tornado of shot and shell which poured from the Confederate batteries on the river front in Vicksburg as soon as the movement was discovered. The *Lafayette* stood up to this fiery christening and successfully ran the gantlet, as did all the other vessels save one transport. She was commanded during the Red River expedition by Lieutenant-Commander J. P. Foster.

THE BATTLE WITH THE RIVER

Colonel Bailey's wonderful dam—which, according to Admiral Porter, no private company would have completed within a year. Bailey's men did it in eleven days and saved a fleet of Union vessels worth $2,000,000. Never was there an instance where such difficulties were overcome so quickly and with so little preparation. The current of the Red River, rushing by at the rate of nine miles an hour, threatened to sweep away the work of the soldiers as fast as it was performed. The work was commenced by building out from the left bank of the river with large trees cross-tied with heavy timber and filled in with brush, brick, and stone. We see the men engaged upon this work at the right of the picture. Coal barges filled with brick and stone were sunk beyond this, while from the right bank cribs filled with stone were built out to meet the barges. In eight days Bailey's men, working like beavers under the broiling sun, up to their necks in water, had backed up the current sufficiently to release three vessels. The very next

THE MEN WHO CAPTURED THE CURRENT

morning two of the barges were swept away.   Admiral Porter, jumping on his horse, rode to the upper falls and ordered the *Lexington* to come down and attempt the passage of the dam.   The water was rapidly falling, and as the *Lexington,* having squeezed through the passage of the falls, approached the opening in the dam through which a torrent was pouring, a breathless silence seized the watchers on the shore.   In another instant she had plunged to safety, and a deafening cheer rose from thirty thousand throats.   Porter was afraid that Colonel Bailey would be too disheartened by the accident to the dam to renew work upon it.   The other three vessels were at once ordered to follow the *Lexington's* example, and came safely through.   But Bailey was undaunted and "his noble-hearted soldiers, seeing their labor swept away in a moment, cheerfully went to work to repair damages, being confident now that all the gunboats would be finally brought over."   Their hopes were realized when the last vessel passed to safety on May 12, 1864.

whole effect of the river scene, are admirably indicated in the cleverly taken photographs.

A view of Fort McAllister recalls a closing incident of Sherman's dramatic march from Atlanta to the sea. The veterans had for weeks been tramping, with an occasional interval of fighting, but with very little opportunity for what the boys called a square meal. By the time the advance had reached the line of the coast, the commissary wagons were practically empty. The soldiers had for days been dependent upon the scattered supplies that could be picked up by the foraging parties, and the foragers, working in a country that had been already exhausted by the demands of the retreating Confederates, gave hardly enough return, in the form of corn on the cob or an occasional razor-backed hog, to offset the "wear and tear of the shoe-leather."

The men in the division of General Hazen, which was the first command to reach the Savannah River, could see down the river the smoke of the Yankee gunboats and of the transports which were bringing from New York, under appointment made months back by General Sherman, the much-needed supplies. But between the boys and the food lay the grim earthworks of Fort McAllister. Before there could be any eating, it was necessary to do a little more fighting. The question came from the commander to General Hazen, "Can your boys take those works?" and the answer was in substance, "Ain't we jest obleeged to take them?"

The assault was made under the immediate inspection of General Sherman, who realized the importance of getting at once into connection with the fleet, and the general was properly appreciative of the energy with which the task was executed.

"See my Bummers," said Old Sherman with most illigant emotion. "Ain't their heads as horizontal as the bosom of the ocean?"

The raising of Old Glory over the fort was the signal for the steaming up-stream of the supply ships, and that evening

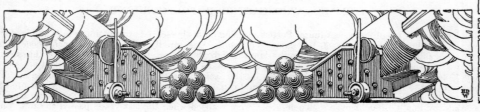

GRANT AND HIS STAFF—DURING THE FINAL CAMPAIGN

Just as the veterans in Blue and Gray were lining up for the final struggle—before Petersburg, June, 1864—this photograph was taken of the future victor, at his City Point headquarters, surrounded by his faithful staff. They are (from left to right, sitting) Colonel John A. Rawlins, Adjutant-General; Colonel C. B. Comstock, A. D. C.; Lieutenant-General U. S. Grant; Major M. M. Morgan, Chief Commissary; Colonel Ely S. Parker, Military Secretary; Colonel O. E. Babcock, A. D. C.; (standing) Captain Henry Janes, Quartermaster for Headquarters; Captain William S. Dunn, A. D. C.; Major Peter Hudson, A. D. C.

witnessed for the advance division a glorious banquet, with real beef and soft bread.

And even this climax was capped when, on the 22d of December, General Sherman was able to report to President Lincoln that he had secured for him, or for the nation, a Christmas present in the shape of the city of Savannah.

The preponderance of capable military leaders was an important factor in giving to the Southern armies the measure of success secured by these armies during the first two years; but even during this earlier period, military capacity developed also on the side of the North, and by the middle of the war the balance of leadership ability may be considered as fairly equal. It may frankly be admitted, however, that no commander of the North had placed upon him so stupendous a burden as that which was carried by Lee, as the commander of the Army of Northern Virginia, through the weary and bloody campaigns of three years. For the last year of that period, Lee was fighting with no forces in reserve and with constantly diminishing resources. With great engineering skill, with ingenuity in utilizing every possible natural advantage for defense, with initiative and enterprise in turning defense at most unexpected moments into attack, with a sublime patience and persistence and with the devotion and magnificent fighting capacity of the men behind him, Lee accomplished with his Army of Northern Virginia a larger task in proportion to the resources at his command than has, I believe, ever been accomplished in modern warfare. The higher we place the ability of the Southern commander and the fighting capacity of the men behind him, the larger, of course, becomes the task of the leaders and armies of the North through whose service the final campaigns were won and the cause of nationality was maintained.

In going to England in the years immediately succeeding the war, I used to meet with some sharp criticism from army men and from others interested in army operations, as to the time that had been taken by the men of the North to overcome

[82]

LEE—WITH HIS SON, G. W. C. LEE, AND COLONEL TAYLOR

No military leader in any country, not even excepting General Washington himself, ever became so universally beloved as Robert E. Lee throughout the South before the close of the war. Rising from the nominal position of Superintendent of Fortifications at Richmond, he became the military adviser of Jefferson Davis and finally the General-in-Chief of the Confederate forces. From the time that Lee began to drive back McClellan's forces from Richmond in the Seven Days' Battles the hopes of the Confederates were centered in their great general. So hastily arranged was that first and final meeting with Grant to discuss the terms of surrender that no photograph was obtained of it, but here are preserved for us the commanding figure, keen eyes, and marvelously moulded features of General Lee as he appeared immediately after that dramatic event. He has just arrived in Richmond from Appomattox, and is seated in the basement of his Franklin Street residence between his son, Major-General G. W. C. Lee, and his aide, Colonel Walter Taylor.

their opponents and to establish their control over the territory in rebellion. Such phrases would be used as: "You had twenty-two millions against nine millions. You must have been able to put two muskets into the field against every one of your opponents. It was absurd that you should have allowed yourselves to be successfully withstood for four years and that you should finally have crushed your plucky and skilful opponents only through the brute force of numbers." I recall the difference of judgment given after the British campaigns of South Africa as to the difficulties of an invading army.

The large armies that were opposed to the plucky and persistent Boers and the people at home came to have a better understanding of the nature and extent of the task of securing control over a wild and well-defended territory, the invaders of which were fighting many miles from their base and with lines of communication that were easily cut. By the constant cutting and harassing of the lines of communication, and a clever disposition of lightly equipped and active marching troops who were often able to crush in detail outlying or separated troops of the invaders, a force of some forty thousand Boers found it possible to keep two hundred thousand well-equipped British troops at bay for nearly two years. The Englishman now understands that when an army originally comprising a hundred thousand men has to come into action at a point some hundred of miles distant from its base, it is not a hundred thousand muskets that are available, but seventy thousand or sixty thousand. The other thousands have been used up on the march or have been left to guard the lines of communication. Without constantly renewed supplies an army is merely a helpless mass of men.

It is probable, in fact, that the history of modern warfare gives no example of so complex, extensive, and difficult a military undertaking as that which was finally brought to a successful close by the armies of the North, armies which were contending against some of the best fighting material and the ablest military leadership that the world has known.

THE SOUTH AND THE FEDERAL NAVY

THE SOUTH AND THE WAR RECORDS

With Many Photographs of '61–'65 Taken Inside the Confederate Lines

THE SOUTHERN FLAG FLOATING OVER SUMTER ON APRIL 16, 1861—SOUTH CAROLINA TROOPS DRILLING ON THE PARADE, TWO DAYS AFTER FORCING OUT ANDERSON AND HIS FEDERAL GARRISON—THE FLAG IS MOUNTED ON THE PARAPET TO THE RIGHT OF THE FORMER FLAGSTAFF, WHICH HAS BEEN SHATTERED IN THE COURSE OF THE BOMBARDMENT FROM CHARLESTON

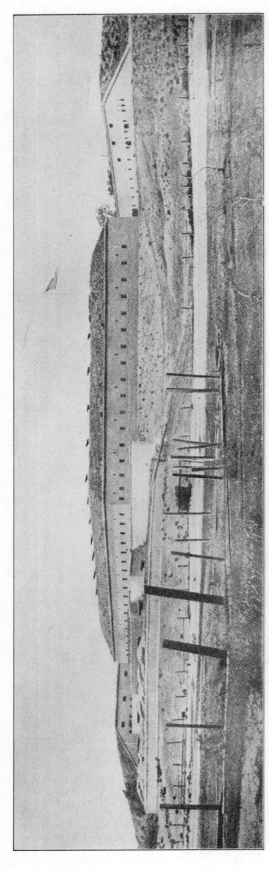

BEGINNING OF THE BLOCKADE, 1861—THE STARS AND BARS OVER BARRANCAS

INSIDE FORT BARRANCAS

In these hitherto unpublished Confederate photographs appear the first guns trained upon the Federal fleet at the beginning of the blockade. The fort lay about a mile west of the United States Navy Yard at Pensacola and commanded the inner channel to Pensacola Bay. When Florida seceded, January 10, 1861, about 550 Florida and Alabama State troops appeared before the barracks of Company G, 1st U. S. Artillery, 60 men. These retired into Fort Barrancas, after an attack upon that fort about midnight had been repelled. This was the first fighting of the war. Meanwhile Lieut. A. J. Slemmer, commander at Fort Pickens across the inlet, was removing the Barrancas garrison and their families. He succeeded in getting all safely across in a vessel to Fort Pickens, and the guns of Fort Barrancas bearing upon the channel were spiked. The Florida and Alabama troops occupied the fort on the 12th and began mounting twenty-five 32-pounders, which threatened Fort Pickens until the Confederates abandoned the works, May 9, 1862.

THE SPIRIT OF RESISTANCE

Here a Confederate camera has caught the spirit of the Southern soldiers at the outbreak of the war. These are Captain G. W. Dowson's Perote Guards manning the Perote Sand Batteries at Mobile, January, 1861. On the 11th of January, 1861, the ordinance of secession was passed by the Alabama convention at Montgomery. Its announcement was received with great excitement throughout the State. In Mobile the Cadets and the Independent Rifles marched to the public square and fired salvos of artillery. Alabama was early active in organizing volunteer militia and gave liberally of her sons to the Confederate cause throughout the war. On January 9th, at the request of the Governor of Florida, two days before Alabama seceded, two regiments of Alabama troops were sent to co-operate in the seizure of the navy yard and forts at Pensacola Bay

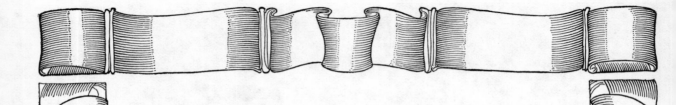

THE FEDERAL NAVY AND THE SOUTH

By French E. Chadwick,
Rear-Admiral, United States Navy

Who shall estimate the value to the United States of the services of its navy which thus isolated the Confederacy, cut it off from communication with the outside world, and at the same time compelled it to guard every point against a raid like that which had destroyed the Capitol of the United States in 1814? Had the Confederacy instead of the United States been able to exercise dominion over the sea; had it been able to keep open its means of communication with the countries of the Old World, to send its cotton abroad and to bring back the supplies of which it stood so much in need; had it been able to blockade Portland, Boston, Newport, New York, the mouth of the Delaware, and the entrance of Chesapeake Bay; had it possessed the sea power to prevent the United States from despatching by water into Virginia its armies and their supplies, it is not too much to say that such a reversal of conditions would have reversed the outcome of the Civil War.—*Hilary A. Herbert, Colonel 8th Alabama Volunteers, C.S.A., ex-Secretary of the Navy, in an address, "The Sea and Sea Power as a Factor in the History of the United States," delivered at the Naval War College, August 10, 1896.*

NOW that half a century has passed since the Civil War, we have come to a point where we can deal calmly with the philosophy of the great contest without too great disturbance of the feeling which came near to wrecking our nationality. The actualities of the struggle will be dealt with in the photographic history. Meanwhile it is not amiss in these pages to look into the causes of the South's failure to set up a nation and thus justify Gladstone's surety of Southern success in his Newcastle speech in 1862.

It has been, as a rule, taken for granted that the South was worsted in a fair fight in the field. This is so in a moderate

[88]

A BLOCKADE RUNNER, THE SWIFTEST CRAFT OF HER DAY

With the regularity of express trains, swift vessels like this one left Nassau and Bermuda and traveled direct for their destination, timed to arrive in the night. So great were the profits of blockade running that in some cases one successful voyage out and back would more than repay the owners for the loss of the vessel. Under these circumstances it can be easily seen that men were tempted to take risks that ordinarily they would avoid.

A CHARLESTON VOLUNTEER COMPANY AT DRILL UNDER THE WALLS OF CASTLE PINCKNEY

In pipe-clayed cross belts and white gloves, with all their accoutrements bright and shining, here we see a volunteer company of young Confederates standing at "Present Arms" and posing before the camera. The four officers standing in front of the line are Captain C. E. Chichester, Lieutenant E. John White, Lieutenant B. M. Walpole and Lieutenant R. C. Gilchrist. Gilchrist is curving his Damascus scimitar—a blade so finely tempered that its point would bend back to form a complete loop.

degree only; for the fight was not wholly a fair one. Difference of forces in the field may be set aside, as the fight being on the ground of the weaker, any disproportion in numbers was largely annulled. But the army of the North was lavishly equipped; there was no want of arms, food, raiment, ammunition, or medical care. Everything an army could have the Federal forces had to overflowing. On the other hand the Southern army was starved of all necessaries, not to speak of the luxuries which the abounding North poured forth for its men in the field. The South was in want of many of these necessaries even in the beginning of the war; toward the end it was in want of all. It was because of this want that it had to yield. General Joseph E. Johnston, writing General Beauregard in 1868, said truly: "We, without the means of purchasing supplies of any kind, or procuring or repairing arms, could continue this war only as robbers or guerillas." The Southern army finally melted away and gave up the fight because it had arrived at the limit of human endurance through the suffering which came of the absolute want brought by the blockade.

Some few historians have recognized and made clear this fact, notably General Charles Francis Adams, himself a valiant soldier of the war. Another is Mr. John Christopher Schwab, professor of political economy in Yale University. The former, analyzing six reasons for the South's failure, given by a British sympathizer in Blackwood's Magazine for July, 1866, says: "We are . . . through elimination brought down to one factor, the blockade, as the controlling condition of Union success. In other words that success was made possible by the undisputed naval and maritime superiority of the North. Cut off from the outer world and all exterior sources of supply, reduced to a state of inanition by the blockade, the Confederacy was pounded to death."[1] The "pounding"

[1] Charles Francis Adams, *Proceedings, Massachusetts Historical Society,* 1905, vol. xix, 224.

THE FIRST TASTE OF CAMP LIFE

This rare Confederate photograph preserves for us the amusements of the Alabama soldiers in camp near Mobile on a spring day in 1861. To the left we see a youth bending eagerly over the shoulder of the man who holds the much-prized newspaper in his hands. To the right a group of youngsters are reading letters from home, while in the background still others are playing the banjo and the violin to relieve the tedium of this inactive waiting for the glorious battles anticipated in imagination when they enlisted. These men are clad in the rough costume of home life, and can boast none of the bright new uniforms with shining brass buttons that made the Federal camps resplendent. Here and there a cap indicates an officer. Yet even these humble accessories were much better than the same troops could show later on, when the ruddy glow on their faces had given place to the sallowness of disease.

ON PARADE

Here a Confederate photographer has caught the Orleans Cadets, Company A, parading before their encampment at Big Bayou, near Pensacola, Florida, April 21, 1861. This was the first volunteer company mustered into service from the State of Louisiana. The Cadets had enlisted on April 11, 1861. Although their uniforms are not such as to make a brilliant display, it was with pride and confidence for the future that their commander, Captain (afterwards Lieut. Colonel) Charles D. Dreux, watched their maneuvers on this spring day, little dreaming that in less than three months he would fall in battle, the first but one among army officers to offer up his life for the Southern cause. The hopes now beating high in the hearts of both officers and men were all to be realized in deeds of bravery but only at further cost of human life here seen at its flood tide.

was mainly done by the army; the conditions which permitted it to be effectively done were mainly established by the navy.

"The blockade," says Mr. Schwab in his "Financial and Industrial History of the South during the Civil War," "constituted the most powerful tool at the command of the Federal Government in its efforts to subdue the South. The relentless and almost uniformly successful operations of the navy have been minimized in importance by the at times more brilliant achievements of the army; but we lean to ascribing to the navy the larger share in undermining the power of resistance on the part of the South. It was the blockade rather than the ravages of the army that sapped the industrial strength of the Confederacy."

The South was thus beaten by want; and not merely by force of arms. A nation of well on to 6,000,000 could never have been conquered on its own ground by even the great forces the North brought against it but for this failure of resources which made it impossible to bring its full fighting strength into the field.

We know that there was a total of 2,841,906 enlistments and reenlistments in the army and navy of the North, representing some 1,600,000 three-year enlistments; we shall, however, never know the actual forces of the South on account of the unfortunate destruction of the Southern records of enlistments and levies. That some 1,100,000 men were available is, of course, patent from the fact that the white population of the seceding states was 5,600,000, and to these were added 125,000 men, who, as sympathizers, joined the Southern army. The South fought as men have rarely fought. Its spirit was the equal of that of any race or time, and if the 325,000 Boers in South Africa could put 80,000 men into the field, the 5,600,-000 of the South would have furnished an equal proportion had there been arms, clothing, food, and the rest of the many accessories which, besides men, go to make an army. The situation which prevented an accomplishment of such results as

CONFEDERATES ENLISTING AT THE NATCHEZ COURTHOUSE, EARLY IN 1861

This rare Confederate photograph preserves a lively scene that was typical of the war preparations in the South in the spring of 1861. The fresh recruits are but scantily supplied with arms and accouterments, for only the Federal arsenals in the South could supply munitions of war. The military population of Mississippi at the opening of the war has been estimated at seventy thousand, and that of Louisiana at eighty thousand. It is believed that nearly a hundred thousand from each State enlisted in the Southern armies. The two scenes on this page were duplicated in hundreds of towns throughout the Southland as the war opened.

Copyright by Review of Reviews Co.

RECRUITING AT BATON ROUGE—1862

those in South Africa, and it was impossible in the circumstances that they could be, was the result of the blockade of the Southern coast, a force the South was powerless to resist.

What has been said shows how clear was the rôle of the navy. The strategic situation was of the simplest; to deprive the South of its intercourse with Europe and in addition to cut the Confederacy in twain through the control of the Mississippi. The latter, gained largely by the battles of Farragut, Porter, Foote, and Davis, was but a part of the great scheme of blockade, as it cut off the supply of food from Texas and the shipments of material which entered that State by way of Matamoras. The question of the military control of Texas could be left aside so long as its communications were cut, for in any case the State would finally have to yield with the rest of the Confederacy. The many thousand troops which would have been an invaluable reenforcement to the Southern armies in the East were to remain west of the Mississippi and were to have no influence in the future events.

The determination to attempt by force to reinstate the Federal authority over a vast territory, eight hundred miles from north to south and seventeen hundred from east to west, defended by such forces as mentioned, was truly a gigantic proposition, to be measured somewhat by the effort put forth by Great Britain to subdue the comparatively very small forces of the South African republic. It was as far from Washington to Atlanta (which may be considered as the heart of the Confederacy) as from London to Vienna. The frontier of the Confederacy, along which operations were to begin, was fifteen hundred miles in length. Within the Confederacy were railways which connected Chattanooga with Lynchburg in Virginia, on the east and with Memphis, on the Mississippi, on the west; two north and south lines ran, the one to New Orleans, the other to Mobile; Atlanta connected with Chattanooga; Mobile and Savannah were in touch with Richmond through the coast line which passed through Wilmington and Charleston. No

WAITING FOR THE SMELL OF POWDER—CONFEDERATES BEFORE SHILOH

Some very youthful Louisiana soldiers waiting for their first taste of battle, a few weeks before Shiloh. These are members of the Washington Artillery of New Orleans. We see them at Camp Louisiana proudly wearing their new boots and their uniforms as yet unfaded by the sun. Louisiana gave liberally of her sons, who distinguished themselves in the fighting throughout the West. The Fifth Company of the Washington Artillery took part in the closely contested Battle of Shiloh. The Confederates defeated Sherman's troops in the early morning, and by night were in possession of all the Federal camps save one. The Washington Artillery served their guns handsomely and helped materially in forcing the Federals back to the bank of the river. The timely arrival of Buell's army the next day at Pittsburg Landing enabled Grant to recover from the reverses suffered on that bloody "first day"—Sunday, April 6, 1862.

part of the South, east of the Mississippi, was very distant from railway transportation, which for a long period the South carried on excepting in that portion which ran from Lynchburg to Chattanooga through the eastern part of Tennessee, where the population was in the main sympathetic with the Union.

Thus the South had the great advantage, which it held for several years, of holding and operating on interior lines. Its communications were held intact, whereas those of the Federals, as in the case of Grant's advance by way of the Wilderness, were often in danger. It was not until Sherman made his great march to the sea across Georgia, a march which Colonel Henderson, the noted English writer on strategy, says " would have been impossible had not a Federal fleet been ready to receive him when he reached the Atlantic," that the South felt its communications hopelessly involved.

To say that at the outset there was any broad and well-considered strategic plan at Washington for army action, would be an error. There was no such thing as a general staff, no central organization to do the planning of campaigns, such as now exists. The commanders of Eastern and Western armies often went their own gait without any effective coordination. It was not until Grant practically came to supreme military command that complete coordination was possible.

Four Unionist objectives, however, were clear. The greatly disaffected border states which had not joined the Confederacy must be secured and the loyal parts of Virginia and Tennessee defended; the southern ports blockaded; the great river which divided the Confederacy into an east and west brought under Federal control, and the army which defended Richmond overcome. At the end of two years all but the last of these objectives had been secured, but it was nearly two years more before the gallant Army of Northern Virginia succumbed through the general misery wrought in the Confederacy by the sealing of its ports and the consequent inability of

OFFICERS OF MISSISSIPPI'S "FIGHTING NINTH."

n this long-lost Confederate photograph we see vividly the simple accoutrements which characterized many of the Southern regiments during the war. These men of Company B of the Ninth Mississippi enlisted as the Home Guards of Marshall County, and were mustered into the State service at Holly Springs, February 16, 1861. Their checked trousers and workday shirts are typical of the simple equipment each man furnished for himself. The boots worn by Colonel Barry, at the right, were good enough for the average Confederate soldier to go through fire to obtain later on in the war. Lacking in the regalia of warfare, the Ninth Mississippi made a glorious record for itself in Chalmers' Brigade at Shiloh, where it lost its gallant Colonel, William A. Rankin. "Never," said General Bragg, "were troops and commander more worthy of each other and their State."

the Southerners to hold their own against the ever increasing, well-fed and well-supplied forces of the North. To quote again the able Englishman just mentioned, "Judicious indeed was the policy which, at the very outset of the war, brought the tremendous pressure of the sea power to bear against the South, and had her statesmen possessed the knowledge of what that pressure meant, they must have realized that Abraham Lincoln was no ordinary foe. In forcing the Confederates to become the aggressors, and to fire on the national ensign, he had created a united North; in establishing a blockade of their coasts he brought into play a force which, like the mills of God, 'grinds slowly, but grinds exceedingly small.'" It was the command of the sea which finally told and made certain the success of the army and the reuniting of the States.

[To the discussion presented above by Admiral Chadwick may be added the following expression of opinion by one of the foremost military students of modern Europe: "The cooperation of the United States navy with their army in producing a decisive effect upon the whole character of the military operations is akin to what happens with us in nearly every war in which we engage. An English general has almost always to make his calculations strictly in accordance with what the navy can do for him. The operations by which the Federal navy, in conjunction with the army, split the Confederacy in two and severed the East from the West, must always, therefore, have for him a profound interest and importance. The great strategical results obtained by this concentration of military and naval power, which were as remarkable as the circumstances under which the successes were gained, deserve our closest study."—*Field-Marshal, the Right Honorable Viscount Wolseley.*—Editors.]

SUMTER BECOMES A FEDERAL TARGET

The eastern barracks inside Fort Sumter during the Bombardment of Sept. 8, 1863.—The guns of the Federal blockading fleet had now been pounding the fort for many weeks. This but recently re-discovered picture s the work of G. S. Cook, the Charleston photographer. The view is to the right of the exploding shell n the picture on page 100. The flag and guns shown in the earlier picture have been swept away. The pper casemate to the left has been demolished. The lower ones remained intact, however, and continued o be used and even armed to the end of the Confederate's defense. The guns here bore on the channel early opposite Fort Moultrie. The bake oven of the barracks—on the chimney of which are a couple of Confederate soldiers—was frequently used for heating solid shot. In one of the lower rooms of the barracks, seen to the right, the ruins later fell upon a detachment of sleeping soldiers.

THE EXPLODING SHELL

A wonderful war photograph preserved by the Daughters of the Confederacy of Charleston, S. C. The picture is fully described in Major John Johnson's authoritative work, "The Defense of Charleston Harbor," where a drawing based on the photograph was published. It is believed that the photograph itself has never been reproduced before its appearance here. All during August, Sumter was subjected to a constant bombardment from the Federal batteries. On September 7th, Admiral Dahlgren sent to demand the surrender of Sumter. Major Stephen Elliott replied: "Inform Admiral Dahlgren that he may have Fort Sumter when he can take and hold it." That night the Admiral sent a boat party. It was disastrously repulsed. The very same night, under cover of the darkness, George S. Cook, a Charleston photographer, was being rowed across to Fort Sumter and the next morning set up his camera. After securing what is probably the most daring photograph

the interior of the fort and luckily caught the one reproduced above. It is quite as successful a picture as could have been made by the instantaneous photographic apparatus of the present day. We see centrally in the parade the explosion of a shell, which has just been dropped over the gorge wall by the stranded monitor *Weehawken.* She, though dangerously exposed, took a vigorous part in the engagement.

NOTE.—The extraordinary conditions under which this photograph was taken made it desirable for the artist to retouch slightly. The photograph is printed here as Cook left it, notwithstanding the rule that none of the illustrations in the PHOTOGRAPHIC HISTORY may be retouched in any way. The retouching in thousands of scenes reproduced are from photographs taken direct from nature. The retouching in this one exception has in no way marred the historical accuracy, as will be seen by comparison with the illustrations on the opposite page and page 99, which are nearer views of the left and right of this picture. They also were taken by George S. Cook. The series forms a faithful and unique presen-

THE FIRST BREACH

Within the Walls of Sumter—September 8, 1863.—The parapet shows the terrific havoc wrought by the almost continuous bombardment by the Federal fleet and land batteries during August. It culminated on September 8th when photographer Cook secured this view, made under more favorable conditions than the one above and consequently much clearer. The breach is seen to the left in the opposite picture. It was probably first made by a shot from the battery on Morris Island, the fire from which passed centrally through the fort. According to an eye witness, "it indicated the focus of all the breaching guns as they were, from all positions on Morris Island, trained upon the mass of the fort." This breach was steadily widened during the day—September 8th. Expecting another boat attack that night, Major Elliott stationed Captain Miles and his company to defend this formidable breach. The attack came an hour after midnight and was handsomely repelled. Sumter, though almost demolished, could not yet be had for the asking.

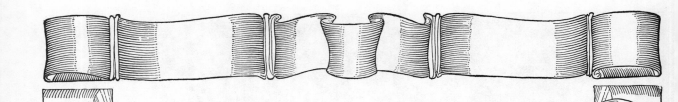

RECORDS OF THE WAR BETWEEN THE STATES

By Marcus J. Wright, Brigadier-General, C.S.A.
Agent of the United States War Department for the Collection of Military Records

THE war which was carried on in the United States in 1861–5, called "The War of the Rebellion," "The Civil War," "The War of Secession," and "The War Between the States," was one of the greatest conflicts of ancient or modern times. Official reports show that 2,865,028 men were mustered into the service of the United States. The report of Provost-Marshal General Fry shows that of these 61,362 were killed in battle, 34,773 died of wounds, 183,287 died of disease, 306 were accidentally killed, and 267 were executed by sentence. The Adjutant-General made a report February 7, 1869, showing the total number of deaths to be 303,504.

The Confederate forces are estimated from 600,000 to 1,000,000 men, and ever since the conclusion of the war there has been no little controversy as to the total number of troops involved. The losses in the Confederate army have never been officially reported, but the United States War Department, which has been assiduously engaged in the collection of all records of both armies, has many Confederate muster-rolls on which the casualties are recorded. The tabulation of these rolls shows that 52,954 Confederate soldiers were killed in action, 21,570 died of wounds, and 59,297 died of disease. This does not include the missing muster-rolls, so that to these figures a substantial percentage must be added. Differences in methods of reporting the strength of commands, the absence of adequate field-records and the destruction of those actually

SOUTH CAROLINA MEN IN BLUE, SPRING 1861

These officers of the Flying Artillery we see here entering the Confederate service at Sullivan's Island, Charleston Harbor, still wearing the blue uniforms of their volunteer organization. It was one of the state militia companies so extensively organized throughout the South previous to the war. South Carolina was particularly active in this line. After the secession of the State the Charleston papers were full of notices for various military companies to assemble for drill or for the distribution of arms and accoutrements. Number 2 of this group is Allen J. Green, then Captain of the Columbia Flying Artillery (later a Major in the Confederate service). No. 4 is W. K. Bachman, then a 4th Lieutenant, later Captain in the German Volunteers, a state infantry organization that finally entered the artillery service and achieved renown as Bachman's Battery. No. 3 is Wilmot D. de Saussure; No. 7 is John Waites, then Lieutenant and later Captain of another company. After 1863, when the Confederate resources were waning, the Confederate soldiers were not ashamed to wear the blue clothing brought in by the blockade runners.

TWO YEARS AFTERWARD

Confederate Uniforms at Gettysburg, July 1–3, 1863.—According to a Northern authority, Lee's veterans in 1863 were "the finest infantry on earth!" In this picture we see three of them taken prisoners at Gettysburg and caught by the camera of a Union photographer. These battle-stained Confederates had no glittering uniforms to wear; they marched and fought in any garb they were fortunate enough to secure and were glad to carry with them the blankets which would enable them to snatch some rest at night. Their shoes—perhaps taken in sheer necessity from the dead on the field—worn and dusty as we see them, were unquestionably the envy of many of their less fortunate comrades. Lee could only make his daring invasion of the North in 1863 by severing his connection with any base of supplies; and, unlike Sherman in his march to the sea, he had no friendly force waiting to receive him should he prove able to overcome the powerful army that opposed him. "Never," says Eggleston, "anywhere did soldiers give a better account of themselves. The memory of their heroism is the common heritage of all the people of the great Republic."

made are responsible for considerable lack of information as to the strength and losses of the Confederate army. Therefore, the matter is involved in considerable controversy and never will be settled satisfactorily; for there is no probability that further data on this subject will be forthcoming.

The immensity and extent of our great Civil War are shown by the fact that there were fought 2,261 battles and engagements, which took place in the following named States: In New York, 1; Pennsylvania, 9; Maryland, 30; District of Columbia, 1; West Virginia, 80; Virginia, 519; North Carolina, 85; South Carolina, 60; Georgia, 108; Florida, 32; Alabama, 78; Mississippi, 186; Louisiana, 118; Texas, 14; Arkansas, 167; Tennessee, 298; Kentucky, 138; Ohio, 3; Indiana, 4; Illinois, 1; Missouri, 244; Minnesota, 6; California, 6; Kansas, 7; Oregon, 4; Nevada, 2; Washington Territory, 1; Utah, 1; New Mexico, 19; Nebraska, 2; Colorado, 4; Indian Territory, 17; Dakota, 11; Arizona, 4; and Idaho, 1.

It soon became evident that the official record of the War of 1861–5 must be compiled for the purposes of Government administration, as well as in the interest of history, and this work was projected near the close of the first administration of President Lincoln. It has continued during the tenure of succeeding Presidents, under the direction of the Secretaries of War, from Edwin M. Stanton, under whom it began, to Secretary Elihu Root, under whose direction it was completed. Colonel Robert N. Scott, U.S.A., who was placed in charge of the work in 1874, prepared a methodical arrangement of the matter which was continued throughout. Officers of the United States army were detailed, and former officers of the Confederate army were also employed in the work. The chief civilian expert who continued with the work from its inception was Mr. Joseph W. Kirkley. The total number of volumes is 70; the total number of books, 128, many of the volumes containing several separate parts. The total cost of publication was $2,-858,514.67.

THE LAST TO LAY DOWN ARMS

Recovered from oblivion only after a long and patient search, this is believed to be the last Confederate war photograph taken.   On May 26, 1865, General E. Kirby Smith surrendered the troops in the Trans-Mississippi Department.   Paroled by that capitulation these officers gathered in Shreveport, Louisiana, early in June to commemorate by means of the camera their long connection with the war.   The oldest of them was but 40.   The clothes in which they fought were worn to tatters, but each has donned the dress coat of an unused uniform carefully saved in some chest in the belief that it was to identify him with a victorious cause and not as here with a lost one.   The names of those standing, from left to right, are: David French Boyd, Major of Engineers; D. C. Proctor, First Louisiana Engineers; unidentified; and William Freret.   The names of those seated are: Richard M. Venable; H. T. Douglas, Colonel of Engineers; and Octave Hopkins, First Louisiana Engineers.

In view of the distrust with which the South for a while naturally regarded the efforts made by the Government to procure the records of the Confederacy, the work of the department to obtain this material at first met with slight success.

In 1878, the writer, a Confederate officer, was appointed as agent of the War Department for the collection of Confederate archives. Through his efforts the attitude of the Southern people became more cordial, and increased records were the result. By provision of Congress, certain sets of the volumes were distributed, and others held for sale at cost.

The history of this official record is mentioned in these pages as it indicates a wide-spread national desire on the part of the people of the United States to have a full and impartial record of the great conflict, which must form, necessarily, the basis of all history concerned with this era. It is the record of the struggle as distinguished from personal recollections and reminiscences, and its fulness and impartial character have never been questioned. The large number of these volumes makes them unavailable for general reading, but in the preparation of " The Photographic History of the Civil War " the editors have not only consulted these official reports, but give the equally permanent testimony of the photographic negative. Therefore, as a successor to and complement of this Government publication, nothing could be more useful or interesting than " The Photographic History of the Civil War." The text does not aim at a statistical record, but is an impartial narrative supplementing the pictures. Nothing gives so clear a conception of a person or an event as a picture. The more intelligent people of the country, North and South, desire the truth put on record, and all bitter feeling eliminated. This work, it is believed, will add greatly to that end.

YOUNG ARTILLERISTS OF THE CONFEDERACY, 1863

This remarkable Confederate photograph instantly recalls Lincoln's oft-quoted saying that "war robbed both the cradle and the grave." Charleston was, throughout the war, active in providing for her own defense, and the women of the city constantly busied themselves in making flags and uniforms for the troops. This home company was much better equipped than the troops in the field at this stage of the war. The youth of some of the men here is noticeable. The standard-bearer is a mere boy— hardly sixteen. As early as April 16, 1862, the Confederate Congress conscripted all men over 18 and under 45 to serve during the war. The Charleston artillery, because Charleston was one of the principal ports for blockade runners, was well equipped with guns and ammunition. At many critical moments, as at Gettysburg, Confederate batteries in the field ran entirely out of ammunition, hence artillerymen stationed near the source of supply were most fortunate.

THE LAST EXCHANGE. CAMP FISK, FOUR MILE BRIDGE (VICKSBURG), APRIL, 1865

At the close of the war, Camp Fisk was established near Vicksburg for the general exchange of prisoners captured during the operations of the armies in the West. Here we see one of the daily meetings of the officers on both sides for this purpose. The Federal transport *Sultana* was busily engaged during the spring of 1865 in carrying the released Federal soldiers from Vicksburg to the North on their way to their homes. In the smaller picture we see her at Helena wharf loaded with the last shipment of paroled Union soldiers to the number of 2,134. The same day, April 27, 1865, she arrived at Memphis. While steering along some 90 miles above that point, her boilers suddenly exploded and she sunk almost immediately. During the war the levees on both sides of the river had been so demolished that all the bottom lands were inundated, and at this point were covered with water to a width of 50 miles. But few of the ill-fated Union soldiers managed to save their lives. About 1,900 of them perished. A survivor relates that while clinging to a log with three other men, one committed suicide rather than endure the agony caused by the icy water. At Memphis the Federal authorities gathered all the floating bodies they could. Many were found as far below the scene of the disaster as Helena.

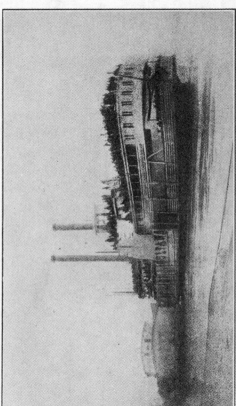

THE ILL-FATED *SULTANA*, HELENA, ARKANSAS, APRIL 27, 1865

THE STRATEGY
OF THE
WAR LEADERS

A CENTRAL STRATEGICAL POINT—THE APPROACH TO RICHMOND *VIA*
JAMES RIVER, AS IT LOOKED IN WAR-TIME, BLOCKED BY THE CONFEDERATE
RAM "VIRGINIA," AND GUNBOATS "PATRICK HENRY" AND "JAMESTOWN,"
SUNK IN THE CHANNEL TO HOLD THE FEDERAL FLEET FROM RICHMOND
(SEE TWO PAGES FOLLOWING FOR ANOTHER VIEW OF THIS SCENE)

OBSTRUCTIONS RENDERED USELESS

The superior navy of the Federals at the beginning and throughout the war enabled them to gain the advantage of penetrating the rivers leading into the interior of the Confederacy and thus support the military forces in many telling movements. To this fact the surrender of Forts Henry and Donelson and the ultimate control of the Mississippi by the Union forces gives eloquent testimony. In the East the regions between Washington and Richmond were traversed by streams, small and large, which made aggressive warfare difficult. For this reason McClellan chose the James River Peninsula for his first advance upon the Confederate Capital. Far more dreaded than the advance of the army was the approach of the powerful *Monitor* and the *Galena* up the James River, and the

JAMES RIVER, VIRGINIA, NEAR DREWRY'S BLUFF.—1862

first thought of the Confederates was to hold this danger in abeyance. Hence the obstructions (shown on the opposite page) sunk in the bend of the James River near Drewry's Bluff, where a powerful battery known as Fort Darling was hastily but effectively constructed. These blocked the attempts of the Federals to invest the Confederate capital until Grant's superior strategy in 1864 rendered them useless by throwing his army across the James in one of his famous flanking movements and advancing toward Richmond in a new direction. The campaign developing into a siege of Petersburg on the Appomattox, the Federal vessels confined their activities to the lower James.

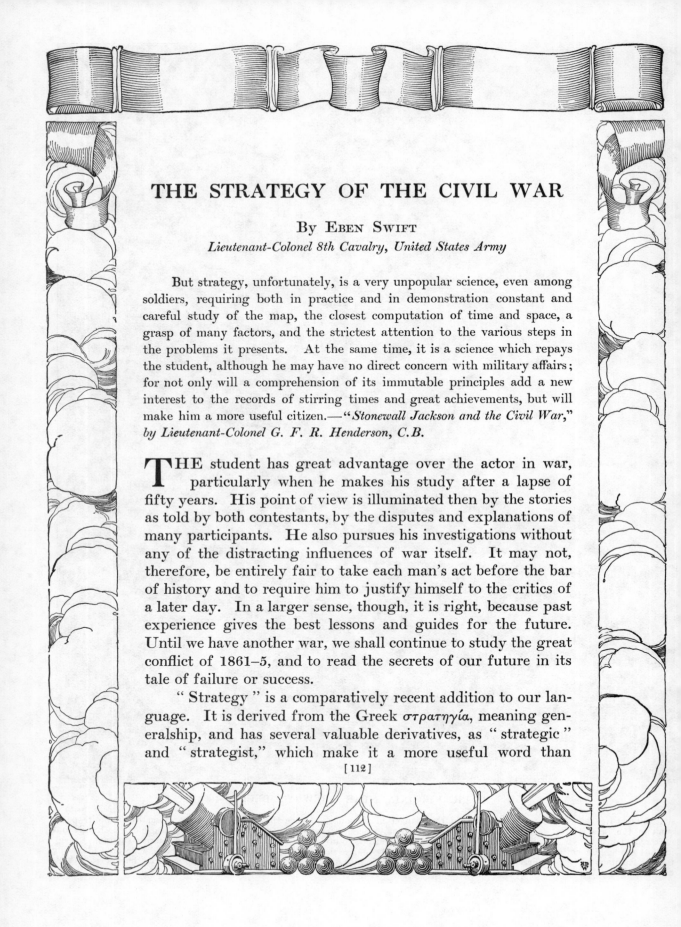

THE STRATEGY OF THE CIVIL WAR

By Eben Swift
Lieutenant-Colonel 8th Cavalry, United States Army

But strategy, unfortunately, is a very unpopular science, even among soldiers, requiring both in practice and in demonstration constant and careful study of the map, the closest computation of time and space, a grasp of many factors, and the strictest attention to the various steps in the problems it presents. At the same time, it is a science which repays the student, although he may have no direct concern with military affairs; for not only will a comprehension of its immutable principles add a new interest to the records of stirring times and great achievements, but will make him a more useful citizen.—*"Stonewall Jackson and the Civil War," by Lieutenant-Colonel G. F. R. Henderson, C.B.*

THE student has great advantage over the actor in war, particularly when he makes his study after a lapse of fifty years. His point of view is illuminated then by the stories as told by both contestants, by the disputes and explanations of many participants. He also pursues his investigations without any of the distracting influences of war itself. It may not, therefore, be entirely fair to take each man's act before the bar of history and to require him to justify himself to the critics of a later day. In a larger sense, though, it is right, because past experience gives the best lessons and guides for the future. Until we have another war, we shall continue to study the great conflict of 1861–5, and to read the secrets of our future in its tale of failure or success.

"Strategy" is a comparatively recent addition to our language. It is derived from the Greek στρατηγία, meaning generalship, and has several valuable derivatives, as "strategic" and "strategist," which make it a more useful word than

WAR STUDENTS OF TWO CONTINENTS

What an excellent example of open-air group portraiture—the work of Gardner's camera! But photography can add nothing to the fame of these men, gathered together in an idle hour to chat about the strategy of the war. Seated in the center is Count Zeppelin, of the Prussian Army, later the winner of honors with his airship and then on a visit to America to observe the Civil War. To his left is Lieutenant Rosencranz, a Swedish officer, on leave of absence, observing the war at close range as General McClellan's personal aide-de-camp. He successively served Burnside, Hooker and Meade in the same capacity. His brave and genial disposition made him a universal favorite. The other men are Americans, conspicuous actors as well as students in the struggle. On the ground, to the left, sits Major Ludlow, who commanded the colored brigade which, and under his direction, in the face of a continual bombardment, dug Dutch Gap Canal on the James. The man in the straw hat is Lieut. Colonel Dickinson, Assistant Adjutant General to Hooker, a position in which he served until the Battle of Gettysburg, where he was wounded. Standing is Captain Ulric Dahlgren, serving at the time on Meade's staff. Even the loss of a leg could not quell his indomitable spirit, and he subsequently sacrificed his life in an effort to release the Federal prisoners at Libby and Belle Isle.

generalship.   It means the art of the general and indicates the time, place, and way to fight battles.

The War of the States was viewed at first with indifference by foreign military men.   For many years past, however, it has claimed their close attention, because they have come to realize that new conditions were tested then, and that new influences, which changed the art of the general even from the respected models of Napoleon fifty years before, were at work. Ironclads, entrenchments, railroads, the breech-loader, a new kind of cavalry were the fresh factors in the problem.

Although hostilities at first began over an area half as large as Europe, the region of decisive operations was, on account of lack of communication, narrowed to the country between the Atlantic and the Mississippi, about seven hundred miles in an air-line.   The line was unequally divided by the towering barrier of the Alleghany Mountains, about two hundred miles wide, over which communication was difficult.   The eastern section of the country beyond the range was about one hundred miles wide and the western section was about four hundred miles wide.   In Maryland, northwestern Virginia, Kentucky, and Missouri sentiment was divided between the Union and the Confederacy.   The Mississippi River separated three of the seceding States from the remaining eight.

The immense amount of supplies needed for a great army caused military operations on a large scale to be confined to rail and water lines.   Of the former, both the North and South had several routes running east and west for lateral communication, and the South had several running north and south in each section, which could be used for lines of military operations.   In respect to water routes, the North soon demonstrated its complete control of the sea and was thus able to choose its points of attack, while interior water routes were available by the Mississippi, Tennessee, Cumberland, and James rivers.   The advantage of the water route over that by rail was at once utilized by the Northern generals.

A KING'S SON IN CAMP

In 1861 there arrived the first great opportunity to study warfare in the field since the campaigns of Napoleon, and these young men of royal blood expected at no distant day to be the leaders of a war of their own to recover the lost Bourbon throne of France. The three distinguished guests of the Army of the Potomac seated at the farther end of the camp dinner-table are, from right to left, the Prince de Joinville, son of King Louis Phillipe, and his two nephews, the Count de Paris and the Duc de Chartres, sons of the Duc d'Orleans. They came to Washington in September, 1861, eager to take some part in the great conflict for the sake of the experience it would give them. President Lincoln welcomed them, bestowed upon each the honorary rank of Captain, and assigned them to the staff of General McClellan. Officially merely guests at headquarters, they acted as aides-de-camp to McClellan, bearing despatches and the like, frequently under fire. They distinguished themselves at the battle of Gaines' Mill. The Prince de Joinville made a painting of that engagement which became widely published.

In the lower picture the Count de Paris and the Duc de Chartres are trying their skill at dominoes after dinner. Captain Leclerc, on the left, and Captain Mohain, on the right, are of their party. A Union officer has taken the place of the Prince de Joinville. It was to perfect their skill in a greater and grimmer game that these young men came to America. At Yorktown they could see the rehabilitated fortifications of Cornwallis, which men of their own blood had helped to seize, now amplified by the latest methods of defensive warfare. Exposed to the fire of the Napoleon field pieces imported by the Confederacy, they could compare their effectiveness with that of the huge rifled Dahlgrens, the invention of an American admiral. General McClellan testified that ever in the thick of things they performed their duties to his entire satisfaction. At the close of the Peninsula Campaign the royal party returned to France, but watched the war with great interest to its close.

LEARNING THE GAME

It was not so vulnerable to attack as the railroad. All navigable rivers within the area of operations were used for this purpose, and McClellan, Burnside, and Grant used the Chesapeake Bay and its tributaries to carry their base of supplies close to Richmond. The operations of the Confederates, on the other hand, were greatly restricted by being confined to railroad lines.

Several natural features which were certain to influence events to a great extent are to be noticed. In Virginia, numerous rivers, running parallel to the direct line of advance, form good lines for defense and also obstacles to an advance. Several mountain valleys leading north at the eastern ranges of the Alleghanies gave opportunities for leading large forces safely into Pennsylvania from Virginia, or vice versa. Within the mountain district, a railroad from Lynchburg, Virginia, to Chattanooga, in Tennessee, about four hundred miles long, gave an opportunity for transferring troops from one section to the other, while the corresponding distance at the North was three times as great. In the western section, the Tennessee and Cumberland rivers are separated at one place by a narrow neck about two miles wide, thus somewhat simplifying the problem of controlling these two important streams. The strategic chess-board, then, gave great opportunities to skilful generalship. The Virginia rivers gave strength to long defensive lines, screened marches from east to west, and forced the Northern generals to seek the flank rather than the front attack. The Shenandoah valley afforded a safe approach to Washington from the rear. This was availed of by Lee, Jackson, and Early to keep many thousand men of the army of the North in idleness. In the West, the long line defended by scattered troops was weak at every point and was quite easily broken by Grant, particularly when the South was slow in grasping the situation there. The advantage of the Richmond-Chattanooga railroad was not used by the Confederates until too late for success.

There is no mistaking the nationality of these Military Attachés with their tartans and Dundreary whiskers. They were accompanying the Army of the Potomac on its Peninsula Campaign. In the center of the group of Englishmen stands the Prince de Joinville. From the observations of these men both France and England were to learn many military lessons from a new conflict on the soil over which the soldiers of both nations had fought in a former generation. The armies of both North and South were being moved and maintained in the field in a manner and upon a scale undreamed of by Napoleon, to say nothing of Howe and Cornwallis. The Count de Paris wrote a very comprehensive and impartial history of the war, and in 1890 revisited America and gathered together some 200 or more surviving officers of the Army of the Potomac at a dinner in the old Hotel Plaza, New York City. Not half the veterans that were his guests more than two decades ago are still alive, and the Duc himself joined the majority in 1894.

WATCHING THE WAR

YORKTOWN EIGHTY YEARS AFTER

Here are some English and other foreign military officers with General Barry and some of his staff before Yorktown in May, 1862. European military opinion was at first indifferent to the importance of the conflict as a school of war. The more progressive, nevertheless, realized that much was to be learned from it. The railroad and the telegraph were two untried elements in strategy. The ironclad gunboat and ram introduced serious complications in naval warfare. At first the influence of Napoleon I was manifest in the field, but as the struggle proceeded both armies developed distinctly new ideas of their own. The sight of Sherman maintaining railroad and telegraphic communications with a base 138 miles away was a new one to the world, while his cutting loose from any base whatever in his March to the Sea was only less remarkable than Lee's invasion of Pennsylvania under similar conditions, to which was added a superior opposing force. In these and many other examples the war set the pace for later development.

The strategy, on account of political and other influences, was not always chosen according to the best military principles. Such influences always exist, and it is the duty of the soldier to conform and to make his plan to suit as best he can.

Under the head of policy would come Lee's several invasions of the North, undertaken with insufficient forces and too far from his base of supplies. Numerous causes have been given for these campaigns, the most plausible of which were of a political and not of a strategic nature. It was thought that a victory won on Northern soil might lead to intervention on the part of foreign nations, or that it would increase the disaffected element in the North to such an extent that the South could dictate a peace.

The policy of making military operations conform to the desire to help Northern sympathizers in eastern Tennessee had a powerful influence on the entire war. In the spring of 1862, it would have taken Buell into eastern Tennessee, instead of to the assistance of Grant and would have changed the course of events in the Mississippi valley. Three months later, it was one of the potent influences that led to the breaking up of Halleck's army at Corinth. It finally caused Buell's relief from command because of his disapproval. It caused Burnside's army to be absent from the battle of Chickamauga.

In 1864, the campaigns of Price in Missouri and Hood in Tennessee are said to have been intended to affect the presidential election at the North by giving encouragement to the party which was claiming that the war was a Federal failure. If that was not the case might not Hood have done better by marching in the track of Longstreet through Knoxville, Tennessee, and Lynchburg, Virginia, to join Lee, while Sherman was marching to the sea, entirely out of reach?

An unreasonable importance, from a military point of view, was given to the capital of each government. The capital of the United States had been captured in two wars without producing more than local effect, but every plan in

SCENE OF A PECULIAR MILITARY SITUATION

A remarkable panoramic view of a scene on James River taken in 1865, fifteen miles from Richmond. Farrar's Island is a point of land enclosed by an almost complete loop of the winding James. It is fifteen miles on a direct line from the former Confederate Capital, and by water, owing to the bends of the stream, some seven or eight miles more. When General Butler's Federal army had retreated from its futile attack on Drewry's Bluff, in May, 1864, to its strong entrenchments at Bermuda Hundred, southward, the military authorities, were in great fear that the Confederate flotilla and the ironclad ram *Virginia No. 2* that was just being completed at Richmond would come down the stream, divide the army and separate it from its base. Much against the advice of many of the naval officers who commanded vessels of the Federal flotilla, obstructions were built across the channel almost from shore to shore at Trent's Reach, a broad stretch of water south of Farrar's Island. Further to strengthen the position, four strong Federal batteries were constructed on the river bank, batteries Wilcox, Parsons, Spofford and Sawyer. Only a mile and a half away to the west was the powerful Confederate Battery "Dantzler," known as "Howlett's" to the Federal forces; from thence could be seen Forts Spofford and Sawyer. A peculiar situation was developed here. The Union obstructions and batteries were intended to prevent the Confederate fleet from coming down, and the Confederate engineers had placed mines and torpedoes in Trent's Reach to hinder the Federal fleet from coming up. The various strong forts along the river were for the same purpose, and at Chaffin's Bluff, less than three miles above Dutch Gap, the neck of Farrar's Island, the Confederate flotilla had penned itself in with obstructions quite as formidable as those below. Grant's later operations farther up the James and before Petersburg rendered much of the Federal work unnecessary.

Virginia was contingent upon the safety of Washington, thus causing the diversion of many thousand soldiers for that single duty. On the Southern side the correct military decision would have been to abandon Richmond as soon as Petersburg was invested, but the Government delayed, for political reasons, until it was too late, and the defending army surrendered as a consequence.

In the distribution of troops the Federal authorities were hampered by the rival claims of the border States, which thought they required protection. Hence, Ohio sent an army into West Virginia; Pennsylvania, into the Shenandoah valley; the national Government concentrated troops for the protection of its capital; the Western States gathered along the Ohio River and in Missouri. This great dispersion existed on both sides and continued more or less till the end of the war. The advantage it gave was in the protection of the friendly portion of the population and in the good recruiting ground thus secured. The great difficulty of holding troops in service, whose home country had been overrun, was appreciated by both sides and exercised a strong influence on the plans of the generals. These conditions dictated much of the strategy which is subject to criticism, and should not be forgotten.

The policy of furloughing great numbers of soldiers during the war, as an inducement to reenlist, was probably unavoidable, but it helped to cause inactivity during many months and in the case of Sherman's Atlanta campaign it caused the absence of two of his divisions. Absenteeism is one of the inevitable consequences of a long war, with troops untrained in time of peace by modern methods. Lincoln complained of it and the generals seemed powerless to limit or prevent it. Probably the latter are entitled to most of the blame. It was not uncommon for a general to call for reenforcements at a time when large numbers of his troops were absent.

The armies were indeed long in getting over the

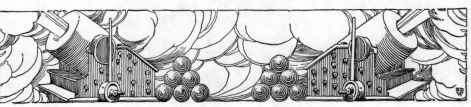

THE KEY TO WASHINGTON

From Chattanooga, Tennessee, to Harper's Ferry, Virginia, lay the Alleghany Mountains, an almost impassable barrier to the movement of armies. Here we see them sloping toward the gap at Harper's Ferry on the Potomac. The approach to this was made easy from the South by the Shenandoah Valley, the facile and favorite avenue of advance by the Confederates when threatening invasion of the enemy's territory. The scene is of the dismantled bridge across Armstrong Run. Driving General Banks' forces up the Valley and forcing him across the Potomac, Jackson saved Richmond from McClellan in 1862. Up the Valley came Lee the following year, striking terror to the North by the invasion that was only checked at Gettysburg. This eastern gap, provided by nature in the Alleghanies, became a veritable gateway of terror to the Federals, for through it lay open the path for sudden approach upon Washington on the part of the Confederates.

characteristics of raw troops, but the generals in their early movements do not appear much better than the troops. Every man who had been graduated from West Point was regarded as a "trained soldier," which was a mistake, because West Point was a preparatory school, and such men as had studied the art of high command had done so by themselves. The trade of the general was new to all, and had to be learned in the hard school of experience.

In four of the early campaigns in which the Federal troops were practically unopposed, they marched on an average of less than seven miles per day, while, in case of opposition by a greatly inferior force, the average was down to a mile a day, as in the Peninsula campaign and the advance on Corinth.

The plans for the early battles were complicated in the extreme, perhaps due to the study of Napoleon and his perfect army opposed by poor generals. Bull Run, Wilson's Creek, Seven Pines, Glendale, Malvern Hill, Shiloh, Gaines' Mill were of this kind, and failed. Even at Gettysburg, July 2, 1863, Lee's failure to execute his echelon attacks showed that his army was not yet ready to perform such a delicate refinement of war.

As an example of improvement, however, take Jackson's march of fourteen miles on a country road and the battle fought on May 2, 1863, all between daylight and dark of one day. In battles, also, we notice the fine play of early campaigns replaced by a savage directness and simplicity at a later period, in the Wilderness by Lee and at Spottsylvania by Grant. Thus it was that both leaders had ceased to count on the inefficiency of the enemy. At the beginning of the movement on Richmond both Lee and Grant seemed reckless in the risks they took. It was not so earlier.

The earliest form of strategy was the practice of ruse, stratagem, and surprise, but they have long been considered as clumsy expedients which are no longer effective against

RICHMOND IN RUINS, OCCUPIED BY THE FEDERALS

POLITICAL OBJECTIVES, WASHINGTON

In these two pictures appear the two capitals that were mistakenly made the goals of the military operations on both sides. The Confederates threatened Washington at the outset of the war, and realizing the effectiveness of such a move in giving moral rather than military support to their cause, similar movements were repeated throughout the war. For a like reason "On to Richmond" was the cry at the North until Grant took command and made the army of Lee and its ultimate reduction to an ineffective state his controlling purpose. With the investment of Petersburg by the Federals, Lee's proper military move would have been the abandonment of Richmond and the opposing of Grant along other lines.

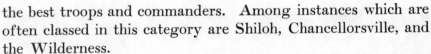

the best troops and commanders. Among instances which are often classed in this category are Shiloh, Chancellorsville, and the Wilderness.

Some forms of strategy have not changed in several thousand years. Sherman, for instance, crossed the Chattahoochee, which was held by Johnston, in 1864, in the same way that Alexander crossed the Hydaspes in the year 326 B. C., by feinting at one flank and crossing at the other.

The Vicksburg campaign gave great fame to General Grant and is really one of the most complete and decisive examples in history. In this campaign, he deliberately crossed the river north of Vicksburg, marched south and crossed again below Vicksburg. Then, relying on the country for supplies, he moved to Jackson, forty-five miles east of Vicksburg, where he interposed between the fractions of the Confederate army under Pemberton and Johnston. He then turned back again toward the Mississippi, drove Pemberton into Vicksburg, established a base of supplies at the North and invested the city. In this case, it is noticeable that the tendency to rate localities at too high a value is shown in Pemberton's retreating to Vicksburg, which was quite certain to be surrendered, instead of joining forces with Johnston to oppose Grant in the interior.

The same point is illustrated by the siege of Petersburg. As soon as Grant's army crossed the James and began this siege the fate of Richmond was sealed, for Grant had a great army and numerous means of extending his fortified lines until they crossed every avenue of approach to Richmond.

Moltke remarked that strategy was nothing more than common sense, but he acknowledged that it was often difficult to decide what was common sense and what was not. He might easily have had our Civil War in his mind. In 1861, the art of war had been greatly complicated by pedantic study, principally by officers of the French school, in attempting to reduce it to an exact science. The true lesson of Napoleon's

A DEFENDER OF THE FEDERAL CAPITAL

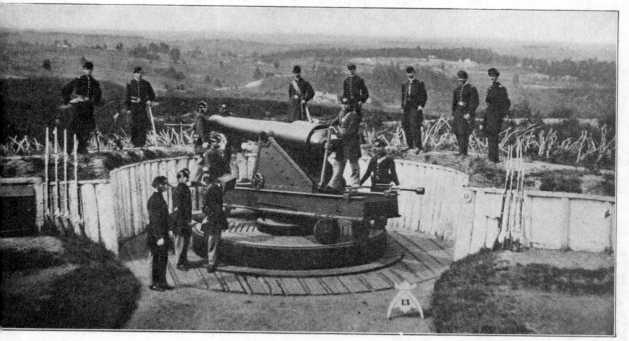

AN IDLE GARRISON

nly once were the elaborate fortifications about Washington seriously threatened. That was when the Confederate General Jubal
. Early, with a force of 10,000 men, marched against the Federal capital in July, 1864, with the intention of capturing it. Rein-
rcements were rushed to these works and Early retreated. The constant compliance with the clamor at the North that Washington
e strongly defended was a serious strategical mistake. The Army of the Potomac was at first superior in number to Lee's army
' Northern Virginia. It could have been made overwhelmingly so at the beginning of the war if the troops around Washington had
en added to it. Grant demonstrated the wisdom of this policy in 1864 by leaving only a few heavy artillery regiments, the "hun-
red days' men," and detachments from the Veteran Reserve to defend Washington. He then outnumbered Lee in the field.

campaigns had either been lost or the effect of new conditions had not been appreciated. It seems rather commonplace to say at this time that the first thing to do in war is to decide on your objective, but in the Civil War an incalculable amount of time was wasted, much treasure expended, and many lives were lost in a blind search for an objective. By objective is meant, of course, a point upon which to concentrate the greatest effort, the gaining of which will mean the success or failure of the cause.

In 1862, when the hostile armies opposed each other in front of Washington, McClellan insisted on attacking Richmond instead of Johnston's army. His plan resulted in the transfer of his army to the Peninsula and carried him to within six miles of Richmond with insignificant loss. For this, great credit has been claimed and unfavorable comment made on later campaigns. But McClellan found the undefeated Confederate army at Richmond, and he was weakened by a vast army which had been kept back to guard Washington. Without entering into this great controversy, we may simply say that to fight the foe as far from Richmond as possible would now be considered the correct solution of that problem. It is well known that Lincoln disapproved of McClellan's plan, whether by the counsel of wise military advisers or by his own common sense we know not.

Again, in 1862, when Halleck with much trouble and skill had collected a great army of one hundred thousand men at Corinth, the army was dispersed, contrary to his desire, it appears, and the true objective was lost. The Confederate leader repaired his losses and soon recovered from his serious defeats. At that time the army could have gone anywhere, whether to Vicksburg to open the Mississippi, or to Chattanooga and even to Richmond. This is the opinion of those best qualified to know. Burnside, also, in the fall of 1862, marched away from Lee's army when he went to Fredericksburg.

WHERE GRANT CROSSED THE JAMES.

When Grant at this point crossed the James and, ignoring the water approaches upon Richmond, proceeded to the investment of Petersburg, Lee was as good as checkmated. For months Grant's brilliant flanking movements had gained him no advantage over his opponent, who persistently remaining on the defensive shifted from one impregnable position to another till at last Grant saw that the railroads were the key to the situation. With Lee's forces entirely disposed for the defense of Richmond, it was but necessary to cut off the communications of the Confederate capital in order to force Lee to come forth and give battle. The investment of Petersburg, successfully prosecuted, would leave but one railroad in the hands of the Confederates. The crossing of the James near Wilcox Landing over the bridge, the remains of which appear in the picture, was the final strategic triumph by which Grant accomplished victory over Lee's army.

So deep-rooted is the idea of choosing a locality as the objective of a campaign instead of a hostile army, that Rosecrans' campaign, in the summer of 1863, has gone into history as the " Campaign for Chattanooga," and it has been claimed by his admirers that the possession of that place was worth what it cost—a heavy defeat at Chickamauga.

In 1864, Grant had authority to lay down a choice of objective, which he had already announced in 1862. For himself it was clearly Lee's army, and it was intended to be the same with other commands as well. General Sherman, however, was not so clear in his manner of execution as was his chief. His strategy creates a suspicion that it was designed to force Johnston to retreat and to relinquish territory. There was an idea that Johnston would not give up Dalton, which he had strongly fortified, but Sherman's heavy turning movement against his rear forced him to retreat without a battle. The same strategy continued until Atlanta was reached, and still Johnston's army was undefeated, while Sherman had weakened his army by guarding a long line of communication. Judging from this, we are disposed to suspect that Atlanta, rather than Johnston's army, was Sherman's main objective.

Later, the historic " March to the Sea " introduces a novel element into the question, for Sherman abandoned Hood's army as a first objective, and chose Lee's army instead. It will be remembered that Sherman had difficulty in getting consent from Grant, who wanted him to ruin Hood's army first. As it turned out, Sherman marched one thousand miles and was several hundred miles from Lee at the end of the campaign. If Lee's army had been his real objective there were other ways of reaching it: first, by sending his army by sea north from Savannah, as was suggested by Grant, which would have taken two months, say until the end of February, 1865; second, by sending the troops by rail, as Schofield was moved with fifteen thousand men and as Hooker was moved with twenty-three thousand men, and, third, by marching on

SHERMAN'S FAMOUS FEINT. RAILROAD BRIDGE OVER THE CHATTAHOOCHEE, 1863

In the foreground we see the formidable defenses behind which Johnston held the railroad bridge over the Chattahoochee against the advance of Sherman upon Atlanta. At this river Sherman exemplified again the strategy of Alexander at the Hydaspes. While Johnston with all his forces save cavalry was lying menacingly at the head of this bridge, Sherman, feinting strongly against his right with Stoneman's cavalry as if determined to gain a crossing, meanwhile quickly shifted the main body of his army to the left of Johnston's position, crossed the river on pontoons and immediately established a *tête du pont* of his own in Johnston's rear capable of withstanding his entire force. There was nothing for Johnston but to retreat upon Atlanta, burning the bridge behind him. In the picture is the bridge as rebuilt by Sherman's engineers, another link in his long line of communication by rail.

Lynchburg by the Knoxville road, which would have been about one-third to one-half the distance actually marched.

Looking upon the war with all the advantage of to-day, it is not difficult to assume that the hopes of both sides rested on two great armies, one in the East and one in the West, and the destruction of either meant the destruction of the other. This clear estimate seems to have come quite naturally and easily to only one man during the war, and that man was Grant. Such a conception clears away a mass of secondary objectives, such as so-called " strategic points " along the coast and west of the Mississippi, which consumed hundreds of thousands of troops and had only a minor effect on the final issue. It must be admitted that Grant used some seventy-five thousand men on secondary objectives which were not successful, in 1864, when these men would have had a great effect either with the armies of Sherman or himself. He probably thought that an army of one hundred and twenty thousand men was large enough for his purposes, but he found it was a mistake.

Equally fallacious with the importance given to " strategic points " was that ascribed to the occupation of territory. The control of Kentucky and Tennessee was given by Grant's Fort Donelson campaign, but the injury inflicted on the Confederate army by the large capture of men at Donelson and Island Number 10 was the real and vital result. The control of territory that was not accompanied by the defeat of the foe often had many disadvantages. Such was the experience of Grant and Sherman, the former in his first advance on Vicksburg, and the latter in the Atlanta campaign.

For the South it was an easier task to decide upon an objective because it was the weaker side and its acts were determined by those of the stronger. The main idea of the strategy of the Southern generals was to divert attention to side issues, to induce the opposing general to weaken his forces at decisive points. Numerous examples of diversions are afforded by Jackson's Valley campaign, in 1862, which kept many

WORK OF THE ENGINEERS AND THE CAVALRY

The great Civil War first introduced the railroad as a strategic factor in military operations. In the upper picture we see the Federal engineers at Vibbard Draw on Long Bridge at Washington busily at work rehabilitating a locomotive for use along the railroad connections of the capital with its army. Extemporized wooden structures of that time seem paltry in comparison with the great steel cranes and derricks which our modern wrecking trains have made familiar. The railroads in control of the North were much better equipped and guarded than those of the South, yet the bold Confederate Cavalry, under such leaders as Stuart, were ever ready for raids to cut communications. How thoroughly they did their work whenever they got the chance, the lower picture tells.

AFTER A RAID ON THE ORANGE AND ALEXANDRIA RAILROAD

thousand men away from McClellan; Early's march on Washington, and many cavalry raids.

The result of a study of objectives shows that, with good troops, and safe, but not brilliant, generals on both sides, the only way to overthrow the opponent is to attack and defeat his main army.

The long periods of inactivity in the several armies of the North seem to have been largely, but not always, due to the frequent change of commanders. The other causes would take long to analyze. Lee made six campaigns in fourteen months, from May, 1862, to July, 1863, a performance unequaled in history. But McClellan's army was inactive for ten months after Bull Run; Rosecrans' army for five months after Murfreesboro, and Grant's army for four months after Vicksburg, while Grant's army was almost in the same class during its ten months before Petersburg.

The concentration of scattered forces at decisive points, which is technically called in the text-book the use of interior lines, and in more homely phrase, "getting there first with the most men," was often skilfully performed on both a large and small scale. Thus, Johnston joined Beauregard at Bull Run in time to win the battle; Jackson alternately attacked the divided forces of his opponents and neutralized their greatly superior forces, and finally joined Lee for another campaign; Longstreet joined Bragg to win Chickamauga; Ewell joined Breckinridge to defeat Sigel. Many opportunities were lost, even in the very campaigns mentioned, as we see them to-day.

The conduct of pursuits confirms the idea that it is the most difficult operation presented to a general. Johnston after Bull Run, McClellan after Antietam, Meade after Gettysburg, Bragg after Chickamauga, Grant after Chattanooga, and Lee after Fredericksburg practically allowed the defeated enemy to escape without further injury. Lee's pursuit of McClellan in the Seven Days' Battles on the Peninsula and of Meade in

MILITARY COMMERCE

This view of the magazine wharf at City Point in 1864 reveals the immensity of the transportation problem that was solved by the North in support of its armies in the field. The Federal army in Virginia, unlike the armies of Napoleon, did not forage off the territory which it occupied. Rail and water transportation made possible the bringing of supplies long distances. Whatever point was chosen for the army base quickly became a bustling center, rivaling the activity of any great commercial city, and giving employment to thousands of men whose business it was to unload and forward the arriving stores and ammunition to the army in the field near by.

CITY POINT, VIRGINIA, JULY, 1864

When Grant finally settled down to the siege of Petersburg, and City Point became the army base, the little village was turned temporarily into a great town. Winter quarters were built in the form of comfortable cabins for the reserve troops and the garrison, and ample hospital buildings were provided. The railroad to Petersburg was controlled and operated by the army for the forwarding of troops and stores. The supply base longest occupied by the Army of the Potomac, City Point, grew up almost in a night. With the coming of peace the importance of the post vanished, and with it soon after the evidences of its aggrandizement.

the operations of October, 1863, had only partial success. Near the end of the war Thomas' pursuit of Hood, after Nashville, showed a much higher efficiency than had yet been reached, and the Appomattox campaign gives the only entirely successful instance in about one hundred years of military history.

The campaigns of Lee and Jackson were models of their kind. Napoleon has said that the general who makes no mistakes never goes to war. The critic of Lee finds it hard to detect mistakes. No general since Hannibal, and perhaps Napoleon, in the last two years of his campaigns, has made war under greater disadvantages and accomplished so much with an inferior force. While all great generals before him inherited a ready-made army, Lee, like Washington, made his own army. He fought soldiers of the same race and generals of the same school as himself. His genius was shown in many ways, but nowhere more than in his ability to calculate chances, even when he was violating the so-called rules of war. He used converging columns which met upon the field of battle; he detached inferior forces against the Federals' rear; he divided his army in the presence of the foe; he uncovered his lines of retreat and fought battles in that position; he did not hesitate to throw his last reserve into the fight.

On two occasions he withdrew his army across the Potomac River, in good order and without loss, in the presence of a powerful hostile army. His use of the ground to compensate for inferior numbers and to hide his movements from the Federals shows how clearly he saw the secrets of Napoleon's generalship, while his battles in the woods were entirely original and his use of entrenchments was effective. The power of the modern fire-arm in the hands of his opponents forced him to accept less decisive results than great soldiers who preceded him. As with other great soldiers, his best success was due to the inefficiency of his opponents in the early days. He was probably the last of the race of generals who, like Napoleon, dominated the field of war by genius alone. He

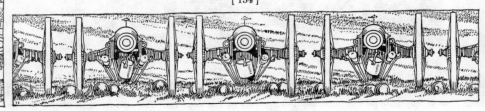

FORMIDABLE FIELDWORKS IN AN ADVANCE

NEW NECESSITIES OF WARFARE

The increased deadliness of firearms taught the commanders in the Civil War the habit of greatly strengthening every new position occupied with earthworks as formidable as possible. The works in the upper picture were thrown up in a night by the Federals near North Anna River, Virginia, in 1864. It is apparent how they would strengthen the resistance of a small force to larger numbers who might advance across the open upon the position. In the lower picture we see the salient of "Fort Hell," with its ditch and abattis and breastworks constructed of gabions, the result of many days' work of the soldiers in anticipation of attack. This was one of the fortifications about Petersburg, where the construction of fieldworks was developed to the highest point of efficiency.

The Strategy of 1861-65   ❖   ❖   ❖   ❖   ❖

The Strategy of 1861-65

will be replaced by the safe leader who is never brilliant, but makes no mistakes and at the same time commands the heaviest battalions.

The absence of a broad and comprehensive plan of operations was particularly noticeable on both sides. It never seemed to have been developed in the North until Grant issued his orders for a general advance, in 1864. In the South, Longstreet seems to have prepared a strategic plan for the movement of all Confederate armies after Chancellorsville, but this was not approved. The immense area occupied by the opposing forces, greater than had ever before been occupied in a single war, may be the excuse for this.

Great fame has come to the various generals who each made some well-planned maneuver, which forced the foe to relinquish territory and retreat to a rear position. McClellan before Manassas, Rosecrans before Shelbyville, and Sherman before Dalton did all this, but it is a debatable question whether the final issue was hastened or delayed.

Sherman gained Atlanta with a loss of thirty-two thousand men, and Rosecrans gained Chattanooga with a loss of eighteen thousand men, but the foe was not defeated. On the other hand, Grant, in his year from the Rapidan to Appomattox accomplished the desired result, but with severe losses, it is true.

After all is said, the subject may be narrowed down to the statement that Lee, Jackson, and perhaps Johnston handled inferior forces with as great skill as any commanders since Hannibal and Napoleon.

On the other side it was also an American soldier, even before Sedan and Mukden, who formulated the modern idea of strategy which has been so closely followed in recent wars— to seek out the foe, get close to him, and fight it out by short-arm jolts.

PART I

THE FIRST OF THE GREAT CAMPAIGNS

BULL RUN

(HERE BEGIN THE CHAPTERS THAT PICTURE BROADLY THE CAMPAIGNS, FROM BULL RUN TO APPOMATTOX, CONTINUING THROUGH VOLUME III—EACH OF THE REMAINING SEVEN VOLUMES IS DEVOTED THROUGHOUT TO A SEPARATE PHASE OF WAR-TIME ACTIVITY.)

VOLUNTEERS ABOUT TO FACE FIRE AT BULL RUN—
McCLELLAN'S TROOPS DRILLING NEAR WASHINGTON

THE TURNING POINT OF THE BATTLE

Across this little stream that was destined to mark the center of the first, and in many respects the most desperate, battle of the Civil War, we see what was left of the bridge after the day had ended in a Federal rout (see "Bull Run," page 142). On the farther side of Bull Run the Confederates under Beauregard had taken their stand with the stream as a contested barrier between them and McDowell's troops. At daylight of July 21, 1861, Tyler's division advanced to this bridge. It was a day of confusion on both sides. First, the Confederates were driven back in disorder by the impetuous onslaught of the Federals. These were congratulating them-

RUINS OF THE STONE BRIDGE—BULL RUN, VIRGINIA

selves upon a victory, when Johnston's reinforcements from Winchester fell upon the rear of their right, and threw the lines into confusion. Back across the field fled the first memorable Federal rout. The little bridge was soon groaning with the weight of the men struggling to get across it. Finally, in frantic haste, it was destroyed by the Federals to delay the dreaded pursuit. Here Federal engineers are rebuilding the bridge, in order to forward supplies to the army that is some thirty miles to the south in the wooded Virginia country, but dependent on communications with the base at Washington.

THE DEFENDER OF WASHINGTON—GENERAL IRVIN McDOWELL AND HIS STAFF

The man who planned the battle of Bull Run for the Northern Army was Brigadier-General Irvin McDowell, then in command of the forces before Washington. When assured that Patterson would hold Johnston in the Shenandoah, he undertook to advance with his raw and unorganized troops on Beauregard at Manassas. The plan for the battle which he adopted on the night of July 18th was, according to General Sherman, one of the best formed during the entire war. But it failed because, even before he began his attack, Johnston with a good part of his troops had already joined Beauregard at Manassas. After the defeat McDowell was placed in charge of the defenses of Washington on the Virginia side of the Potomac. This picture was taken the next year at General Robert E. Lee's former home in Arlington.

TROOPS THAT FOUGHT AT BULL RUN—A THREE MONTHS' COMPANY

When Lincoln issued his call for volunteers on the evacuation of Sumter, Rhode Island was one of the first to respond. We here see Company "D" of the First Regiment (organized April, 1861), as it looked during its encampment at Camp Sprague, Washington, from April 24th to July 16th, 1861. The care-free faces of the men lack all the gravity of veterans. In the famous first battle of the war, the regiment was in Burnside's Brigade of Hunter's Division, which marched some miles to the north, crossed Bull Run at Sudley Ford, met the Confederates north of Young's Branch, and drove them south across the stream to the Henry house plateau. Later it yielded to the panic which seized upon the Union army. On August 2, 1861, Company "D" closed its brief career in the conflict that was to fill four years with continuous combat.

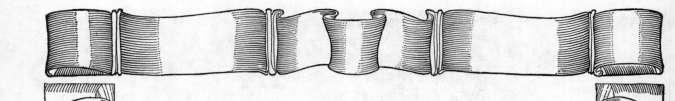

BULL RUN—THE VOLUNTEERS
FACE FIRE

THERE had been strife, a bloodless, political strife, for forty years between the two great sections of the American nation. No efforts to reconcile the estranged brethren of the same household had been successful. The ties that bound the great sections of the country had severed one by one; their contention had grown stronger through all these years, until at last there was nothing left but a final appeal to the arbitrament of the sword—then came the great war, the greatest civil war in the annals of mankind.

For the first time in the nation's history the newly-elected President had entered the capital city by night and in secret, in the fear of the assassin's plots. For the first time he had been inaugurated under a military guard. Then came the opening shots, and the ruined walls of the noble fort in Charleston harbor told the story of the beginnings of the fratricidal war. The fall of Sumter, on April 14, 1861, had aroused the North to the imminence of the crisis, revealing the danger that threatened the Union and calling forth a determination to preserve it. The same event had unified the South; four additional States cast their lot with the seven which had already seceded from the Union. Virginia, the Old Dominion, the first born of the sisterhood of States, swung into the secession column but three days after the fall of Sumter; the next day, April 18th, she seized the arsenal at Harper's Ferry and on the 20th the great navy-yard at Norfolk.

Two governments, each representing a different economic

[A complete record of leading events and the various engagements, giving the troops involved and casualties between January, 1861, and August, 1862, appears on page 346. —THE EDITORS.]

THE SOUTHERNER OF THE HOUR IN '61.

Born in New Orleans on May 28, 1818, the Southern leader upon whom at first all eyes were turned, Pierre Gustave Toutant Beauregard, was graduated from the U. S. Military Academy in 1838. Gallant and dashing, he won the brevets of Captain and Major in the war with Mexico and was wounded at Chapultepec. Early in '61 he resigned from the army, and joined the Confederacy, being in command of the Confederate forces in the firing on Fort Sumter in April. Owing to his forceful personality, he became a popular and noted leader in the Confederacy. After the Union defeat at Manassas, he was looked upon as the coming Napoleon. He was confirmed as Major-General in the Confederate army on July 30, 1861, but he had held the provisional rank of Brigadier-General since February 20th, before a shot was fired. After his promotion to Major-General, he commanded the Army of the Mississippi under General A. S. Johnston, whom he succeeded at Shiloh. He defended Charleston, S. C., in 1862–3 and afterward commanded the Department of North Carolina and Southeastern Virginia. He died at New Orleans in 1893.

and political idea, now stood where there had been but one—the North, with its powerful industrial organization and wealth; the South, with its rich agricultural empire. Both were calling upon the valor of their sons.

At the nation's capital all was confusion and disorder. The tramp of infantry and the galloping of horsemen through the streets could be heard day and night. Throughout the country anxiety and uncertainty reigned on all sides. Would the South return to its allegiance, would the Union be divided, or would there be war? The religious world called unto the heavens in earnest prayer for peace; but the rushing torrent of events swept on toward war, to dreadful internecine war.

The first call of the President for troops, for seventy-five thousand men, was answered with surprising alacrity. Citizens left their farms, their workshops, their counting rooms, and hurried to the nation's capital to take up arms in defense of the Union. A similar call by the Southern President was answered with equal eagerness. Each side believed itself in the right. Both were profoundly sincere and deeply in earnest. Both have won the respect of history.

After the fall of Fort Sumter, the two sides spent the spring months marshaling their forces for the fierce conflict that was to follow. President Lincoln had called for three-months' volunteers; at the beginning of July some thirty thousand of these men were encamped along the Potomac about the heights of Arlington. As the weeks passed, the great Northern public grew impatient at the inaction and demanded that Sumter be avenged, that a blow be struck for the Union.

The "call to arms" rang through the nation and aroused the people. No less earnest was the feeling of the South, and soon two formidable armies were arrayed against each other, only a hundred miles apart—at Washington and at Richmond.

The commander of the United States Army was Lieut.-General Winfield Scott, whose military career had begun before most of the men of '61 had been born. Aged and infirm,

YOUNG SOUTHERNERS AT RICHMOND MAKING LIGHT OF WAR

Skylarking before the lens of the Confederate photographer, we see the Boys in Gray just before Bull Run had taught them the meaning of a battle and elated them with the conviction of their own prowess. The young and confident troops on both sides approached this first severe lesson of the war in the same jocular spirit. There is not a serious face in the picture. The man flourishing the sword bayonet and the one with the drawn dagger are marking with mock heroics their bravado toward the coming struggle, while the one with the musket stands debonair as a comic-opera soldier. The pipe-clay cross belt and breast plate, the cock plumes in the "shapo" of the officer, indicate that the group is of a uniformed military organization already in existence at the beginning of the war. There was no such paraphernalia in the outfit of Southern troops organized later, when simplicity was the order of the day in camp.

he remained in Washington. The immediate command of the army was entrusted to Brigadier-General Irvin McDowell.

Another Union army, twenty thousand strong, lay at Martinsburg, Virginia, under the command of Major-General Patterson, who, like General Scott, was a veteran of the War of 1812 and of the Mexican War.

Opposite McDowell, at Manassas Junction, about thirty miles from Washington, lay a Confederate army under Brigadier-General Beauregard who, three months before, had won the homage of the South by reducing Fort Sumter. Opposed to Patterson in the Shenandoah valley was Joseph E. Johnston with a force of nine thousand men. The plans of the President and General Scott were to send McDowell against Beauregard, while Patterson was to detain Johnston in the Valley and prevent him from joining Beauregard. It was confidently believed that, if the two Confederate forces could be kept apart, the "Grand Army" could win a signal victory over the force at Manassas; and on July 16th, with waving banners and lively hopes of victory, amid the cheers of the multitude, it moved out from the banks of the Potomac toward the interior of Virginia. It was a motley crowd, dressed in the varied uniforms of the different State militias. The best disciplined troops were those of the regular army, represented by infantry, cavalry, and artillery. Even the navy was drawn upon and a battalion of marines was included in the Union forces. In addition to the regulars were volunteers from all the New England States, from New York and Pennsylvania and from Ohio, Michigan, and Minnesota, organizations which, in answer to the President's call for troops, had volunteered for three months' service. Many were boys in their teens with the fresh glow of youth on their cheeks, wholly ignorant of the exhilaration, the fear, the horrors of the battle-field. Onward through the Virginia plains and uplands they marched to the strains of martial music. Unused to the rigid discipline of war, many of the men would drop out of line to gather

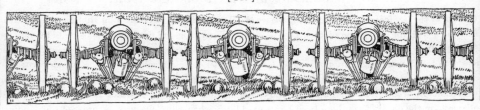

ONE OF THE FIRST UNION VOLUNTEER REGIMENTS.

The First Minnesota, a regiment that fought in the flanking column at Bull Run. On April 14, 1861, the day after Sumter's surrender, the Federal Government received an offer of a volunteer regiment from Minnesota, and on April 29, the First Minnesota was mustered into service by Lieutenant W. W. Sanders, U. S. A. Under Colonel William O. Gorman the regiment proceeded to Washington in June and, attached to Franklin's Brigade, Heintzelman's Division of McDowell's Army, at Bull Run gave an excellent account of itself, finally retiring from the field in good order. A record for conspicuous bravery was sustained by the First Minnesota throughout the war, notably its famous charge on the field of Gettysburg, July 2, 1863.

The photograph was taken just before the regiment left Fort Snelling in 1861. In the front line the first from the left is Lieut. Colonel Stephen Miller, the next is Colonel Gorman. On his left hand is Major Dyke and next to him is Adjutant W. B. Leach. Between the last two and behind them is Captain William Colvill, while at the left hand of Adjutant Leach is Captain Mark Downie. At the extreme right of the picture stands General J. B. Sanborn with Lieutenant Sanders (mustering officer) on his right hand, and on Sanders' right is the Honorable Morton S. Wilkinson. Colvill, as Colonel, led the regiment in its Gettysburg charge.

berries or tempting fruits along the roadside, or to refill their canteens at every fresh stream of water, and frequent halts were necessary to allow the stragglers to regain their lines.

After a two days' march, with "On to Richmond" as their battle-cry, the army halted at the quiet hamlet of Centreville, twenty-seven miles from Washington and seven miles from Manassas Junction where lay the waiting Confederate army of similar composition—untrained men and boys. Men from Virginia, from North and South Carolina, from the mountains of Tennessee, from Alabama, Mississippi, and Georgia, even from distant Arkansas, had gathered on the soil of the Old Dominion State to do battle for the Southern cause. Between the two armies flowed the stream of Bull Run, destined to give its name to the first great battle of the impending conflict. The opposing commanders, McDowell and Beauregard, had been long-time friends; twenty-three years before, they had been graduated in the same class at West Point.

Beauregard knew of the coming of the Federal army. The news had been conveyed to him by a young man, a former government clerk at Washington, whose sympathies, however, lay with the cause of the South. He won the confidence of Beauregard. The latter sent him to the capital city bearing a paper with two words in cipher, "Trust Bearer." With this he was to call at a certain house, present it to the lady within, and wait a reply. Traveling all night, he crossed the Potomac below Alexandria, and reached the city at dawn, when the newsboys were calling out in the empty streets the latest intelligence of the army. The messenger rang the doorbell at a house within a stone's throw of the White House and delivered the scrap of paper to the only one in the city to whom it was intelligible. She hurriedly gave the youth his breakfast, wrote in cipher the words, "Order issued for McDowell to march upon Manassas to-night," and giving him the scrap of paper, sent him on his way. That night the momentous bit of news was in the hands of General Beauregard. He instantly wired

EVE OF THE CONFLICT

Stone Church, Centreville, Virginia.—Past this little stone church on the night of July 20, 1861, and long into the morning of the twenty-first marched lines of hurrying troops. Their blue uniforms were new, their muskets bright and polished, and though some faces were pale their spirits were elated, for after their short training they were going to take part, for the first time, in the great game of war. It was the first move of the citizen soldier of the North toward actual conflict. Not one knew exactly what lay before him. The men were mostly from New England and the Middle States. They had left desk and shop and farm and forge, and with the thought in their minds that the war would last for three months the majority had been mustered in. Only the very wise and farseeing had prophesied the immensity of the struggle, and these were regarded as extremists. Their ideas were laughed at. So on they went in long lines down the road in the darkness of the night, chattering, laughing and talking carelessly, hardly realizing in the contagion of their patriotic ardor the grim meaning of real war. The battle had been well planned, but who had had the experience, even among the leaders, to be sure of the details and the absolute carrying out of orders? With the exception of the veterans of the Mexican War, who were regulars, there was not one who had ever maneuvered a thousand men in the field. A lesson lay before them and it was soon to come. The surprising battle that opened early in the morning, and whose results spread such consternation through the North, was really the result of popular clamor. The press and the politicians demanded action, and throughout the South the same confident and reckless spirit prevailed, the same urging to see something done.

President Davis at Richmond and asked that he be reenforced by Johnston's army.

As we have seen, General Scott had arranged that Patterson detain Johnston in the Valley. He had even advised McDowell that "if Johnston joins Beauregard he shall have Patterson on his heels." But the aged Patterson was unequal to the task before him. Believing false reports, he was convinced that Johnston had an army of thirty-five thousand men, and instead of marching upon Johnston at Winchester he led his army to Charlestown, twenty miles in the opposite direction. Johnston thereupon was free to join Beauregard at Manassas, and he promptly proceeded to do so.

McDowell's eager troops had rested at Centreville for two days. The time for them to test their mettle in a general engagement was at hand. Sunday, July 21st, was selected as the day on which to offer battle. At half-past two in the morning the sleeping men were roused for the coming conflict. Their dream of an easy victory had already received a rude shock, for on the day after their arrival a skirmish between two minor divisions of the opposing armies had resulted in the retreat of the Union forces after nineteen of their number lay dead upon the plain. The Confederates, too, had suffered and fifteen of their army were killed. But patriotic enthusiasm was too ardent to be quenched by such an incident, and eagerly, in the early dawn of the sultry July morning, they marched toward the banks of the stream on which they were to offer their lives in the cause of their country.

The army moved out in three divisions commanded by Generals Daniel Tyler, David Hunter, and S. P. Heintzelman. Among the subordinate officers was Ambrose E. Burnside, who, a year and five months later, was to figure in a far greater and far more disastrous battle, not many miles from this same spot; and William T. Sherman, who was to achieve a greater renown in the coming war.

On the Southern side we find equally striking characters.

PRELUDE TO THE COMBAT—BLACKBURN'S FORD

This crossing of Bull Run, was on July 18, 1861, the scene of a lively prelude to the first great combat. General Daniel Tyler, commanding a division of McDowell's army, pushed a reconnaissance to the north bank of the stream near this Ford. Confederates posted on the opposite bank fired upon Tyler's advance line, driving it back in disorder. Tyler then withdrew "satisfied that the enemy was in force" at this point. This picture was taken the next year, while Rickett's division of the McDowell Corps was encamped at Manassas.

A THREE MONTHS' REGIMENT—THE THIRD CONNECTICUT

The Third Connecticut was present on the field of Bull Run. The men had enlisted in April, 1861, and their time was all but up in July, for they were three months' men. Their drilling had taken place for a short time in their home State and afterward in the camps around Washington. They were mostly artisans and farmer boys with a sprinkling of mill hands and men of business from the larger towns. The regiment was attached to Tyler's division, of McDowell's army, and suffered little in the battle. The total losses, including deaths from sickness, in this regiment, which was mustered out at the end of its service, amounted to five all told. It goes without saying, however, that many re-enlisted and again went to the front, where they stayed until the conflict ended.

General Joseph E. Johnston was not held by Patterson in the Valley and with a portion of his army had reached Manassas on the afternoon of the 20th. In the Indian wars of Jackson's time Johnston had served his country; like McDowell and Beauregard, he had battled at the gates of Mexico; and like the latter he chose to cast his lot with the fortunes of the South. There, too, was Longstreet, who after the war was over, was to spend many years in the service of the country he was now seeking to divide. Most striking of all was "Stonewall" Jackson, whose brilliant military career was to astonish the world.

The Union plan for this fateful July day was that Tyler should lead his division westward by way of the Warrenton turnpike to a stone bridge that crossed Bull Run, about four miles from Centreville. At the same time the main army under Hunter and Heintzelman was to make a detour of several miles northward through a dense forest to a ford of Bull Run, known as Sudley's Ford. Here they were to cross the stream, march down its right bank and, while Tyler guarded the Stone Bridge, engage the foe on the west side of Bull Run. The plan of the battle was admirably drawn, but the march around to Sudley's Ford was slower than had been expected, and it was ten o'clock before the main army reached the point west of the Stone Bridge. While the Federals were making their plans to attack the Confederate left wing, Generals Beauregard and Johnston were planning an aggressive movement against the left wing of the Federal army. They were to cross Bull Run by fords several miles below the Stone Bridge and attack the Northern troops on the weaker wing of the Union force in an effort to rout them before relief could be sent from the Federal right. The Confederate attack was planned to take place a few hours later than McDowell had decided to move. The Southern troops were preparing to cross the stream when the boom of cannon at the Stone Bridge told that the Federals had taken the aggressive and that the

BULL RUN—BATTLEFIELD OF THE MORNING, JULY 21, 1861

Along Bull Run Creek on the morning of July 21st Tyler's division vigorously attacked from the east the Confederates under Longstreet and Beauregard on the western bank. By this attack McDowell hoped to succeed in falling unexpectedly on the rear of the Confederate left with the force sent on a detour of some three miles to the north. A charge of fresh troops brought forward by Beauregard in person in the late afternoon started the panic of the raw Union volunteers. . . . "Men who had fought courageously an hour before, had become as hares fleeing from pursuing hounds. The confusion was increased and multiplied by the presence among the fugitives of a multitude of panic-stricken picnickers, Congressmen, civilians of every sort, and lavishly dressed women—who had gone out in carriages and carryalls to see the spectacle of a Federal army walking over the Confederates. The Confederates fed fat for days afterward upon the provisions that the picnickers abandoned in their flight."

GENERAL BEAUREGARD'S HEADQUARTERS

The handsome old colonial mansion known as the McLean House was near Manassas station, not far from Blackburn's Ford, the scene of a sharp encounter preliminary to the battle of Bull Run. Tyler's division of McDowell's army, finding the Confederates had retreated from Centreville, attacked near here on the morning of July 18th. A vigorous cannonade opened the action, and a shell landing in the fireplace of the McLean house deprived General Beauregard of his dinner.

weak Confederate left was in danger of being overwhelmed by the superior numbers of the Union right wing. Orders countermanding the command to attack were quickly sent to the Southerners at the lower fords, and preparations were hurriedly made to repulse the attack of the Northern force.

Tyler reached the Stone Bridge before six in the morning and opened fire on a Confederate force under Colonel Evans on the other side of the run. For some time this was kept up, and Evans was much puzzled that the Federals did not attempt to cross the bridge; they merely kept up a desultory fire. The failure of the Union troops to advance led Evans to believe that Tyler's attack was only a feint and that the real attacking force would approach from some other direction. This belief was confirmed when he descried a lengthening line of dust above the tree-tops far in the distance, north of the Warrenton turnpike. Evans was now convinced (and he was right) that the main Union army was marching to Sudley's Ford, three miles above the Stone Bridge, and would reach the field from that direction. Quickly then he turned about with six companies of brave South Carolinians and a battalion of "Louisiana Tigers" and posted them on a plateau overlooking the valley of Young's Branch, a small tributary of Bull Run. Here, not far from the Matthews and Carter houses, he awaited the coming of the Federals.

His force was stationed overlooking the Sudley and Newmarket road and an open field through which the Federal troops would be forced to pass to reach the higher ground held by the Confederates. Two 6-pound howitzers were placed to sweep the field of approach, one at each end of Evans' line of defense.

With guns loaded, and howitzers ready to pour their charges into an advancing force, the Southerners stood and watched the line of dust that arose above the trees. It moved slowly to the westward. Then, where the Sudley road turns to the southward to cross the Sudley Ford, it followed the

WHERE A FEDERAL VICTORY SEEMED ASSURED

udley Church—July 21, 1861.—This Methodist Episcopal church stood a half mile south of the ford by which Hunter and Heintzelman crossed Bull Run. These troops crossed Cat Harpin Run, seen in the foreground, by the ford at the left, and marched southward
ast the church. A mile farther south Burnside's brigade engaged the Confederate troops led by Colonel Evans. As Evans' men fell
ack, Johnston deemed the situation "critical." The remains at the right of the picture are of the Sudley Sulphur Spring House.

THORNTON'S HOUSE—BULL RUN—JULY 21, 1861

his house, which stood some three miles north of the battlefield of the afternoon, marked the northern point of the detour of the
visions of Hunter and Heintzelman. The Confederate Colonel Evans, who held the extreme left of Beauregard's line, and whose
spicions had been aroused, marched upstream with half a brigade and confronted the turning column beyond the turnpike. Instead
deploying a line of battle, Hunter sent successive detached regiments and brigades against it. Evans, heavily reinforced, took up a
w position in the rear.

trend of the highway. It reached the crossing of Bull Run, and the line of dust faded as the Federals spread into battle-line behind the expanse of woodland that hid each column from the other's view.

It was nearing ten o'clock. The rays of the summer sun were beating in sweltering heat upon the waiting troops. Those who could find shelter beneath the trees moved from their places into the shade. Heavy banks of storm clouds were gathering on the horizon, giving promise of relief from oppressive warmth. A silence settled over the ranks of the Confederates as they watched the edge of the woodland for the first appearance of the approaching troops.

Suddenly there was a glimmer of the sunlight reflected from burnished steel among the trees. Then, in open battle array, the Federal advance guard, under the command of Colonel Burnside, emerged from the wood on a neighboring hill, and for the first time in the nation's history two hostile American armies faced each other in battle array. At Fort Sumter only the stone walls had suffered; not a drop of human blood was shed. But here was to be a gigantic conflict, and thousands of people believed that here on this field on this day would be decided the fate of the Union and the fate of the Confederacy. The whole country awaited in breathless expectancy the news of this initial conflict, to become known as the battle of Bull Run.

With little delay the battle opened. The Federals had a clear advantage in numbers as their outlying forces came up; but they met with a brave resistance. General Bee, of South Carolina, with two brigades, crossed a valley to the south of Evans in the face of a heavy artillery fire to a point within one hundred yards of the Federal lines. At this short range thousands of shots were fired and many brave men and boys were stretched upon the green. The outcome at this point was uncertain until the Union forces were joined by Heintzelman with heavy reenforcements and by Sherman with a portion of

HERE "STONEWALL" JACKSON WON HIS NAME

Robinson House, Bull Run.—"Stonewall" Jackson won his name near this house early in the afternoon of July 21st. Meeting General Bee's troops retreating in increasing disorder, he advanced with a battery to the ridge behind the Robinson House and held the position until Bee's troops had rallied in his rear. "Look at Jackson standing there like a stone wall," was the sentence that gave birth to his historic nickname. It was General Bee who uttered these words, just before he fell, adding, "Rally on the Virginians."

WHERE THE CONFEDERATES WAVERED

Center of Battle of Morning—July 21, 1861.—North of this house, about a mile, the Confederate Colonel Evans met the columns of Burnside and Porter in their advance south from Sudley Ford. Though reinforced by General Bee, he was driven back at noon to this house in the valley near Young's Branch. Here a vigorous Union charge swept the whole battle to the hill south of the stream. General Bee sent for reinforcements, saying that unless he could be supported "all was lost."

Tyler's division. Bee could now do nothing but withdraw, and in doing so his men fell into great disorder. Cheer after cheer arose from the ranks of the Union army.

Meanwhile, Generals Beauregard and Johnston had remained at the right of their line, near Manassas, nearly four miles from the scene of action, still determined to press their attack on the Federal left if the opportunity was offered. As the morning passed and the sounds of conflict became louder and extended further to the westward, it became evident to the Confederate leaders that the Federals were massing all their strength in an effort to crush the left of the Southern army. Plans for an aggressive movement were then abandoned, the commanders withdrawing all their reserve forces from the positions where they had been held to follow up the Confederate attack, and sending them to the support of the small force that was holding back the Federals. After dispatching troops to threaten the Union left, Johnston and Beauregard galloped at full speed to the scene of the battle. They arrived about noon—at the moment when Bee's brigade was fleeing across the valley from the hail of Federal bullets. As the frightened men were running in the utmost disorder, General Bee, seeing Thomas J. Jackson's brigade calmly waiting the onset, exclaimed to his men, "Look at Jackson; there he stands like a stone wall!" The expression spread to the army and to the world, and that invincible soldier has since been known as "Stonewall" Jackson.

Beauregard and Johnston found it a herculean task to rally the fleeing men and re-form the lines, but they succeeded at length; the battle was renewed, and from noon till nearly three o'clock it raged with greater fury than before. The fight was chiefly for the possession of the plateau called the Henry hill. Up and down the slopes the two armies surged in the broiling sun. Beauregard, like McDowell on the other side, led his men in the thickest of the fight. A bursting shell killed his horse under him and tore the heel from his boot; he mounted

THE STORM CENTER OF THE BATTLE, BULL RUN, JULY 21, 1861

Near where the ruins of this house (the Henry House) are shown, in the middle of the afternoon, the raw, undisciplined volunteers of both sides surged back and forward with the heroism and determined courage of rugged veterans until the arrival of fresh Confederate troops turned the tide, and in the crowning hour of Union victory precipitated the flight and contagious panic. The Union batteries commanded by Ricketts and Griffin had moved across Young's Branch and taken up a position on the Henry Hill. Confederate sharpshooters from bushes, fences and buildings picked off cannoneers and horses. Thirteen Confederate and eleven Federal guns engaged in a stubborn duel till the Confederate regiments swarmed from cover and captured the Union position. The City of Washington was now threatened.

another horse and continued the battle. At half-past two the Confederates had been entirely driven from the plateau, had been pressed back for a mile and a half, and for the second time within three or four hours the Union troops raised the shout of victory.

At three o'clock, while McDowell and his men were congratulating themselves on having won the battle, a faint cheering was heard from a Confederate army far across the hills. It grew louder and nearer, and presently the gray lines were seen marching gallantly back toward the scene of the battle from which they had been driven. The thrilling cry then passed through the Union ranks, "Johnston has come, Johnston has come!" and there was terror in the cry. They did not know that Johnston, with two-thirds of his army, had arrived the day before; but it was true that the remaining third, twenty-three hundred fresh troops, had reached Manassas at noon by rail, and after a forced march of three hours, under the command of Kirby Smith, had just united with the army of Beauregard. It was this that caused the cheering and determined Beauregard to make another attack on the Henry plateau.

The Union men had fought valiantly in this, their first battle, untrained and unused to warfare as they were; they had braved the hail of lead and of bursting shells; they had witnessed their comrades, their friends, and neighbors fall at their feet to rise no more. They nevertheless rejoiced in their success. But with the long march and the five hours' fighting in the scorching July sun they were weary to exhaustion, and when they saw the Confederates again approaching, reenforced with fresh troops, their courage failed and they began to retreat down the hill. With waving colors the Confederates pressed on, opening a volley of musketry on the retreating Federals, and following it with another and another.

In vain McDowell and his officers attempted to rally his panic-stricken men and re-form his lines. Only the regulars,

THE LOST CHANCE. CONFEDERATE FORTIFICATIONS AT MANASSAS.

Winter 1861–2. The Confederates did not follow up their success at Bull Run. "Having won the completest and most conspicuous victory of modern times, they set to work to fortify themselves for defence against the enemy they had so disastrously overthrown, precisely as if they had been beaten in the fight, and were called upon to defend themselves against aggression at the hands of an enemy to be feared." It was the lost chance—many military writers aver they could have swept on to Washington. The Federals fully expected them to do so and all was alarm and confusion within the city. The North never quite got over the haunting fear that the Confederate army would some day redeem that error and the defenses of the capital were made well nigh impregnable.

THE ROAD THAT CHANGED HANDS TWICE

The Orange & Alexandria R. R. Manassas Station. Part of the eastern defenses constructed by the Confederates after "Bull Run" during the winter of 1861-2. Confederate troops had been withdrawn in March, 1862, as the first move in the spring campaign. This view, taken in August, 1862, after the Union occupation of the abandoned works, looks down the road towards Union Mills Ford. At the close of Pope's disastrous campaign against Richmond the railroad again fell into the hands of Lee's army.

about sixteen hundred in number, were subject to the orders of their superiors, and they made a brave stand against the oncoming foe while they covered the retreat of the disorganized mass. On the Henry hill were the two powerful batteries of Griffin and Ricketts. They had done most valiant service while the tide of battle ebbed and flowed. But at last their hour had come. A Confederate regiment, dashing from a neighboring hill, poured in a deadly volley, cut down the cannoneers almost to a man, killed their horses, and captured the guns. A few minutes later General Beauregard rode up to the spot and noticed Captain Ricketts lying on the ground, desperately wounded. The two men had been friends in the years gone by. Beauregard, recognizing his old friend, asked him if he could be of any service. He then sent his own surgeons to care for the wounded captain and detailed one of his staff to make him comfortable when he was carried to Richmond as a prisoner of war.

There is little more to relate of the battle of Bull Run. In his report McDowell stated that after providing for the protection of the retreat from the battlefield by Porter's and Blenker's volunteer brigades, he took command in person of the force previously stationed for holding the road back to Centreville and made such disposition " as would best serve to check the enemy," at the Centreville ridge. Some hundreds of civilians, members of Congress and others, had come out from Washington to witness a victory for the Grand Army, and they saw that army scattered in wild flight to escape an imaginary pursuer. The Confederates made no serious effort to follow after them, for the routed Federals had destroyed the Stone Bridge as they passed it in their retreat, and had obstructed the other avenues of pursuit. As darkness settled over the field the Confederates returned to their camps.

McDowell made a desperate effort to check and reorganize his army at Centreville, but he was powerless. The troops refused to listen to any commands; they rushed on and

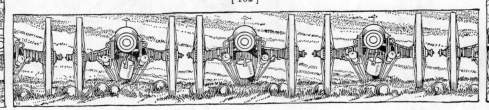

THE PRINCIPAL FORT AT CENTREVILLE, 1861-2

This almost circular fort was constructed in the village of Centreville, Va., by the Confederates during the winter of 1861-2. All about it on the North can be seen the quarters in which the Confederate troops wintered after their victory at Bull Run. This picture was taken in March, 1862, when the Federals had occupied the abandoned works. From Centreville McDowell sent a reconnaisance in force July 18, 1861, under General D. Tyler to feel for the Confederate position. A strong force under Longstreet was encountered at Blackburn's Ford and a spirited engagement followed. This was the prelude to the battle of July 21st.

THE DUMMY GUNS

Here is another well-built field work of the Confederates at Centreville, Va. We are looking north along the line of the earthworks east of the town and can see the abandoned Confederate winter quarters on the left. When the Confederates evacuated this line dummy guns of rough hewn logs were placed in position to deceive the Federals into the belief that the works were still occupied in force. Centreville did not fall into the hands of the Federals until the Peninsula Campaign caused its abandonment. In the lower picture we see the dummy guns in position, and in the upper two of them are lying on the ground.

great numbers of them traveled all night, reaching Washington in the morning.

These raw troops had now received their first baptism of blood and fire. Nearly five hundred of their number were left dead on the field of battle, and fourteen hundred were wounded. The captured and missing brought the Federal loss to nearly three thousand men. The Confederate loss in killed, wounded, and missing was less than two thousand. The Federal forces engaged were nearly nineteen thousand, while the Confederates had more than eighteen thousand men on the field.

The Confederate victory at Bull Run did the South great injury in that it led vast numbers to believe the war was over and that the South had won. Many soldiers went home in this belief, and for months thereafter it was not easy to recruit the Southern armies. The North, on the other hand, was taught a needed lesson—was awakened to a sense of the magnitude of the task before it.

The first great battle of the American Civil War brought joy to the Confederacy and grief to the States of the North. As the Federal troops marched into Washington through a drenching downpour of rain, on July 22d, the North was shrouded in gloom. But the defeated army had not lost its courage. The remnants of the shattered forces were gathered, and from the fragments a mightier host was to be rallied under the Stars and Stripes to meet the now victorious foe on future battle-grounds.

AFTER BULL RUN—GUARDING THE PRISONERS.

Inside Castle Pinckney, Charleston Harbor, August, 1861.—In these hitherto unpublished Confederate photographs we see one of the earliest volunteer military organizations of South Carolina and some of the first Federal prisoners taken in the war. The Charleston Zouave Cadets were organized in the summer of 1860, and were recruited from among the patriotic young men of Charleston. We see in the picture how very young they were. The company first went into active service on Morris Island, January 1, 1861, and was there on the 9th when the guns of the battery turned back the *Star of the West* arriving with reinforcements for Sumter. The company was also stationed on Sullivan's Island during the bombardment of Sumter, April 12–13, 1861. After the first fateful clash at Bull Run, July 21, 1861, had taught the North that the war was on in earnest, a number of Federal prisoners were brought to Charleston and placed for safe-keeping in Castle Pinckney, then garrisoned by the Charleston Zouave Cadets. To break the monotony of guard duty Captain Chichester, some time in August, engaged a photographer to take some pictures about the fort showing his men. Gray uniforms with red stripes, red fatigue caps, and white cross belts were a novelty. The casemates of the fort had been fitted up with bunks and doors as sleeping quarters

THE PRISONERS—11TH NEW YORK ZOUAVES

for the prisoners. Casemate No. 1 was occupied by prisoners from the 11th New York Zouaves, who had been recruited almost entirely from the New York Fire Department. The smaller picture is a nearer view of their quarters, over which they have placed the sign "Hotel de Zouave." We see them still wearing the uniform of the battlefield: wide dark-blue trousers with socks covering the bottoms, red flannel shirts with the silver badge of the New York Fire Department, blue jackets elaborately trimmed with braid, red fez caps with blue tassels, and a blue sash around the waist. Their regiment, the famous "Ellsworth's Zouaves," was posted at Bull Run as a support for Rickett's and Griffin's Batteries during the fierce fighting of the afternoon on the Henry House hill. They gave way before the charge of the Confederates, leaving 48 dead and 75 wounded on the field. About 65 of them were taken prisoners, some of whom we see here a month after the battle. The following October the prisoners were exchanged. At the beginning of the war the possession of prisoners did not mean as much to the South as it did later in the struggle, when exchanges became almost the last resource for recruiting the dwindling ranks. Almost every Southerner capable of bearing arms had already joined the colors.

WORK THROWN AWAY—CONFEDERATE ENTRENCHMENTS AT CENTREVILLE

A big gun of the kind now mounted in any of the coast defenses of the United States could have dropped a shot from these entrenchments within a short distance of the heart of Washington. Yet here the Southern army remained after the battle of Bull Run. It is a moot question whether Johnston's victorious troops could ever have reached the Federal capital. Judging from the awful panic into which the city and its defenders had been thrown, the disorganization of army divisions, brigades and regiments due to defeat, perhaps a vigorous Confederate advance might have succeeded. At all events there is no gainsaying that the Confederate batteries could have reached the Virginia shores of the Potomac

given to either side the very men themselves would have gone forward. Nothing could have stopped them. But the Confederates, like their opponents, had it all to learn. So, content with what they had done, they constructed elaborate defenses around Manassas, then rested. Meanwhile Washington became one huge fortress and the city was surrounded on all sides by fortifications and soldiers at drill. Ceaseless and untiring were the preparations. There is no doubt that in the lull that followed before the opening of the Peninsula Campaign the Federal cause gained momentum. When all was ready and the time ripe for a forward movement the Confederate works at Centreville and Manassas were abandoned. Here we see some Union soldiers viewing the deserted forts.

A SCHOOL FOR SOLDIERS, McCLELLAN'S ARDUOUS TASK

Five days after the disastrous battle of Bull Run, on July 26, 1861, Major-General George B. McClellan was called from his successes in West Virginia to take charge of the raw dispirited troops huddled near Washington. All during the fall and the winter he applied himself to the herculean task of forging the broken regiments and new levies into the powerful weapon that became famous as the Army of the Potomac. Besides, this young leader exerted his abilities as an engineer to devise in all its details the system of defensive works from Alexandria to Georgetown, and employed his unrivaled talents for organization in supplying the newly created army with all the material indispensable for an army in the field. This picture shows the Christmas Day parade of the Second Maine Infantry at Camp James near Washington, 1861. The regiment, with others, took part in the incessant drilling required to give the raw "thinking soldier" the "blind unquestioning obedience" necessary to military success. The Second Maine served in the Army of the Potomac two years and lost 139 men. After Chancellorsville, it was ordered home and the three-year men were transferred to the Twentieth Maine Infantry.

MAKING AN ARMY—THE TWENTY-SIXTH NEW YORK

Passing before us is a regiment that is yet to taste war in its reality. The regimental drum corps is in position, and, as the marching men step out smartly, the camera catches them as perfectly as would the instantaneous photography of to-day. The scene is within Fort Lyon—one of the outlying defenses of Washington below Alexandria. To the defenses established about the capital came the raw recruits who flocked to the standard of the Union at the call of President Lincoln. Not only were they to serve as defenders of the capital, but here, during the winter of 1861–2, they were made into soldiers for service in the field. McClellan is said to have created an army out of a mob during this period, but the men we see before us—the Twenty-Sixth New York—although green at the game of war when they enlisted, came from stock that makes good soldiers, and from the State which furnished the most men to the Federal cause and suffered the heaviest losses in battle during the struggle. The Twenty-Sixth was one of the two-years regiments and its term of service covered some of the hardest fighting in the war. It went into the battle of Fredericksburg 300 strong, and came out with a loss of 170, nearly sixty per cent.

DRILLING THE 96TH PENNSYLVANIA AT CAMP NORTHUMBERLAND, NEAR WASHINGTON—1861

Along this sloping hillside, well suited for a camp, we see a Federal regiment at its full strength, before bullets and sickness had lowered its numbers to a mere skeleton of its former self. The band is out in front, the men are standing at "shoulder arms;" the Colonel and his Major and Adjutant, mounted on their sleek, well-fed horses, are grouped at one side, conscious that the eye of the camera is upon them. There is an old adage among military men that "a straight shot takes the best." When a freshly joined regiment, recruited to its full strength, reached the army corps to which it had been assigned and which had been for a long time actively engaged, it caused comment that well may be understood. "Hello, here comes a new brigade!" cried a veteran of the Potomac who had seen eight months' continuous service, calling the attention of a companion to a new regiment just marching into camp. "Brigade!" exclaimed the other, "I'll bet my hat it's a division!" There are instances in plenty where a company commander found himself at the head of less than a score of men; where regiments that had started a 1,000 strong could muster but some 200 odd, and where, in a single action, the loss in killed, wounded and missing was over sixty per cent. of those engaged. We begin to understand what war is when we stop to think of this.

SCOTT—THE FIRST LIEUTENANT–GENERAL AFTER WASHINGTON.

Upon Winfield Scott, hero of the Mexican War, fell the responsibility of directing the Union armies at the outbreak of the Civil War. Sitting here with his staff in Washington, second in command only to President Lincoln, his fine countenance and bearing betoken the soldierly qualities which made him one of the first commanders of his age. In active service for half a century, he had never lost a battle. Born in Petersburg, Virginia, in 1786, he was now in his seventy-fifth year. On his left in the picture stands Colonel E. D. Townsend; on his right, Henry Van Rensselaer. General Scott retired on October 31, 1861.

PART II
DOWN THE MISSISSIPPI VALLEY

———

FORT HENRY
AND
FORT DONELSON

———

THE FIRST CLASH WEST OF THE MISSISSIPPI

Near here the citizens of St. Louis saw the first blood spilled in Missouri at the outbreak of the War. By order of Governor Jackson, a camp had been formed in the western suburbs of the city for drilling the militia. It was named in honor of the Governor, and was in command of General D. M. Frost. Captain Nathaniel Lyon was in command of the United States troops at the Arsenal in St. Louis. Lyon, on May 10th, marched nearly five thousand strong, toward Camp Jackson, surrounded it, planted batteries on all the heights overlooking it, and set guards with fixed bayonets and muskets at half cock. Meanwhile the inhabitants of St. Louis had gathered in great crowds in the vicinity, hurrying thither in carriages, baggage-wagons, on horses and afoot. Many of the men had seized their rifles and shotguns and had come too late to the assistance of the State troops. Greatly outnumbered by Lyon, General Frost surrendered his command, 689 in all. The prisoners, surrounded by a line of United States soldiers, at half-past five in the afternoon

CAMP JACKSON, ST. LOUIS, MISSOURI, MAY, 1861

were marched out of camp, on the road leading to St. Louis, and halted. After a short wait the ominous silence was suddenly broken by shots from the head of the column. Some of Lyon's soldiers had been pressed and struck by the crowd, and had discharged their pieces. No one was injured. Tranquillity was apparently restored when volley after volley broke out from the rear ranks, and men, women, and children were seen running frantically from the scene. It was said that Lyon's troops were attacked with stones and that two shots were fired at them before they replied. Twenty-eight citizens—chiefly bystanders including women and children—were killed. As Lyon, with his prisoners, marched through the city to the Arsenal, excitement ran high in St. Louis. A clash occurred next day between troops and citizens and it was many weeks before the uproar over Lyon's seizure quieted down. Meanwhile Camp Jackson became a drill-ground for Federal troops, as we see it in the picture.

WHERE WESTERN SOLDIERS WERE TRAINED BY GRANT

Here, under Ulysses S. Grant, many a Western raw recruit was whipped into shape for active service. Grant, who served under Taylor and Scott, through the Mexican War, had resigned his commission of captain in 1854 and settled in St. Louis. He was among the first to offer his services to his country in 1861. He went to Springfield, Illinois, and Governor Yates gave him a desk in the Adjutant General's office. He soon impressed the Governor with his efficiency and was made drill officer at Camp Butler. Many Illinois regiments, infantry, artillery, and especially cavalry, were organized and trained at Camp Butler under the watchful eye of Grant. By

CAMP BUTLER, NEAR SPRINGFIELD, ILLINOIS, IN 1862

May, 1861, his usefulness had become so apparent that he was made mustering officer and aide, with the complimentary rank of colonel. In June he was appointed Colonel of the Seventh District Regiment, then at Camp Yates on the State Fair Grounds at the western edge of Springfield. On June 28th this regiment became the Twenty-first Illinois Volunteers, and on July 3d started for northern Missouri. This photograph was taken in 1862, after Grant had left Camp Butler and was winning laurels for himself as Commander of the District and Army of West Tennessee.

MOUNTING ARTILLERY IN FORT DARLING AT CAMP DEFIANCE

REACHING OUT FOR THE RIVER

These busy scenes were enacted in the late spring of 1861, by five regiments under Brig.-General Swift, who had been ordered by Secretary of War Cameron to occupy Cairo at the junction of the Mississippi and Ohio Rivers and save it from the fate of Sumter, which it was anticipated the Confederate gunboats coming up the Mississippi might visit upon it, and thus gain access to the Ohio. It was tedious work for the men of the Eighth, Ninth, Tenth, Eleventh, and Twelfth Illinois Volunteers, who, began the building of barracks, cleared parade grounds, mounted guns, and threw up fortifications against the attack which never came. In the upper

UNCOMPLETED EARTHWORKS, CAMP DEFIANCE

DRILL GROUNDS OF THE DEFENDERS OF CAIRO, ILL.

pictures the men are at work rushing to completion the unfinished Fort Darling, which was situated to the left of the drill grounds seen in the lower panorama. In the latter we see one of the innumerable drills with which the troops were kept occupied and tuned up for the active service before them. Across the Mississippi was the battery at Bird's Point, on the Missouri shore. This and Fort Darling were occupied by the First and Second Illinois Light Artillery, but their labors were chiefly confined to the prevention of contraband traffic on the river. The troops at Cairo did not see any campaigning till Grant led them to Paducah, Ky., September 5-6, 1861.

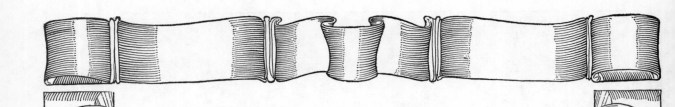

FORT HENRY AND FORT DONELSON

By this brilliant and important victory Grant's fame sprang suddenly into full and universal recognition. President Lincoln nominated him major-general of volunteers, and the Senate at once confirmed the appointment. The whole military service felt the inspiring event. —*Nicolay and Hay, in "Life of Lincoln."*

THE grasp of a great section of western Kentucky and Tennessee by the Northern armies, the capture of a stronghold that was thought impregnable, the forced surrender of a great army, and the bringing into public notice of a new commander who was destined to outshine all his fellows— these were the achievements of the short, vigorous campaign of Fort Donelson.

There were two great battle-grounds of the Civil War, nearly a thousand miles apart—Virginia and the valley of the great river that divides the continent—and the two definite objects of the Northern armies during the first half of the war period were to capture Richmond and to open the Mississippi. All other movements and engagements were subordinate to the dramas of these two great theaters, incidental and contributory. The South, on the other hand, except for the early threatening of Washington, the Gettysburg campaign, the raid of Morgan in Ohio, and the expeditions of Bragg and Hood into Kentucky and Tennessee, was on the defensive from the beginning of the war to the end.

In the East after the initial engagement at Bull Run "all was quiet along the Potomac" for some months. McClellan had loomed large as the rising hero of the war; but McClellan did not move with the celerity that was expected of him; the North became impatient and demanded that

CAIRO CITIZENS WHO MAY HAVE RECALLED THIS DAY

With his hands thrust in his pockets stands General Grant, next to General McClernand, who is directly in front of the pillar of the Cairo post-office. The future military leader had yet his great name to make, for the photograph of this gathering was taken in September, 1861, and when, later, the whole world was ringing with his praises the citizens who chanced to be in the group must have recalled that day with pride. Young Al Sloo, the postmaster's son, leans against the doorway on Grant's right, and next to him is Bob Jennings; then comes Dr. Taggart, then Thomas, the mason, and Jaques, the butcher. On the extreme right, facing the camera, is young Bill Thomas. Up in the windows sit George Olmstead and Will Smith. In his shirt sleeves, on General McClernand's left, is C. C. Davidson. In the group about him are Benjamin Munn, Fred Theobold, John Maxey, and Phil. Howard. Perhaps these men told their children of the morning that Grant left his headquarters at the St. Charles Hotel and met them here. Who knows?

something be done. But while the public was still waiting there were two occurrences in the West that riveted the attention of the nation, sending a thrill of gladness through the North and a wave of depression over the Southland. These were the fall of Fort Henry and of Fort Donelson.

After Missouri had been saved to the Union in spite of the disaster at Wilson's Creek in August, 1861, a Union army slowly gathered in southern Illinois. Its purpose was to dispute with the Confederates their hold on Kentucky, which had not seceded, and to regain control of the Mississippi. To secure the latter end a flank movement was decided upon—to open the mighty river by moving up the Cumberland and Tennessee—the greatest flanking movement in the history of warfare. It began at Fort Henry and ended at Vicksburg, covered a year and five months, and cost tens of thousands of human lives and millions of dollars' worth of property—but it was successful.

Eastern Kentucky, in the early days of 1862, was also in considerable ferment. Colonel James A. Garfield had driven the Confederate commander, General Humphrey Marshall, and a superior force into the Cumberland Mountains, after a series of slight encounters, terminating at Paintsville on the Big Sandy River, on January 10th. But one later event gave great encouragement to the North. It was the first substantial victory for the Union arms. General Zollicoffer held the extreme Confederate right at Cumberland Gap and he now joined General George B. Crittenden near Mill Springs in central Kentucky. General Buell, in charge of the Army of the Ohio, had placed General George H. Thomas at Lebanon, and the latter promptly moved against this threatening Confederate force. A sharp engagement took place at Logan's Cross Roads near Mill Springs on January 19th. The Confederate army was utterly routed and Zollicoffer was killed. The Union loss was about two hundred and sixty, and the Confederate over twice that number. It was not a great

CAPTAIN CLARK B. LAGOW

DR. JAMES SIMONS.

WINNING HIS SPURS AT CAIRO.

Few will recognize in this early and unusual photograph the man who at Appomattox, wore plain fatigue dress in striking contrast with the fully uniformed Lee. Here Grant appears in his full-dress Brigadier-General's uniform as he came to Cairo to assume command of a military district including southern Illinois, September 4, 1861. Grasping at once the problems of his new post he began the work of reorganization, assisted by a well-chosen staff. Without waiting for permission from Frémont, his immediate superior, Commander of the Department of the West, Grant pushed forward a

BRIGADIER-GENERAL U. S. GRANT

force and occupied Paducah, Kentucky, before the Confederates, approaching with the same purpose, could arrive. Grant was impatient to drive back the Confederate lines in Kentucky and Tennessee and began early to importune Washington to be allowed to carry out maneuvers. His keen judgment convinced him that these must quickly be made in order to secure the advantage in this outlying arena of the war. Captain Rawlins was made Assistant Adjutant-General by Grant, and lifted from his shoulders much of the routine of the post. Captain Lagow and Captain Hillyer were two of the General's aides-de-camp. Dr. James Simons was Medical Director of the District.

CAPTAIN WILLIAM S. HILLYER

CAPTAIN JOHN A. RAWLINS.

battle, but its effect on the North was most stimulating, and the people first learned to appreciate the abilities of their great general, George H. Thomas.

It was now February, 1862. General U. S. Grant was in command of the Union forces in western Kentucky and Tennessee. The opposing commander was Albert Sidney Johnston, then reputed the ablest general of the South. At Bowling Green, Kentucky, he had thirty thousand men. Believing, perhaps, that he could not hold Kentucky, he determined to save Tennessee for the South and took his stand at Nashville.

On February 2d, 1862, General Grant left Cairo with his army of seventeen thousand men and on transports moved up the Ohio and the Tennessee to attack Fort Henry. Accompanying him was Flag-Officer Foote with his fleet of seven gunboats, four of them ironclads.

Fort Henry was garrisoned by an army of about three thousand men under the command of General Lloyd Tilghman, a brave officer who was destined to give his life for the Confederate cause, the following year, near Vicksburg. It covered about three acres and mounted seventeen heavy guns. Grant's plan of attack was to land his army four miles below the fort, to move across the country and seize the road leading to Fort Donelson, while Foote should move up the river with his fleet and turn his guns on the Confederate batteries.

On February 6th, Foote formed his vessels into two lines, the ironclads—the *Cincinnati,* the *Carondelet,* the *Essex,* and the *St. Louis*—forming a front rank. Slowly and cautiously he approached the fort, firing as he went, the guns on the parapet answering those of the fleet. Several of the Confederate guns were disabled. The fleet was yet unhurt when the first hour had passed. Then a 24-pound shot struck the *Essex,* crashed through her side and penetrated her boiler, instantly killing both her pilots and flooding the vessel from stem to stern with scalding steam. The *Essex,* wholly disabled, drifted

THE UNLUCKY *ESSEX* AFTER FORT HENRY

The thousand-ton ironclad *Essex* received the severest punishment at Fort Henry. Fighting blood surged in the veins of Commander W. D. Porter, son of Admiral David Porter and brother of Admiral David D. Porter. The gunboat which he led into action at Fort Henry was named after the famous *Essex* which his father commanded in the War of 1812. Fifteen of the shots from Fort Henry struck and told upon the *Essex*, the last one penetrating her armor and piercing her middle boiler. Commander Porter, standing among his men directing the fight, was terribly scalded by the escaping steam, as were twenty-seven others. Wrongly suspected of disloyalty at the outbreak of the war, Commander Porter's conduct during the struggle gave the lie to such calumny. He recovered after Fort Henry, and was made Commodore in July, 1862. Again in command of the *Essex* he attempted unsuccessfully to destroy the dread Confederate ram *Arkansas* at Vicksburg on July 22d. Porter and the *Essex* then joined Farragut's fleet. His shells helped the Union forces to repulse the Confederates at Baton Rouge, August 5th, and he witnessed the blowing up of the *Arkansas* the following day. He died May 1, 1864.

COMMANDER W. D. PORTER

THE *ESSEX* TWO YEARS LATER

down stream, while her companion ships continued their advance and increased their fire.

Presently, a sound exceeding the roar of cannon was heard above the tumult. A great gun in the fort had exploded, killing or disabling every man who served it. A great 10-inch columbiad was also destroyed. Tilghman, seeing that he had no hope of holding the fort, decided to save his army by sending it to Fort Donelson, on the Cumberland River. This he did, reserving fewer than a hundred men to work the guns. He then raised the white flag and surrendered the seventy-eight that remained. Grant had failed to reach the road to Fort Donelson until the Confederates had escaped. The Southerners hastened across the country and added their numbers to the defenders of Donelson—and by so doing they deferred surrender for ten days.

Fort Donelson was a fortified enclosure of a hundred acres that crowned a plateau on the Cumberland River. It was just south of the boundary between Kentucky and Tennessee and close by the little village of Dover, consisting of a court-house, a two-story tavern, and a few houses scattered about. Beneath the bluff and on the river bank were two powerful batteries commanding the approach to the river. Outside the fort and stretching far along the ridges that enclosed it were rifle-pits, lines of logs covered with yellow clay. Farther beyond, the hillsides were covered with felled trees whose interlacing branches were supposed to render the approach of the foe impossible under fire.

At this moment Donelson was held by eighteen thousand men under the command of General John B. Floyd, late Secretary of War in the cabinet of Buchanan. Next to him were Gideon J. Pillow and Simon B. Buckner. The Union army under Grant was divided into three parts under the respective commands of Charles F. Smith, a veteran of the regular army; John A. McClernand, an Illinois lawyer and member of Congress, and Lew Wallace, the future author of " Ben Hur."

THE GUNBOAT THAT FIRED THE FIRST SHOT AT FORT HENRY

Here, riding at anchor, lies the flagship of Foote, which opened the attack on Fort Henry in the first movement to break the backbone of the Confederacy, and won a victory before the arrival of the army. This gunboat, the *Cincinnati*, was one of the seven flat-bottom iron-clads built by Captain Eads at Carondelet, Missouri, and Mound City, Illinois, during the latter half of 1861. When Grant finally obtained permission from General Halleck to advance the attack upon Fort Henry on the Tennessee River, near the border of Kentucky, Flag Officer Foote started up the river, February 2, 1862, convoying the transports, loaded with the advance detachment of Grant's seventeen thousand troops. Arriving before Fort Henry on

FLAG-OFFICER FOOTE

February 6th, the intrepid naval commander at once began the bombardment with a well-aimed shot from the *Cincinnati*. The eleven heavy guns of the fort responded in chorus, and an iron rain began to fall with telling effect upon the *Cincinnati*, the *Essex*, the *Carondelet*, and the *St. Louis*, which were steaming forward half a mile in advance of the rear division of the squadron. At a range of 1,700 yards the *Cincinnati* opened the engagement. After a little over an hour of heavy firing the colors on Fort Henry were lowered and General Tilghman surrendered it to Flag-Officer Foote. When General Grant arrived an hour later, Foote turned over the fort to him and returned to Cairo with his disabled gunboats.

With waving banners the divisions of Smith and McClernand marched across country on February 12th, arriving at noon and encircling the doomed fort ere nightfall. Smith was stationed on the left and McClernand on the extreme right, near the village of Dover. This left an open space in the center, to be filled by Lew Wallace, who arrived with his division the next day. On the 13th there was a continuous bombardment from morning till night, punctuated by the sharp crack of the sharpshooter's rifle.

The chief action of the day that involved the infantry was an attempt to capture a battery on a hill, near the center of the Confederate line of battle, known as Maney's Battery, commanded by Captain Maney, of Tennessee. This battery had annoyed McClernand greatly, and he delegated his third brigade to capture it. The charge was led by Colonel Morrison of Illinois, and a braver one never was made throughout the whole period of the war. The men who made it were chiefly youths from the farms and workshops of Illinois. With no apparent thought of danger they sallied forth, determined at all hazards to capture the battery on the hill, which stood out in relief against the sky. As they ran up the hill, firing as they went, their numbers were rapidly thinned by the terrific cross-fire from this battery and two others on adjoining hills. Still the survivors pushed on and their deadly fire thinned the ranks of the men at the battery. At length when they came within forty yards of the goal a long line of Confederate musketry beside the battery suddenly burst into flame and a storm of bullets cut down the brave boys of Illinois, with fearful slaughter. Even then they stood for fifteen minutes, returning volley for volley, before retreating. Reaching the foot of the hill, they rallied under the Stars and Stripes, and returned to the assault. Even a third time they charged, but the dry leaves on the ground now caught fire, the smoke stifled them, and they had to retreat. As they returned down the hill, Lew Wallace tells us, "their ears and souls were

A GALLANT GUNBOAT—THE *ST. LOUIS.*

With the shots from the Confederate batteries ringing and bounding off her iron plates, this gallant gunboat that Foote had chosen for his flag-ship, entered the zone of fire at Fort Donelson. In the confined space of her smoke-filled gun-deck, the river sailors were loading and firing the heavy broadsides as fast as the great guns could be run out and aimed at the frowning line of entrenchments on the river bank. From them the concentrated hail of iron was poured upon her and the marksman-ship was good. Fifty-nine times was this brave vessel struck. But her armored sides withstood the heavy shocks although the plating, dented and bent, bore record of each impact. Nearer and nearer grew the forts as up the narrow channel the flag-ship led the way, the *Louis-ville,* the *Carondelet,* and the *Pittsburgh* belching their fire at the wooded heights, as though endeavoring to attract the attention of the Con-federate gunners to themselves and save the flag-ship from receiving more than her share. Up in the pilot-house the brave man who knew the channel stood at the wheel, his eyes firmly fixed ahead; and on the "texas," as the upper deck was called, within speaking distance of him, stood Foote himself. A great shot, aimed accurately as a minie ball, struck the frail pilot-house. It was as if the vessel's heart was pierced. The wheel was swept away from the pilot's hand and the brave river guide was hurled into the corner, mangled, bleeding and soon to die. Flag Officer Foote did not escape. He fell badly wounded in the leg

THE FLAG–SHIP *ST. LOUIS* VIEWED FROM ASTERN

by a fragment of the shell—a wound from which he never fully re-covered. Helpless now, the current swept the *St. Louis'* bow around, and past her consorts that were still fighting, she drifted down the stream and out of action; later, in convoy of the *Louisville,* she returned to Cairo, leaving the *Carondelet* and *Pittsburgh* to escort the transports. Meanwhile on shore, Grant was earning his first laurels as a soldier in a big battle. The disabling of the gunboats caused the Confederates to make the fatal attack that resulted so disastrously for them. Assail-ing Grant's right wing that held a strong position, on the 15th of February, 19,000 men were hurled against a force 8,000 greater in number. But the repulse was complete. Shattered they retreated to their works, and in the morning of the 16th, the Confederate general, Buckner, surrendered. About 14,000 prisoners were taken. The Federal loss was nearly 3,000, and that of the Southern cause about 1,000 less. For the capture of Fort Donelson Grant was made major-general. The first step to the conquest of the Mississippi had been achieved. In October, 1862, the river fleet was transferred from the Army to the Navy Department, and as there was another vessel in the service, bear-ing the same name the *St. Louis* was renamed the *Baron de Kalb.* At Fort Henry, she went into action lashed to the *Carondelet* on account of the narrowness of the stream; and later again, the gallant gunboat won laurels at Island No. 10, Fort Pillow, Memphis, and Vicksburg.

LOUISVILLE—A FIGHTER AT THE FORT

riven with the shrieks of their wounded comrades, upon whom the flames crept and smothered and charred where they lay."

Thus ended the 13th of February. That night the river gunboats, six in number, four of them ironclads, under the command of Andrew H. Foote, arrived. Grant had sent them down the Tennessee to the Ohio and up the Cumberland, to support his army at Fort Donelson. On the 14th, about three in the afternoon, Foote steamed with his four ironclads to a point in the river within four hundred yards of the two powerful batteries on the river bank under the fort and opened fire with his cannon while continuing to advance. The reply from the Confederate batteries was terrific and many of their shots struck home. In a short time the decks of the vessels were slippery with human blood. Foote himself was severely wounded. At length a solid shot struck the pilot house of the flagship and tore away the pilot wheel. At almost the same moment another gunboat was disabled. The two vessels, one of which had been struck fifty-nine times, could no longer be managed; they turned about with the eddies of the river and floated down with the current. The others followed.

The Confederates raised a wild shout of joy at this, their second victory since the coming of the Union army. But what will be the story of the morrow? With the reenforcements brought by Foote, Lew Wallace's division, Grant's army was now swelled to twenty-seven thousand, and in spite of the initial repulse the Federals felt confident of ultimate victory. But a dreary night was before them. The springlike weather had changed. All that fearful night of February 14th there was a fierce, pitiless wind with driving sleet and snow. Thousands of the men, weary of the burden of their overcoats and blankets during the warm preceding days, had thrown them away. Now they spent the night lying behind logs or in ditches or wherever they could find a little protection from the wintry blasts. General Floyd, knowing that Grant's army was much

THE ADVENTUROUS GUNBOAT *CONESTOGA*

Lying at anchor in the Ohio River this little wooden gunboat is having the finishing touches put to her equipment while her officers and men are impatiently waiting for the opportunity to bring her into action. A side-wheel river steamer originally, she was purchased at Cincinnati by Commander John Rodgers in the spring of 1861 and speedily converted into a gunboat. Her boilers and steam pipes were lowered into the hold and the oaken bulwarks five inches thick which we see were put on her and pierced for guns. She got her first taste of fighting when, at Lucas Bend, she engaged the land batteries and a Confederate gunboat, September 10, 1861. She was present at Fort Henry in the second division of the attacking fleet, and also at Fort Donelson.

THE *TYLER*

A sister-ship of the *Conestoga*. She was present both at Fort Henry and Fort Donelson.

stronger than his own, decided, after consulting with Pillow and Buckner, to attack the Union right at dawn on the 15th.

The night was spent in preparing for this, and in the morning Pillow with ten thousand men fell upon McClernand, and Buckner soon joined him with an additional force. Toward noon many of McClernand's men ran short of powder and he was forced to recede from his position. Pillow seems then to have lost his head. He felt that the whole Union army was defeated, and though the road to Nashville was open, the Confederates made no attempt to escape. Just then General Grant rode upon the scene. He had been absent all morning down the river consulting Foote, not knowing that the Confederates had planned an escape. This moment, says Lew Wallace, was the crisis in the life of Grant.

Hearing the disastrous news, his face flushed for a moment; he crushed some papers in his hand. Next instant he was calm, and said in his ordinary tone, to McClernand and Wallace, "Gentlemen, the position on the right must be retaken." Then he galloped away to General Smith. In a short time the Union lines were in motion. General Smith made a grand assault on the Confederate outworks and rifle-pits. When his lines hesitated Smith waved his cap on the point of his sword and rode in front, up the hill, in the hottest fire of the foe, toward the rifle-pits—and they were carried. At the same moment Lew Wallace was leading his division up another slope with equal gallantry. Here again the Confederates retired, and the road to Nashville was no longer open. Furthermore, Smith held a position from which he could shell the fort on the inside, and nothing was left to the inmates but surrender or slaughter on the morrow.

A council was held by Floyd, Pillow, and Buckner. Buckner, who was a master in the art of warfare, declared that he could not hold his position for half an hour in the morning. The situation was hopeless. Floyd was under indictment at Washington for maladministration in the Buchanan cabinet.

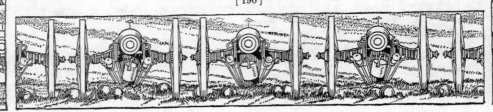

The Captured Commanders of Forts Henry and Donelson.—It requires as much moral courage to decide upon a surrender, even when odds are overwhelming, as it does physical bravery, in maintaining a useless fight to the death. Brigadier-General Tilghman, who commanded the Confederate Fort Henry on the Tennessee and General Simon Bolivar Buckner in command of the Confederate Fort Donelson —a much stronger position on the Cumberland only a few miles away—were men who possessed this kind of courage. Both had the misfortune to hold untenable positions. Each displayed generalship and sagacity and only gave up to the inevitable when holding out meant nothing but wasted slaughter and the sacrifice of men who had been called upon to exert every human effort. Fort Henry, on the banks of the Tennessee, was held by a few thousand men and strongly armed with twenty guns including one 10-inch Columbiad. But on the 6th of February it fairly lay in the possession of the Federals before a shot had actually been fired, for Grant with 17,000 men had gained the rear of the fortification after his move from Cairo on the 30th of the previous month. The actual reduction of the fort was left to the gunboat flotilla under Flag Officer Foote, whose heavy bombardment began early in the morning. General Tilghman had seen from the first that the position could not be held. He was trapped on all sides, but he would not give way without a display of resistance. Before the firing began, he had sent off most of the garrison and maintained the unequal combat with the gunboats for an hour and a quarter with less than a hundred men, of whom he lost twenty-one. Well did this handful serve the guns on the river bank. One shot struck the gunboat *Essex*, piercing her boilers, and wounding and scalding twenty-eight men. But at last, enveloped on all sides, his retreat cut off —the troops who had been ordered to depart in the morning, some three thousand in number, had reached Fort Donelson, twelve miles away—General Tilghman hauled down his flag, surrendering himself and eighty-four men as prisoners of war. Here we see him—a brave figure of a man—clad in the uniform of a Southern Colonel. There was never the slightest doubt of his courage or his proper discretion in making this surrender. Only for a short time was he held prisoner, when he was exchanged and welcomed back with all honor into the ranks of the Confederacy, and given an important command. He did not, however, live long to serve his cause, for shortly after joining the army he was killed at the battle of Baker's Creek, Mississippi, on the 16th of May, 1863.

GENERAL LLOYD TILGHMAN.

TWO UNWILLING GUESTS OF THE NORTH

It is not often that on the battlefield ties of friendship are cemented that last a lifetime, and especially is this so between conqueror and conquered. Fort Donelson, that was, in a measure, a repetition of Fort Henry, saw two fighting foes become thus united. It was impossible for the garrison of Fort Donelson to make its escape after the flotilla of gunboats had once appeared in the river, although General Floyd, its senior commander, the former Secretary of War under President Buchanan, had withdrawn himself from the scene tendering the command to General Pillow, who in his turn, after escaping with his own brigade, left the desperate situation to be coped with by General Buckner. Assailed in the rear by an army that outnumbered the defenders of the fort by nearly eight thousand and with the formidable gunboats hammering his entrenchments from the river, Buckner decided to cut his way out in a desperate charge, but being repulsed, saw his men flung back once more into the fort. There was nothing for it but to make terms. On February 16th, in a note to Grant he asked what might be granted him. Here, the coming leader won his nickname of "Unconditional Surrender" Grant. Buckner was informed that the Federal army was about to move upon his works. Hurt and smarting under his position, he sent back a reply that in a few short hours he would, perhaps, have been willing to recall. Yielding to circumstances he accepted what he bluntly pronounced, "ungenerous and unchivalrous terms." But when the capitulation had taken place and nearly fifteen thousand men had surrendered, a greater number than ever before laid down their arms upon the continent, Grant was so generous, that then and there began the friendship that grew as close as if the two men were brothers of the blood. Most of the prisoners were paroled. Each one was allowed to retain his personal baggage, and the officers to keep their side arms. Grant had known Buckner in the Mexican War, and received him after the battle as his guest. For a short time General Buckner was kept a prisoner at Fort Warren until he was exchanged. But the friendship between the two leaders continued. When General Grant, after having been twice President, failed in his business career, Buckner sent him a check, trusting that it might be of use in his time of trouble. Grant, shortly before his death, wrote his old-time comrade and antagonist requesting that Buckner do him the final honors by becoming one of his pallbearers.

BUCKNER, THE DEFENDER OF DONELSON

He declared that he must not be taken, and that with his Virginia troops he would escape on two little boats that were to arrive from Nashville in the morning. He passed the command to Pillow, and Pillow, declaring that he too would escape, passed it on to Buckner. Floyd and Pillow with their men made good their escape; so did Colonel Forrest, the cavalry leader, and his mounted force.

In the early morning Buckner sent a note to Grant offering to capitulate. The answer is well known. Grant demanded "unconditional surrender," and added, "I propose to move immediately on your works." Buckner was too good a soldier to sacrifice his men in needless slaughter. His men were so worn with eighty-four hours of fighting and watching that many of them had fallen asleep while standing in battle-line and under fire. He accepted the "ungenerous and unchivalrous terms," as he pronounced them, and surrendered Fort Donelson and the army, consisting of at least fourteen thousand men, with all its stores of ammunition. The Union loss was over twenty-eight hundred men. The Confederate loss, killed and wounded, was about two thousand.

The capture of Fort Donelson did three things. First, it opened up the way for the Federal army to penetrate the heart of the western South and gave it control of Kentucky and of western Tennessee. Second, it electrified the North with confident hopes of ultimate success. It was the first great victory for the North in the war. Bull Run had been a moral victory to the South, but the vanquished were weakened scarcely more than the victors. At Donelson, the victors gained control of an extensive territory and captured a noble army which could ill be spared by the South and which could not be replaced. Third, the capture of Donelson forced before the nation a new man—Ulysses S. Grant.

SHILOH
THE FIRST
GRAND BATTLE

THE PLUCKY LITTLE WOODEN GUNBOAT "TYLER"—ITS FLANKING FIRE
ON THE CONFEDERATE TROOPS CHARGING ACROSS THE RAVINE OF DILL'S
BRANCH, CLOSE BY THE RIVER, GREATLY ASSISTED HURLBUT, COMMANDER
OF THE FEDERAL LEFT, IN HOLDING OFF WITHERS' GALLANT ATTACK

THE DEFENDERS OF GRANT'S LAST LINE AT SHILOH

These heavy guns when this picture was taken had not been moved from the actual position they held in the afternoon of the battle of Shiloh, April 6, 1862. In one of the backward movements of Grant's forces in the afternoon of that day General Prentiss, isolated by the retirement of troops in his flanks, fought till overwhelmed by the Confederates, then surrendered the remnant of his division. Encouraged by this success General Bragg ordered a last desperate charge in an effort to turn the left of the re-formed Federal line. Onward swept the Confederates toward a grim line of batteries, which Colonel Webster, of Grant's staff, had ranged along the top of the bluff from a quarter to a half a mile from Pittsburg Landing. The line of artillery overlooked a deep ravine opening into the

GUNS THAT HELD THEIR GROUND AT PITTSBURG LANDING

Tennessee River. Into this and up its precipitous side General Withers dashed with two brigades. The gunboats *Tyler* and *Lexington* in the river joined with Webster's batteries upon the ridge and a frightful fire was poured into the ranks of the advancing Confederates. In the face of this, although finding himself unsupported save by Gage's battery, Withers led on his men. The division that he had expected to reenforce him had been withdrawn by the order of General Beauregard. To his men working their way up the slope came the order to retire. General Chalmers, of Withers Division, did not get the word. Down in the ravine his men alone of the whole Confederate army were continuing the battle. Only after nightfall did he retire.

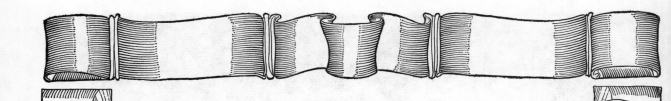

SHILOH—THE FIRST GRAND BATTLE

No Confederate who fought at Shiloh has ever said that he found any point on that bloody field easy to assail.—*Colonel William Preston Johnston (Son of the Confederate General, Albert Sidney Johnston, killed at Shiloh).*

IN the history of America many battles had been fought, but the greatest of them were skirmishes compared with the gigantic conflicts of the Old World under Marlborough and Napoleon. On the field of Shiloh, for the first time, two great American armies were to engage in a mighty struggle that would measure up to the most important in the annals of Europe. And the pity of it was that the contestants were brethren of the same household, not hereditary and unrelenting enemies.

At Fort Donelson the western South was not slain—it was only wounded. The chief commander of that part of the country, Albert Sidney Johnston, determined to concentrate the scattered forces and to make a desperate effort to retrieve the disaster of Donelson. He had abandoned Bowling Green, had given up Nashville, and now decided to collect his troops at Corinth, Mississippi. Next in command to Johnston was General Beauregard who fought at Bull Run, and who had come from Virginia to aid Johnston. There also came Braxton Bragg, whose name had become famous through the laconic expression, " A little more grape, Captain Bragg," uttered by Zachary Taylor at Buena Vista; Leonidas Polk who, though a graduate of West Point, had entered the church and for twenty years before the war had been Episcopal bishop of Louisiana, and John C. Breckinridge, former Vice President of the United States. The legions of the South were gathered at Corinth until, by the 1st of April, 1862, they numbered forty thousand.

A brilliant Southern leader, whose early loss was a hard blow to the Confederacy. Albert Sidney Johnston was a born fighter with a natural genius for war. A West Pointer of the Class of '26, he had led a strenuous and adventurous life. In the early Indian wars, in the border conflicts in Texas, and in the advance into Mexico, he had always proved his worth, his bravery and his knowledge as a soldier. At the outbreak of the Civil War he had already been brevetted Brigadier-General, and had been commander of the military district of Utah. An ardent Southerner, he made his choice, dictated by heart and conscience, and the Federal authorities

GENERAL A. S. JOHNSTON, C. S. A.

knew the loss they would sustain and the gain that would be given to the cause of the Confederacy. In '61 he was assigned to a district including Kentucky and Tennessee with the rank of General. At once he displayed his gifts as an organizer, but Shiloh cut short a career that would have led him to a high place in fame and history. The early Confederate successes of the 6th of April were due to his leadership. His manner of death and his way of meeting it attested to his bravery. Struck by a minie ball, he kept in the saddle, falling exhausted and dying from the loss of blood. His death put the whole South into mourning.

Copyright by Review of Reviews Co.

CAMP OF THE NINTH MISSISSIPPI
The story of this regiment is told on page 201.

To no one who was close to him in the stirring scenes of the early conflict in the West did Grant pay higher tribute than to this veteran of the Mexican War who was his Chief of Staff. He was a man to be relied upon in counsel and in emergency, a fact that the coming leader recognized from the very outset. An artillery officer and engineer, his military training and practical experience made him a most valuable executive. He had also the gift of leading men and inspiring confidence. Always cool and collected in the face of danger, and gifted with a personality that won friends everywhere, the reports of all of his superiors show the trust and confidence that were reposed in him. In

BRIG.-GEN. J. D. WEBSTER

April, 1861, he had taken charge of the fortifications at Cairo, Illinois. He was with Grant at Paducah, at Forts Henry and Donelson, and at Shiloh where he collected the artillery near the Landing that repelled the final Confederate attack on April 6th. He remained Chief of Staff until October, 1862. On October 14th, he was made a Brigadier-General of Volunteers, and was appointed superintendent of military railroads in the Department of Tennessee. Later he was Chief of Staff to General Sherman, and again proved his worth when he was with General Thomas at Hood's defeat before Nashville in December, 1864. On March 13, 1865, he received the brevet of Major-General of Volunteers.

Meantime, the Union army had moved southward and was concentrating at Pittsburg Landing, on the Tennessee River, an obscure stopping place for boats in southern Tennessee, and some twenty miles northeast from Corinth. The name means more now than merely a landing place for river craft. It was clear that two mighty, hostile forces were drawing together and that ere long there would be a battle of tremendous proportions, such as this Western hemisphere had not then known.

General Grant had no idea that the Confederates would meet him at Pittsburg Landing. He believed that they would wait for an attack on their entrenchments at Corinth. The position his army occupied at the Landing was a kind of quadrilateral, enclosed on three sides by the river and several small streams that flow into it. As the early days of April passed there were ominous rumors of the coming storm; but Grant was so sure that Johnston would not attack that he spent the night of the 5th of April at Savannah, some miles down the Tennessee River.

It was Saturday night. For two weeks the Union troops had occupied the undulating tableland that stretched away from the river at the Landing. There was the sound of the plashing streams overflowing from recent rains, there were revelry and mirth around the thousand camp-fires; but there was no sound to give warning of the coming of forty thousand men, who had for two days been drawing nearer with a steady tread, and during this night were deploying around the Union camp, only a mile away. There was nothing to indicate that the inevitable clash of arms was but a few hours in the future.

At the dawn of day on Sunday, April 6th, magnificent battle-lines, under the Confederate battle-flag, emerged from the woods on the neighboring hills within gunshot of the Federal camps. Whether the Union army was really surprised has been the subject of long controversy, which we need not

BRAVE SOUTHERNERS AT SHILOH

In the Southern record of the battle of Shiloh, the name of the Washington Artillery, of New Orleans, stands out in red letters. It was composed of the best blood of the city, the dandies of their day. Here we see the officers of the Fifth Company, in the first year of the war while uniforms were bright, sword-belts pipe-clayed, and buttons glistening. Under the command of Captain W. Irving Hodgson, this company made its name from the very first.

SOUTHERN BOYS IN BATTLE

Here we see plainly shown the extreme youth of some of the enlisted men of the Washington Artillery of New Orleans. Not one of the lads here pictured is within a year of his majority. We hardly realize how young the fighters on both sides were; only their faces and the records can show it. At Shiloh, with Anderson's brigade of brave fighters, these young cannoneers answered to the call. Anderson was first in the second line of battle at the beginning. Before the action was twenty minutes old he was at the front; and with the advance, galloping over the rough ground, came the Washington Artillery.

enter. Certainly, the attack on it was most sudden, and in consequence it fought on the defensive and at a disadvantage throughout the day.

General Hardee's corps, forming the first line of battle, moved against the outlying division of the Union army, which was commanded by General Benjamin Prentiss, of West Virginia. Before Prentiss could form his lines Hardee's shells began bursting around him, but he was soon ready and, though pressed back for half a mile in the next two or three hours, his men fought like heroes. Meanwhile the further Confederate advance under Bragg, Polk, and Breckinridge was extending all along the line in front of the Federal camps. The second Federal force to encounter the fury of the oncoming foe was the division of General W. T. Sherman, which was cut to pieces and disorganized, but only after it had inflicted frightful loss on the Confederate army.

General Grant, as we have noted, spent the night at Savannah, a town nine miles by way of the river from Pittsburg Landing. As he sat at breakfast, he heard the distant boom of cannon and he quickly realized that Johnston's army had attacked his own at the Landing. Instantly he took a boat and started for the scene of the conflict. At Crump's Landing, about half way between the two, General Lew Wallace was stationed with a division of seven thousand men. As Grant passed Crump's Landing, he met Wallace and ordered him to be ready for instant marching when he was called for. When Grant arrived at Pittsburg Landing, about eight o'clock in the morning, he found a tremendous battle raging, and he spent the day riding from one division commander to another, giving directions and cheering them on as best he could.

About two and a half miles from the Landing stood a little log church among the trees, in which for years the simple folk of the countryside had been wont to gather for worship every Sunday morning. But on this fateful Sunday, the demon of war reigned supreme. The little church was known

UNUNIFORMED BUT FEARLESS SOUTHERN SOLDIERS

A photograph of the Ninth Mississippi taken a few months before it fought at Shiloh. In this military line of coatless men we see as brave a fighting unit as ever, with all the glitter and panoply of war, swept into the tide of battle. Here they stand, ununiformed but fearless. Attached to Chalmers' Brigade on the extreme right at the opening of Shiloh these soldiers were commanded by Lieut.-Col. William A. Rankin. They dashed forward in the fierce attack that caused the surrender of Prentiss' division. General Chalmers wrote of the bravery of these Mississippians when attacked in turn next day. "As a last resort, I seized a battle-flag from the color-bearer of the Ninth Mississippi and called them to follow. With a wild shout the whole regiment rallied to the charge, and we drove the enemy back and reoccupied our first position of the morning, which we held until the order of retreat was received." Bragg reported: "Brigadier-General James Chalmers, at the head of the gallant Mississippians, filled—he could not have exceeded—the measure of my expectations."

as Shiloh to all the country around, and it gave its name to the great battle that raged near it on that memorable day.

General Prentiss had borne the first onset of the morning. He had been pressed back half a mile. But about nine o'clock, after being reenforced, he made a stand on a wooded spot with a dense undergrowth, and here he held his ground for eight long hours, until five in the afternoon, when he and a large portion of his division were surrounded and compelled to surrender. Time after time the Confederates rushed upon his position, but only to be repulsed with fearful slaughter. This spot came to be known as the " Hornet's Nest." It was not far from here that the Confederates suffered the irreparable loss of the day. Their noble commander, Albert Sidney Johnston, received his death wound as he was urging his troops to force back Hurlbut's men. He was riding in the center of the fight, cheering his men, when a minie ball cut an artery of his thigh. The wound was not necessarily fatal. A surgeon could easily have saved him. But he thought only of victory and continued in the saddle, raising his voice in encouragement above the din of battle. Presently his voice became faint, a deadly pallor blanched his cheek. He was lifted from his horse, but it was too late. In a few minutes the great commander was dead, from loss of blood.

The death of Johnston, in the belief of many, changed the result at Shiloh and prevented the utter rout or capture of Grant's army. One of Johnston's subordinates wrote: " Johnston's death was a tremendous catastrophe. Sometimes the hopes of millions of people depend upon one head and one arm. The West perished with Albert Sidney Johnston and the Southern country followed." Jefferson Davis afterward declared that " the fortunes of a country hung by a single thread on the life that was yielded on the field of Shiloh."

Beauregard succeeded to the command on the fall of Johnston and the carnage continued all the day—till darkness was falling over the valleys and the hills. The final charge

THE BOATS THAT TURNED THE TIDE AT SHILOH
PHOTOGRAPHED A FEW DAYS AFTER THE BATTLE

The assistance rendered by these Tennessee River boats that had been pressed from their peaceful occupations into the service of the army, was of such immense importance as to become a great factor in the turning of the battle tide that saved the Federal cause. General Grant's headquarters in the early morning of April 6th was some miles from where the fight began. It was at Savannah, on the Tennessee, and as soon as the cannonade announced the opening of the battle, Grant transferred his headquarters to the *Tigress*, which lies between the other vessels in the photograph. The steamer on the right is the *Universe*, the largest of the transports present. At one o'clock General Buell, pushing ahead of his troops, reached the river bank, and the two leaders held a conference on the upper deck of the *Tigress*. It was touch and go whether the troops fighting in the forest, beyond the landing, could hold their ground. The Confederate General Johnston, in forming his plans, had intended to leave an opening that would tempt the hard-pressed Federal army to retreat down the river. But, instead, they massed solidly back on Pittsburg Landing, huddled together so closely that brigades, and even regiments, were overlapping. As soon as Buell's hastening troops came up, the transports were turned into ferry-boats, and all night long they plied across the river loaded within an inch of their gunwales with the reënforcements. Later, as the picture shows, they brought supplies.

of the evening was made by three Confederate brigades close to the Landing, in the hope of gaining that important point. But by means of a battery of many guns on the bluff of Dill's Branch, aided by the gunboats in the river, the charge was repulsed. Beauregard then gave orders to desist from further attack all along his lines, to suspend operations till morning. When General Bragg heard this he was furious with rage. He had counted on making an immediate grand assault in the darkness, believing that he could capture a large part of the Federal army.

When the messenger informed him of Beauregard's order, he inquired if he had already delivered it to the other commanders. "Yes," was the reply. "If you had not," rejoined the angry Bragg, "I would not obey it. The battle is lost." But Bragg's fears were not shared by his compatriots.

Further mention is due the two little wooden gunboats, *Tyler* and *Lexington,* for their share in the great fight. The *Tyler* had lain all day opposite the mouth of Dill's Branch which flowed through a deep, marshy ravine, into the Tennessee just above the Landing. Her commander, Lieutenant Gwin, was eager for a part in the battle, and when he saw the Confederate right pushing its way toward the Landing, he received permission to open fire. For an hour his guns increased the difficulties of Jackson's and Chalmers' brigades as they made their way to the surrounding of Prentiss. Later on the *Lexington* joined her sister, and the two vessels gave valuable support to the Union cannon at the edge of the ravine and to Hurlbut's troops until the contest ended. All that night, in the downpour of rain, Lieutenant Gwin, at the request of General Nelson, sent shot crashing through the trees in the direction where the Confederates had bivouacked. This completely broke the rest of the exhausted troops, and had a decided effect upon the next day's result.

Southern hopes were high at the close of this first bloody day at Shiloh. Whatever of victory there was at the end of the

THE *LEXINGTON*

Copyright by Review of Reviews Co.

In the river near Pittsburg Landing, where the Federal transports lay, were two small gunboats, and what they did during the battle of April 6th makes a separate chapter in the action. In the early morning they were out of sight, though within sound of the continuous firing. How the battle was going, however, was evident. The masses of the blue-clad troops appeared through the trees on the river bank, showing that under the continuous and fierce assaults they were falling back upon the Landing. The *Tyler*, commanded by Lieutenant Gwin, and afterward the *Lexington*, commanded by Lieutenant Shirk, which arrived at four o'clock, strove to keep the Confederate army from the Landing. After the surrender of Prentiss, General Withers set his division in motion to the right toward this point. Chalmers' and Jackson's brigades marched into the ravine of Dill's Branch and into the range of the Federal gunboats and batteries which silenced Gage's battery, the only one Withers had, and played havoc with the Confederate skirmishers. All the rest of the afternoon, until nightfall, the river sailors kept up their continuous bombardment, and in connection with the field batteries on the bank checked General Withers' desperate attempt on the Landing. The dauntless brigade of Chalmers, whose brave Southerners held their ground near the foot of the ravine and maintained the conflict after the

battle was ended elsewhere, was swept by the gunboats' fire. When Buell's army, that had been hurrying up to Grant's assistance, reached the battle-field, Gwin sent a messenger ashore in the evening to General Nelson, who had just arrived, and asked in what manner he could now be of service. It was pitch dark; except for the occasional firing of the pickets the armies were resting after the terrific combat. In reply to Gwin's inquiry, General Nelson requested that the gunboats keep on firing during the night, and that every ten minutes an 8-inch shell should be launched in the direction of the Confederate camp. With great precision Gwin followed out this course. Through the forest the shells shrieked and exploded over the exhausted Confederates, showering branches and limbs upon them where they slept, and tearing great gashes in the earth. The result was that they got little rest, and rest was necessary. Slowly a certain demoralization became evident—results that bore fruit in the action that opened on the morrow. Here we see pictured—in the lower part of the page—the captain's gig and crew near the *Lexington*, ready to row their commander out into the stream.

day belonged to the Confederates. They had pressed the Federals back more than a mile and now occupied their ground and tents of the night before. They had captured General Prentiss with some thousands of his men as a result of his brave stand at the "Hornet's Nest."

But their hopes were mingled with grave fears. General Van Dorn with an army of twenty thousand men was hastening from Arkansas to join the Confederate forces at Shiloh; but the roads were bad and he was yet far away. On the other hand, Buell was coming from Nashville to join Grant's army. Should he arrive during the night, the contest of the next day would be unequal and the Confederates would risk losing all that they had gained. Moreover, Beauregard's army, with its long, muddy march from Corinth and its more than twelve hours' continuous fighting, was worn and weary almost to exhaustion.

The Union army was stunned and bleeding, but not disabled, at the close of the first day's battle. Caught unawares, the men had made a noble stand. Though pressed back from their position and obliged to huddle for the night around the Landing, while thousands of their comrades had fallen on the gory field, they had hopes of heavy reenforcements during the night. And, indeed, early in the evening the cry ran along the Union lines that Buell's army had come. The advance guard had arrived late in the afternoon and had assisted Hurlbut in the closing scene on the bluff of Dill's ravine; others continued to pour in during the night. And, furthermore, General Lew Wallace's division, though it had taken a wrong road from Crump's Landing and had not reached the field in time for the fighting of the 6th, now at last had arrived. Buell and Wallace had brought with them twenty-five thousand fresh troops to be hurled on the Confederates on the morning of the 7th. But Van Dorn had not come. The preponderance of numbers now was with the Union army.

Everyone knew that the battle was not over, that the issue

A GALLANT REGIMENT FROM THE HOOSIER STATE

To the Ninth Indiana belongs the banner record, on the Federal side, at bloody Shiloh. It seldom happens to any unit of a fighting force, while still engaged in action, to receive words of thanks and congratulation while still on the firing-line. Flags have been decorated with the medal of honor, individuals have been so rewarded for deeds of bravery and prowess, but to the Ninth Regiment from the Hoosier State fell the unique honor of having the word "well done" given them under fire. General Nelson, on April 7th, rode up and thanked them, and well was it deserved, for they saved the flank of Hazen's brigade by stubborn bravery that has hardly ever been equaled. Posted on the line of a rail fence that offered little or no protection, they held their ground against a force that outnumbered them two to one—able and determined fighters, too, who charged time and again up to the muzzles of their rifles, only to be beaten back by the steady and continuous volleys. Colonel William B. Hazen, in command of the Nineteenth Brigade, two or three times found himself so fiercely assailed that it looked as if the flank would be crumbled in, but the Ninth was there. And when the cost was footed up, it made a sad but gallant showing. The Ninth had suffered the heaviest loss in numbers of any regiment in the Army of the Ohio at that battle. The percentage of officers killed and wounded left many vacancies for promotion; no less than eight positions there were to fill in the depleted companies. And along that thin rail fence, in the battle, one hundred and seventy men had been killed or wounded. The Fourth Division, which General Nelson commanded, points with pride to the scroll of Hazen's Nineteenth Brigade, and first on the list stands the never faltering Ninth. In November it was transferred to the Second Brigade of the Second Division, Fourteenth Corps, Army of the Cumberland, and at Stone's River it lost one hundred and nine men, all told.

must be decided on the coming day, and the weary thousands of both sides sank down on the ground in a drenching rain to get a little rest and to gain a little strength for the desperate struggle that was sure to come on the morrow.

Beauregard rested hopes upon a fresh dispatch announcing that Buell was delayed and the dreaded junction of two Federal armies therefore impossible. Meanwhile Grant and Buell were together in Sherman's camp and it was decided that Buell's troops should attack Beauregard next morning. One division of Buell stood to arms all night.

At the break of day on Monday, April 7th, all was astir in both camps on the field of Shiloh, and the dawn was greeted with the roar of cannon. The troops that Grant now advanced into the contest were all, except about ten thousand, the fresh recruits that Wallace and Buell had brought, while the Confederates had not a single company that had not been on the ground the day before. Some military historians believe that Beauregard would have won a signal victory if neither army had been reenforced during the night. But now under the changed conditions the Confederates were at a great disadvantage, and yet they fought for eight long hours with heroic valor.

The deafening roar of the cannon that characterized the beginning of the day's battle was followed by the rattle of musketry, so continuous that no ear could distinguish one shot from another. Nelson's division of Buell's army was the first to engage the Confederates. Nelson commanded the Federal left wing, with Hardee and Breckinridge immediately opposed to him. The Union center was under the command of Generals McCook and Crittenden; the right wing was commanded by McClernand, with Hurlbut next, while Sherman and Lew Wallace occupied the extreme right. The Confederate left wing was commanded by the doughty Bragg and next to him was General Polk.

Shiloh Church was again the storm center and in it

THE MOUNTED POLICE OF THE WEST

Stalwart horsemen such as these bore the brunt of keeping order in the turbulent regions fought over by the armies in the West. The bugle call, "Boots and Saddles!" might summon them to fight, or to watch the movements of the active Confederates, Van Dorn and Price. It was largely due to their daring and bravery that the Confederate forces were held back from the Mississippi so as not to embarrass the movements of Grant and the gunboats. Of this unattached cavalry of the Army of the Ohio were the men in the upper picture—Company D, Fourth Kentucky Volunteers, enlisted at Louisville, December, 1861.

OFFICERS OF THE FOURTH KENTUCKY CAVALRY

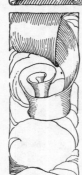

General Beauregard made his headquarters. Hour after hour the columns in blue and gray surged to and fro, first one then the other gaining the advantage and presently losing it. At times the smoke of burning powder enveloped the whole field and hid both armies from view. The interesting incidents of this day of blood would fill a volume. General Hindman of the Southern side had a novel experience. His horse was struck by a bursting shell and torn to a thousand fragments. The general, thrown ten feet high, fell to the ground, but leaped to his feet unhurt and asked for another horse.

Early in the afternoon, Beauregard became convinced that he was fighting a losing battle and that it would be the part of prudence to withdraw the army before losing all. He thereupon sent the members of his staff to the various corps commanders ordering them to prepare to retreat from the field, at the same time making a show of resuming the offensive. The retreat was so skilfully made, the front firing-line being kept intact, that the Federals did not suspect it for some time. Some hours before nightfall the fighting had ceased. The Federals remained in possession of the field and the Confederates were wading through the mud on the road to Corinth.

It was a dreary march for the bleeding and battered Confederate army. An eye-witness described it in the following language:

"I made a detour from the road on which the army was retreating that I might travel faster and get ahead of the main body. In this ride of twelve miles alongside of the routed army, I saw more of human agony and woe than I trust I will ever again be called upon to witness. The retreating host wound along a narrow and almost impassable road, extending some seven or eight miles in length. Here was a line of wagons loaded with wounded, piled in like bags of grain, groaning and cursing; while the mules plunged on in mud and water belly-deep, the water sometimes coming into the wagons. Next came a straggling regiment of infantry, pressing on past the

BUELL'S TROOPS CROSSING THE BIG BARREN

When the Confederate General Braxton Bragg made his masterly march into Kentucky and succeeded in getting in the rear of General Buell in Middle Tennessee in September, there followed a series of movements that demanded the utmost exertions of the engineers to keep the Federal Army in touch with its base and at the same time to oppose a front to General Bragg. In the first Confederate retreat through Kentucky almost all of the causeways had been destroyed, and when Buell arrived at Bowling Green, which is north of Nashville and on the bank of the Big Barren River, that stream was found to be almost flooding its banks. Here the nineteenth Regiment Michigan Engineers rebuilt the bridge almost at the place where General Mitchell had crossed early in the year. The middle part of the bridge was composed of fourteen pontoons.

FEDERALS ADVANCING INTO TENNESSEE—1862

Incessantly, through rain or shine, the work on this bridge over the Elk River, near Pulaski, Tennesse[e] on the Central Alabama Railroad, went on during the months of June and July. The engineers had b[e]fore them an enormous task. The Federal General Buell's army was short of supplies and ammunitio[n] and the completion of this bridge, and other bridges, was a matter of vital necessity. Supplies had to [b]e brought from Nashville. The roads were heavy with mud and the incessant rains had swollen the stream[s] making it not only slow but almost impossible for wagon trains to keep in touch with the base. Over th[e] Central Alabama (Nashville and Decatur Railroad) food and other necessities for the army's very exis[tence]

ENGINEERS AND INFANTRY BUSY AT THE ELK RIVER BRIDGE

ence had to be transported. Among those workers who labored uncomplainingly and whose work bore fruit, was the First Regiment, Michigan Engineers, that numbered among its enlisted men mechanics and artisans of the first class. They built this bridge pictured here. Four companies were employed in its construction, aided by an infantry detail working as laborers. The bridge was 700 feet long, 58 feet high, and crossed the Elk River at a point where the water was over 20 feet deep. At the right of the picture three of the engineer officers are consulting together, and to the left a squad of infantry are marching to their position as bridge guards. Here is the daily business of war—to which fighting is the occasional exception.

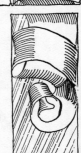

wagons; then a stretcher borne on the shoulders of four men, carrying a wounded officer; then soldiers staggering along, with an arm broken and hanging down, or other fearful wounds, which were enough to destroy life. And, to add to the horrors of the scene, the elements of heaven marshaled their forces—a fitting accompaniment of the tempest of human desolation and passion which was raging. A cold, drizzling rain commenced about nightfall, and soon came harder and faster, then turned to pitiless, blinding hail. This storm raged with violence for three hours. I passed long wagon trains filled with wounded and dying soldiers, without even a blanket to shelter them from the driving sleet and hail, which fell in stones as large as partridge eggs, until it lay on the ground two inches deep.

"Some three hundred men died during that awful retreat, and their bodies were thrown out to make room for others who, although wounded, had struggled on through the storm, hoping to find shelter, rest, and medical care."

Four days after the battle, however, Beauregard reported to his government, "this army is more confident of ultimate success than before its encounter with the enemy." Addressing the soldiers, he said: "You have done your duty. . . . Your countrymen are proud of your deeds on the bloody field of Shiloh; confident in the ultimate result of your valor."

The news of these two fearful days at Shiloh was astounding to the American people. Never before on the continent had there been anything approaching it. Bull Run was a skirmish in comparison with this gigantic conflict. The losses on each side exceeded ten thousand men. General Grant tells us that after the second day he saw an open field so covered with dead that it would have been possible to walk across it in any direction stepping on dead bodies, without a foot touching the ground. American valor was tried to the full on both sides at Shiloh, and the record shows that it was equal to the test.

NEW MADRID
ISLAND No. 10
NEW ORLEANS

CAIRO IN 1862—ON THE EXTREME RIGHT IS THE CHURCH WHERE FLAG-OFFICER
FOOTE PREACHED A SERMON AFTER THE FALL OF FORT HENRY—NEXT
HE LED THE GUNBOATS AT ISLAND NO. 10.

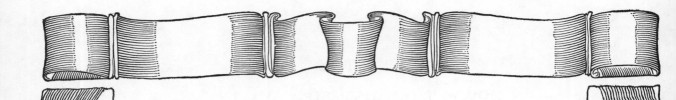

NEW MADRID AND ISLAND NO. 10

IT has been truly said that without the American navy, insignificant as it was in the early sixties, the North could hardly have succeeded in the great war. The blockade was necessary to success, and without the navy the blockade would have been impossible. It may further be said that without the gunboats on the winding rivers of the middle West success in that quarter would have been equally impossible. It was these floating fortresses that reduced Fort Henry and that gave indispensable aid at Fort Donelson. At Shiloh, when at the close of the first day's conflict the Confederates made a wild, impetuous dash on the Union camp, it was the two little wooden gunboats that aided in preserving the camp from capture or complete demoralization.

We have now to relate a series of operations down the Mississippi, in which the gunboats were the alpha and omega and almost all that falls between them. The creator of the fleet of gunboats with which we now have to deal was that master-builder, James B. Eads. It was on August 7, 1861, that Eads signed a contract with the Government to build and deliver seven ironclads, each one hundred and seventy-five feet long, fifty-one feet wide, drawing six feet of water, and carrying thirteen guns. In a week or two four thousand men were at work on the contract; sawmills were busy in five States cutting the timber; machine shops and iron foundries in several cities were running day and night. The places of building were Carondelet, near St. Louis, and Mound City, Illinois.

But the time was too short. The boats were unfinished at the end of sixty-five days. The Government refused to pay for them. And the builder, Eads—what did he do? He went ahead and used up his own fortune to finish those gunboats,

On the night of April 4, 1862, the Confederate garrison of the battery on Island No. 10, peering through the darkness out on the Mississippi, caught sight of the flicker of flames from the smoke-stacks of a steamer proceeding down the river. They knew at once that the attempt of the Federal gunboats to pass down to the support of General Pope's crossing of the river below had begun. The men on shore leaped to their guns, and the crash of cannon and the rattle of musketry broke forth across the bosom of the river. Aiming through the darkness at the luminous tops of the smoke-stacks the gunners poured in their vindictive fire, but the Confederates had elevated their guns too high and only two of their shots sped home. The *Carondelet*, for it was she, held on her way, and her commander, Henry Walke, would not permit his men to send a single answering shot. Walke had begged to be the first to take his vessel by the dreaded batteries on Island No. 10. In the pilot-house he directed the daring attempt, catching glimpses of the tortuous channel amid the fitful lightning of a storm which suddenly descended on the river and added the reverberations of Heaven to those of the battery below. At one moment the *Carondelet*

COMMANDER HENRY WALKE

grazed the bank of the island itself, but hastily backing off, made good her escape past a dreaded floating battery below the Island, which offered little opposition. She arrived at New Madrid without a man having received a single scratch. The *Carondelet* and her commander had made good, and the next morning lay ready to support the army after having achieved one of the greatest feats in the record of the inland navy. On April 6th, her elated and plucky crew captured and spiked the guns of the battery opposite Point Pleasant, an event which convinced the Confederates that Island No. 10 must be evacuated. That very night, encouraged by the success of the *Carondelet*, Commander Thompson, with the *Pittsburgh*, ran by the disheartened gunners on Island No. 10 and joined Commander Walke. The crossing of Pope's forces then proceeded, and the Confederates, in full retreat, were hemmed in by Paine's division and surrendered, before dawn of April 8th. Colonel Cook's troops cut off in their retreat from Island No. 10, were also compelled to surrender. The daring of Commander Walke in the face of this great danger had accomplished the first step in the opening of the Mississippi since the expedition left Cairo.

THE *CARONDELET*—FIRST TO RUN THE GANTLET AT ISLAND NO. 10

then handed them over to the Government and waited for his pay until after they had won their famous victories down the river.

Their first commander was Andrew H. Foote, who was called "the 'Stonewall' Jackson of the West." He had won fame in the waters of the Orient and had spent years in the suppression of the slave trade. Like "Stonewall" Jackson, he was a man of deep religious principles. On the Sunday after the fall of Fort Henry he preached a sermon in a church at Cairo. The next year the aged admiral lay sick in New York. His physician dreaded to tell him that his illness would be fatal, but did so. "Well," answered the admiral, "I am glad to be done with guns and war."

We must get to our story. Fort Henry and Fort Donelson had fallen. General Polk had occupied Columbus, Kentucky, a powerful stronghold from which one hundred and fifty cannon pointed over the bluff. But why hold Columbus in its isolation when Henry and Donelson were lost? So thought the good bishop-general and he broke camp on February 25, 1862, transferring one hundred and thirty of his big guns to Island No. 10, and rolling the remainder down the one hundred and fifty foot embankment into the Mississippi. That nothing might be left for the foe, he burned eighteen thousand bushels of corn and five thousand tons of hay, and when the Federals reached Columbus on March 4th they found only charred remains.

Island No. 10 was situated at the upper bend of a great double curve of the Mississippi, about forty miles below Columbus. It had been strongly fortified by General Beauregard, but Beauregard was called to Corinth and Shiloh and he turned the command over to General Mackall with about seven thousand men. It was confidently believed by its defenders that this fortified island would be the final stopping place of all hostile vessels on the great river, that none could pass it without being blown out of the water by the powerful batteries.

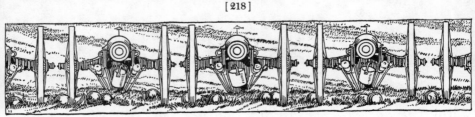

THE RETREAT DOWN THE RIVER.

The Flag-ship of the Confederate Fleet at Island No. 10.—Below the dreaded battery at Island No. 10, lay Commodore George N. Hollins, with his flag-ship, the *McRae* and seven other Confederate gunboats, holding in check the Federal troops chafing to cross the river and get at the inferior force of the enemy on the other side. This opposing fleet was further strengthened by a powerful floating battery which could be pushed about by the gunboats and anchored at the most effective points. When the *Carondelet* accomplished her daring feat of passing Island No. 10 on the night of April 4th, creeping stealthily by this boasted battery and cutting it off from its convoys, the men who manned it cut loose from their moorings and drifted down to the protection of Commodore

COMMODORE GEORGE N. HOLLINS, C.S.N.

Hollins' vigilant fleet. All was at once activity on board the Confederate vessels. Commodore Hollins did not court a meeting to try conclusions with the powerful Eads gunboats and the mortar boats, which he supposed were all making their way down upon him. The flag at the masthead of the *McRae* quickly signaled the order to weigh anchor, and the Confederate squadron, dropping slowly downstream, confined its activities to storming Pope's batteries on the Missouri shore below New Madrid. Farragut, threatening New Orleans, had caused the withdrawal of every available Confederate gunboat from the upper river, and the remaining river defense fleet under Commodore Hollins was not equal to the task of standing up to the determined and aggressive attempt of the Federals to seize and hold possession of the upper Mississippi.

Copyright by Review of Reviews Co.

THE *McRAE*

Below this island, a few miles, was the town of New Madrid on the Missouri shore, held also by the Confederates and protected by heavy guns behind breastworks.

On the west bank of the river, General John Pope commanded a Federal army of twenty thousand men. His object was to capture New Madrid. First he occupied Point Pleasant, twelve miles below, erected batteries and cut off supplies from New Madrid. He then slowly approached the town and meantime sent to Cairo for siege-guns. They arrived on the 12th of March, and all through the next day the cannonading was incessant. At night it ceased, and as Pope was about to renew the attack he discovered that the town had been abandoned during the night. The Confederates had not even delayed to destroy the supply stores, and they fell into the hands of the besiegers, together with all the guns and some thousands of small arms.

Island No. 10 was now isolated, indeed. Above it the river was aswarm with Federal gunboats; below it and along the Missouri shore was Pope's army. Southward was Reelfoot Lake, and eastward were impenetrable swamps. The only possible way of escape was by a road to the southward between the river and Reelfoot Lake to Tiptonville. But the brave defenders of the island were not ready to give up or to flee. They determined to remain and dispute the possession of the river at all hazards. At this time the river was very high. The whole wooded peninsula made by the great bend was covered with water. Houses, fences, trees—every movable thing—had been swept down the current.

General Pope's great desideratum was to secure boats to ferry his army across the river that he might capture Island No. 10. But the threatening cannon on the island forbade, in language without words, any attempt to pass them. The overflow of water on the peninsula was deep enough to float the transports, but a dense forest six miles in width prevented any such passage. At length a novel plan was devised—to cut a

THE FLAG–OFFICER'S GOOD–BYE

The decks of this staunch gunboat, the *Benton*, were crowded on the morning of May 9, 1862, by her officers and men waiting solemnly for the appearance of Commodore A. H. Foote. The *Benton* had been his flag-ship in the operations around Island No. 10 and Fort Pillow; but the wound he had received at Fort Donelson continued to undermine his health until now, supported by Captain Phelps, he feebly made his way on deck to bid good-bye to his brave and faithful comrades and resign his command to Captain Charles H. Davis. At sight of him the old tars swung their hats and burst into loud huzzas, which quickly gave place to moist eyes and saddened countenances, as Foote, with tears trickling down his cheeks, addressed to them some simple, heartfelt words of farewell. The men leaned forward to catch every syllable uttered by the beloved commander's failing voice. An hour later the *De Soto* dropped down to the *Benton*. Foote was assisted to the transport's deck by his successor, Captain Davis, and Captain Phelps. Sitting in a chair on her guards, his breast filled with emotion, he gazed across the rapidly widening space separating him forever from the *Benton*, while the men on her deck continued to look longingly after him, till distance and tears hid each from the other's sight.

channel through the forest. Six hundred skilled engineers were in the army and they were soon at work in relays of three hundred. After cutting off the trees above the water they cut the stumps beneath the water and just above the ground by means of hand-saws attached to pivots. After nineteen days of vigorous toil a channel was cut through the forest six miles long, fifty feet wide, and four and a half feet deep. The flat-bottomed transports could pass through this channel and they quickly did so—quickly, because the river was falling and the opportunity would soon pass. They were soon safely lodged at New Madrid without having come within range of the heavy guns of Island No. 10.

But the ironclad gunboats—what could be done with them? They drew too much water to be taken through the newly-made channel. Above the fortified island lay the Eads fleet, as it should be called (for the patriotic engineer still owned it in part), restless, eager for a fight. There were the *Benton,* the flag-ship, the *Carondelet,* the *St. Louis,* the *Cincinnati,* the *Pittsburgh,* the *Mound City,* and eleven mortar-boats. But these vessels could do something: they could shoot, and they did on March 17th. On that day they trained their guns on the island; for nine long hours the boom of cannon was continuous. The results were slight. Beauregard, who had not yet departed for Corinth, wired to Richmond that his batteries were not damaged and but one man was killed.

General Pope was sorely in need of a gunboat or two to silence a number of batteries guarding the Tiptonville road, on the east side of the river. Could he get possession of that road the last hope of escape from the island would be lost and ere long its defenders must surrender. Pope believed it possible for the gunboats to run the gantlet of the batteries of Island No. 10. But Foote thought it impossible, in the face of the mouths of half a hundred cannon that yawned across the channel. He refused to force anyone to so perilous an undertaking, and the commanders of the vessels all agreed

A VETERAN OF MANY RIVER FIGHTS

The *St. Louis* was the earliest of the Eads iron-clad gunboats to be completed and is first mentioned in despatches on January 14, 1862, when with the *Essex* and *Tyler* she engaged the Confederate batteries at Columbus, Kentucky. The *St. Louis*, commanded by Lieutenant Leonard Paulding, participated in the capture of Fort Henry, going into action lashed to the *Carondelet*. At Fort Donelson she was Foote's flagship. She was struck seven times. Island No. 10, Fort Pillow, Memphis—at all these places the *St. Louis* distinguished herself. On October 1, 1862, the *St. Louis* was renamed the *Baron de Kalb*. All through the Vicksburg operations the *De Kalb* saw service with Admiral Porter. On July 12, 1863, after the fall of Vicksburg, she was sunk by a torpedo in the Yazoo River. This photograph was a gift to the present owner from James B. Eads, the builder.

with him that the running of the batteries was too great a risk, except one—Henry Walke, commander of the *Carondelet*.

"Are you willing to try it with your vessel?" asked Foote, of Commander Walke, in the presence of the other officers. "Yes," answered Walke, and it was agreed that the *Carondelet* should attempt to run the batteries. The next few days were spent in preparing the vessel for the ordeal. Chains, hawsers, and cables were wound around the pilot-house and other vulnerable parts of the vessel. A coal barge loaded with coal and hay was lashed to the side where there was no iron protection for the magazine. The steam escape was led through the wheel-house so as to avoid the puffing sound through the smokestack. The sailors were armed to resist boarding parties, and sharpshooters were placed on board.

The night of April 4th was chosen for this daring adventure. At ten o'clock the moon had set and the sky was overcast with dark clouds. The *Carondelet* began her perilous journey in total darkness. But presently a terrific thunderstorm swept up the river and the vivid flashes of lightning rendered it impossible for the gunboat to pass the island unseen. Presently when near the hostile island the vessel was discovered. Next moment the heavy guns began to roar, as if to answer the thunders of the sky; the flashes from the burning powder commingled with the vivid lightning, the whole presenting a scene of indescribable grandeur.

The *Carondelet* was saved, chiefly, no doubt, through the fact that she ran so near the island that the great guns could not be sufficiently depressed, and they overshot the mark. About midnight the gunboat reached New Madrid uninjured.

Two nights later the *Pittsburgh* ran the gantlet of Island No. 10. The two vessels soon reduced the batteries along the east bank of the river to silence. Pope's army crossed and occupied the Tiptonville road. The Confederate garrison of several thousand men could only surrender, and this they did, while the second day's battle was raging at Shiloh—April 7, 1862.

A GUNBOAT OF FIGHTING FAME, THE CAIRO

The first engagement of the *Cairo*, a third-rate ironclad of 512 tons, mounting six 42-pounders, six 32-pounders, three 8-inch guns and one 12-lb. howitzer, was under the command of Lieutenant N. C. Bryant on February 19th, in the Cumberland River in Tennessee. At Clarksville with the gunboat *Conestoga* the *Cairo* engaged three forts, capturing the town. On May 10th the *Cairo*, still commanded by Lieutenant Bryant, participated in the action at Fort Pillow and the river combat with the Confederate "River Defense" fleet. While being rammed the *Cincinnati* was so injured that she sank. The *Mound City* also was injured and three of the Confederate vessels were disabled. Once more the *Cairo*, on June 6th, with four other ironclad gunboats and two of the Ellet rams, engaged the Confederate flotilla off the city of Memphis. On December 12, 1862, the *Cairo*, then under the command of Lieutenant T. O. Selfridge, was destroyed by a torpedo in the Yazoo River.

NEW ORLEANS—THE ENTERING WEDGE WHERE THE NAVY HELPED THE ARMY

By James Barnes

THE capture of Forts Jackson and St. Philip and the surrender of New Orleans was the first great blow that the Confederacy received from the south. Coming but two months after the fall of Fort Donelson, it was the thunderous stroke on the wedge that started the ensuing separation of the seceding States into two halves. It was the action that shortened the war by months, if not by years; and though performed by the navy alone, its vital connection with the operations of the army in the West and along the great highway of the Mississippi was paramount. The military history of the war could not be written without touching upon it. The inborn genius of President Lincoln was never more clearly shown than when, on November 12, 1861, he ordered a naval expedition to be fitted out for the capture of New Orleans, the real key to the Mississippi; and never was clearer judgment proved than by the appointment of Captain David G. Farragut to the supreme command as flag-officer. To his fleet was attached a mortar flotilla under Commander David D. Porter, and here again was found the right man for the hour.

All through November, December and early January of 1862, the preparations were hurried without waste of energy. On the 2d of February, Farragut sailed from Hampton Roads, with orders to rendezvous at Key West, where Porter's mortar-boats were to join him. Such vessels as could be spared

THE STEAM FRIGATE *BROOKLYN*

The Vessel that Followed the Flagship Past the Forts at New Orleans. When David Glasgow Farragut chose the *Hartford* as the ship to fly his flag, he picked out a craft that for her type (a steam frigate of the second class) was as fine as could be found in any navy in the world; and as much could be said for the *Brooklyn*, the second ship of the center division. She marked the transition period between sail and steam. Her tall masts were the inheritance of former days; her engines were merely auxiliary factors, for she could sail with all her canvas set and the proper wind to drive her faster than she could steam under the best conditions. Here we see her with royal, top-gallant sails, top-sails, and courses clewed up, and her funnel lowered to a level with her bulwarks. In passing the forts at New Orleans, she presented no such appearance—her upper yards had been sent down, and with her engines doing their utmost, her funnel belching smoke, she swept slowly on into the line of fire. The first division, composed of eight vessels under command of Captain Theodorus Bailey on the *Cayuga*, was ahead. But every gunner in Fort Jackson and in Fort St. Philip had been told to "look out for the *Hartford* and the *Brooklyn*." It was dark, but the fire-rafts, the soaring shells, and the flames from the guns afloat and ashore made everything as bright as day. By some mistake, the reports that were first sent to Washington of the passing of the forts contained an erroneous plan. It was the first or discarded drawing, showing the fleet in two divisions abreast. This was afterwards changed into the three-division plan in which Captain Bailey with the *Cayuga* led. It was not until four years after the closing of the war that this mistake was rectified, and many of the histories and contemporary accounts of the passing of the forts are entirely in error. The center division was composed of only three vessels, all of them steam frigates of the first class: the *Hartford*, flying Farragut's flag, under Commander Wainwright; the *Brooklyn*, under Captain T. T. Craven, and the *Richmond*, under Commander J. Alden. In the first division were also the steam sloops-of-war *Pensacola* and *Mississippi*, and they already had been under fire for twenty minutes when the center division neared Fort Jackson. The flagship (really the ninth in line) steered in close to the shore, but was obliged to sheer across the stream in an attempt to dodge a fire-raft that was pushed by the Confederate tug *Mosher*. It was a daring act performed by a little crew of half a dozen men, and as a deed of desperate courage has hardly any equal in naval warfare. The *Mosher* all but succeeded in setting the flag-ship in flames, and was sunk by a well-directed shot. The *Brooklyn*, after a slight collision with the *Kineo*, one of the vessels of Bailey's division, and almost colliding with the hulks in the obstructions, was hit by the ram *Manassas* a glancing blow—a little more and this would have sunk her, as both her inner and outer planking were crushed. But, like the flag-ship, she succeeded in passing safely.

from the blockade, whose pinch upon the South Atlantic ports had already begun to be felt, were detached to aid the expedition. No such great plans and actions could be carried on in secrecy. Almost from its incipiency, the object of all this preparation became known throughout the South. Every effort was made by the Confederate military commanders to strengthen the defenses at New Orleans, which consisted of the formidable forts St. Philip and Jackson that faced one another, the former on the north bank and the latter on the south bank of the river below the city. Once these were passed, New Orleans would fall. Not only were the forts strengthened, but every effort was made by the Confederates to gain supremacy afloat; and in this they all but succeeded. In addition to the formidable obstructions placed in the river, the iron-clad ram, *Manassas*, was strengthened and further protected to prepare her for conflict. The *Louisiana*, then building at New Orleans, was rushed toward completion. If she had been ready, perhaps New Orleans would have told a different story, for she was designed to be the most powerful ironclad of her day—4,000 tons rating and mounting sixteen heavy guns, well protected by armor. Up the river, at Memphis, the *Arkansas* was being prepared for active service; and on the various tributaries were being built several iron-clad vessels.

No ship in Farragut's fleet possessed any more powers of resistance than the old wooden walls of Nelson's time. Against this attacking fleet were the well-placed guns ashore, seventy-four in Fort Jackson and fifty-two pieces of ordnance in Fort St. Philip. The garrisons were made up of about seven hundred well-trained cannoneers apiece. As Admiral Porter has observed, "Assuming upon the general concession of military men that one gun in a fort was equal to about three afloat, and considering the disadvantage of a contrary three-and-a-half-knot current to the Federal vessels (with additional channel obstructions of fire-rafts and

THE *RICHMOND*

The Third Ship of the Center Division at the Passing of the Forts.—There was a current in the Mississippi that had to be taken into account in estimating the time that Farragut's fleet would be under fire from the forts. The larger vessels were all so slow when under steam that, taking the rule that "a fleet is no faster than the slowest ship," caused them literally to crawl past the danger points. The *Richmond* was the slowest of them all. Just as she neared the passageway through the obstructions her boilers began to foam, and she could just about stem the current and no more. The vessels of the third division passed her; but at last, with her bow pointed up the river, she was able to engage Fort Jackson. Opening with her port batteries, she hammered hard at the fort, and with small loss got by, followed by the little gunboat *Sciota* that had equal good fortune. When day dawned, the *Richmond* kept up to the anchored fleet and reported. It was feared at first that she had been lost or sunk. The battle of New Orleans was probably the most successful, and certainly the boldest, attempt ever made to match wooden ships against forts at close range. Although the Confederate gunboats were inferior to the Federal fleet, they also have to be taken into consideration for their brave and almost blind assault. If they had been assisted by the unfinished ironclads they might have borne different results, for the *Louisiana*, owing to her unfinished condition never entered the fight. She was considered to be more powerful than the *Merrimac*. Certainly her armament would prove it, for she mounted two 7-inch rifles, three 9-inch shell guns, four 8-inch smooth-bores, and even 100-pounder rifles—in all sixteen guns. At the city of New Orleans was an unfinished ironclad that was expected to be even more powerful than the *Louisiana*. Only the arrival of Farragut's fleet at this timely hour for the Federal cause prevented her from being finished. It was believed by her builders—and apparently, in view of the immunity of ironclads, with reason—that not only would the *Mississippi* drive the Federal fleet out of the river, but that she would be able to paralyze the whole of the wooden navy of the North, and might possibly go so far as to lay the Northern Atlantic cities under contribution. In order to prevent her from falling into the Federal hands she, like the *Louisiana*, was set on fire and drifted a wreck down the stream. Commander J. Alden, of the *Richmond*, was on the quarterdeck throughout the action and had seen to it that his vessel, like the others, was prepared in every way to render the chances of success more favorable. Cables were slung over the side to protect her vulnerable parts, sand bags and coal had been piled up around her engines, hammocks and splinter-nettings were spread and rigged, and as the attempt to run the forts would be at night, no lights were allowed. Decks and gun-breeches were whitewashed to make them more visible in the darkness. Farragut's orders had concluded with the following weighty sentence: "I shall expect the most prompt attention to signals and verbal orders either from myself or the Captain of the fleet, who, it will be understood in all cases, acts by my authority." The *Richmond* lost two men killed and four men wounded in the action.

chains), the odds were greatly in favor of the Confederate defenses.''

The defenders of the old city, New Orleans, were confident that the fleet would never pass. On the 16th of April, the mortar-boats were in position along what was, owing to the bend of the river, really the southern bank (one division, on the first day, was across the river), and in the morning they opened, each vessel firing at the rate of one shell every ten minutes. Organized into three divisions, they were anchored close to the shore, the furthest up stream, only 2,850 yards from Fort Jackson, and 3,680 from Fort St. Philip. They were near a stretch of woods and their tall masts—they were mostly schooners—were dressed with branches of trees in order to disguise their position from the Confederate guns. For almost eight days, at varying intervals even at night, the twenty boats of this flotilla rained their hail of death and destruction on the forts. Brave and hardy must have been the men who stood that terrific bombardment! The commanders of the Confederate forts bore witness to the demoralization of both the men and defenses that ensued. Nearly every shell of the many thousand fired lodged inside the works; magazines were threatened, conflagrations started, and destruction was reaped on all sides. Long after the memorable day of the 24th of April when the fleet swept past, Colonel Edward Higgins, the brave defender of Fort Jackson, wrote as follows:

" I was obliged to confine the men most rigidly to the casemates, or we should have lost the best part of the garrison. A shell, striking the parapet over one of the magazines, the wall of which was seven feet thick, penetrated five feet and failed to burst. If that shell had exploded, the work would have ended.

" Another burst near the magazine door, opening the earth and burying the sentinel and another man five feet in the same grave.

" The parapet and interior of the fort were completely

David G. Farragut, Who Commanded the Fleets at New Orleans. No man ever succeeded in impressing his own personality and infusing his confidence and enthusiasm upon those under his command better than did David Glasgow Farragut. In drawing up the plans and assuming the responsibility of what seemed to be a desperate and almost foolhardy deed, Farragut showed his genius and courage. His attack was not a blind rush, trusting to suddenness for its effect; it was a well-studied, well-thought-out plan. Nothing was neglected "which prudence could suggest, foresight provide, or skill and science devise." Farragut was well aware of the results that would follow. The control of the lower Mississippi, if complete, would have enabled the Confederate Government to draw almost unlimited supplies from the vast country to the west of the river, and undoubtedly would have prolonged the war. The failure of Farragut's plan and his defeat would have meant a most crushing blow to the North. But in his trust in his officers and his own fearless courage there was small chance of failure. Calm and collected he went through the ordeal, and when safe above the forts he saw Bailey's vessels waiting, and one by one his other ships coming up, he knew that his stupendous undertaking was a success.

DAVID GLASGOW FARRAGUT

THE MAN WHO DARED

The whole of the North rose in elation at the news of the capture of New Orleans; but the surrender of the city at the mouth of the river did not mean complete possession. From Vicksburg southward, the long line of the river and the land on either side was yet in the possession of the Confederates. Baton Rouge and Natchez surrendered on demand. On May 29th, transports carrying the troops of General Williams came down the river after a reconnaissance at Vicksburg. Farragut was anchored off the town of Baton Rouge. He reported to Williams that a body of irregular Confederate cavalry had fired into one of his boats, wounding an officer and two men, and that he had been compelled to open his batteries upon the shore. Williams at once occupied the town in force.

A FLAGSHIP IN UNFRIENDLY WATERS

The *Hartford* Lying Close to the Levee at Baton Rouge

honeycombed, and the large number of sand bags with which we were supplied alone saved us from being blown to pieces a hundred times, our magazine doors being much exposed.

"On the morning of the 24th, when the fleet passed, the terrible precision with which the formidable vessels hailed down their tons of bursting shell upon the devoted fort made it impossible for us to obtain either rapidity or accuracy of fire, and thus rendered the passage comparatively easy."

Although all the foregoing proves the accuracy and value of the mortar fire, it alone could not reduce the forts. They had to be passed to lay the city at the mercy of the fleet. But there were the obstructions yet to deal with. 'Twas a brave deed that was done by the two gunboats, *Itasca* and *Pinola*, which, after great difficulties, broke the great link-chain that, buoyed by logs and hulks, closed up the channel. General M. L. Smith, the engineer of the department, in his report, in referring to the fall of New Orleans, wrote, "While the obstruction existed, the city was safe; when it was swept away, as the defenses then existed, it was in the enemy's power."

By 2 o'clock A.M. in the morning of the 24th, the intrepid Lieutenant Caldwell, who had suggested the expedition of the two gunboats that had broken up the obstruction, returned to the fleet after a daring survey of the channel, and the flag-ship hoisted the appointed signal. In two divisions, the fleet passed through the broken barriers and steamed into the zone of fire. It was an enfilading fire, as soon the guns of both forts were brought into play. There is not space here to go into the details of the naval battle that followed with the bravely fought Confederate gunboats and the ram *Manassas*. That belongs to naval history. There were deeds of prowess performed by vessels that flew either flag; there were small separate actions whose relating would make separate stories in themselves. Amid burning fire-rafts and a continuous roar from the opposing forts, the first division of the fleet under the command of Captain Theodorus Bailey held its course,

Coaling Farragut's Fleet at Baton Rouge. If "a ship without a captain is like a man without a soul," as runs an old naval saying, a vessel dependent upon steam power with empty bunkers is as a man deprived of heart-blood, nerves, or muscles; and a few days after New Orleans, Farragut's vessels faced a serious crisis. Captain A. T. Mahan has summed it up in the following words: " . . . The maintenance of the coal supply for a large squadron, five hundred miles up a crooked river in a hostile country, was in itself no small anxiety, involving as it did carriage of the coal against the current, the provision of convoys to protect the supply vessels against guerillas, and the employment of pilots, few of whom were to be found, as they naturally favored the enemy, and had gone away. The river was drawing near the time of lowest water, and the flag-ship herself got aground under very critical circumstances, having had to take out her coal and shot, and had even begun on her guns, two of which were out when she floated off." Many of the up-river gun-boats could burn wood, and so, at a pinch and for a short time, could the smaller steamers with Farragut. But the larger vessels required coal, and at first there was not much of it to be had, although there were some colliers with the fleet and more were dispatched later. In the two pictures of this page we are shown scenes along the levee in 1862, at Baton Rouge, and out in the river, a part of the fleet. The vessel with sails let down to dry is the sloop-of-war *Mississippi;* ahead of her and a little inshore, about to drop her anchor, is one of the smaller steamers that composed the third division of the fleet. Nearby lies a mortar schooner and a vessel laden with coal. Baton Rouge, where Farragut had hoisted his flag over the arsenal, was policed by a body of foreigners employed by the municipal authority. The mayor had declared that the guerilla bands which had annoyed the fleet were beyond his jurisdiction, saying that he was responsible only for order within the city limits. There was some coal found in the city belonging to private owners, and the lower picture shows the yards of Messrs. Hill and Markham, who, through the medium of Mr. Bryan, the Mayor, opened negotiations with Farragut for its sale.

his ship, the *Cayuga*, leading the van. The second division, under the fleet's commander, followed. The powerful steam ram, *Manassas,* had struck the *Brooklyn,* doing some slight damage. But when the *Mississippi* turned her wooden prow upon her, in order to avoid being turned over like a log, the ram took to the shore, where her crew escaped. Subsequently, having received two broadsides from the *Mississippi,* she slid off the bank and drifted in flames down with the current.

By daybreak nine of the Confederate vessels that had fought so gallantly and dauntlessly were destroyed. The forts lay some five miles downstream. The little batteries that protected the outskirts of the city were silenced. On the 25th, New Orleans lay powerless under Farragut's guns. The dreaded *Louisiana* was set on fire and blew up with tremendous explosion. Another, and still more powerful ironclad, the *Mississippi* (not to be confused with the vessel in Farragut's fleet of the same name), suffered the same fate. She had been launched only six days before. On the 27th, Porter, who was down the river, demanded the surrender of the forts; and General Duncan, the Confederate commander-in-chief, accepted the terms on the 28th. At 2.30 P.M. on that day, Fort St. Philip and Fort Jackson were formally delivered, and the United States flag was hoisted over them. On May 1st, General Butler arrived and the captured city was handed over to the army. The wedge having been driven home, the opening of the Mississippi from the south had begun.

FORT PILLOW
AND
MEMPHIS

THE CONFEDERATE RAM "GENERAL PRICE"—ACCIDENTALLY STRUCK BY HER CONSORT "GENERAL BEAUREGARD" AT THE BATTLE OF MEMPHIS, RUN ASHORE, AND CAPTURED BY THE FEDERALS

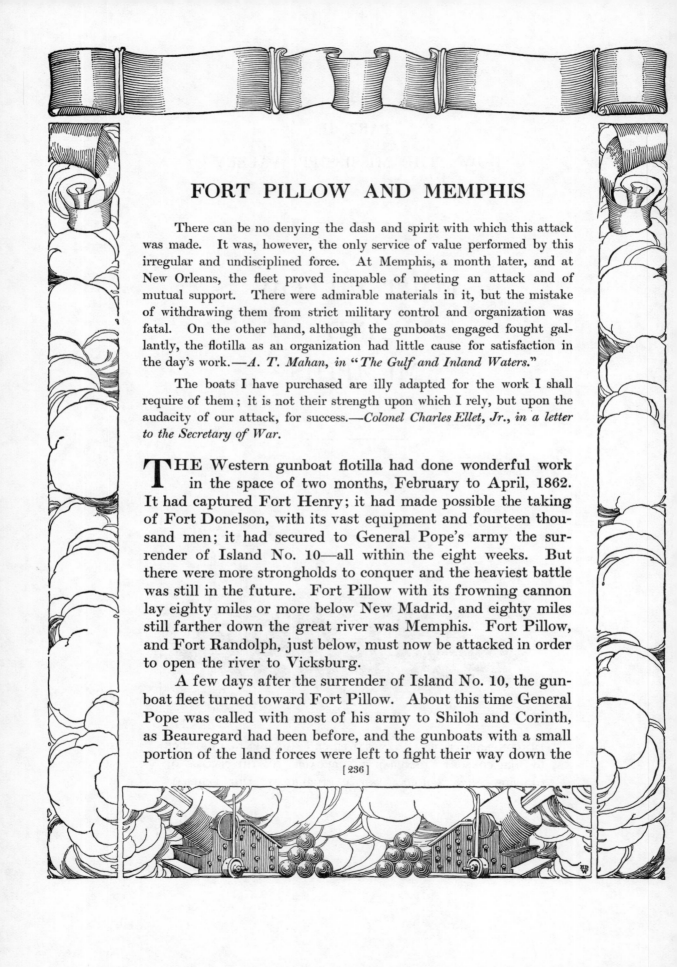

FORT PILLOW AND MEMPHIS

There can be no denying the dash and spirit with which this attack was made. It was, however, the only service of value performed by this irregular and undisciplined force. At Memphis, a month later, and at New Orleans, the fleet proved incapable of meeting an attack and of mutual support. There were admirable materials in it, but the mistake of withdrawing them from strict military control and organization was fatal. On the other hand, although the gunboats engaged fought gallantly, the flotilla as an organization had little cause for satisfaction in the day's work.—*A. T. Mahan, in "The Gulf and Inland Waters."*

The boats I have purchased are illy adapted for the work I shall require of them; it is not their strength upon which I rely, but upon the audacity of our attack, for success.—*Colonel Charles Ellet, Jr., in a letter to the Secretary of War.*

THE Western gunboat flotilla had done wonderful work in the space of two months, February to April, 1862. It had captured Fort Henry; it had made possible the taking of Fort Donelson, with its vast equipment and fourteen thousand men; it had secured to General Pope's army the surrender of Island No. 10—all within the eight weeks. But there were more strongholds to conquer and the heaviest battle was still in the future. Fort Pillow with its frowning cannon lay eighty miles or more below New Madrid, and eighty miles still farther down the great river was Memphis. Fort Pillow, and Fort Randolph, just below, must now be attacked in order to open the river to Vicksburg.

A few days after the surrender of Island No. 10, the gunboat fleet turned toward Fort Pillow. About this time General Pope was called with most of his army to Shiloh and Corinth, as Beauregard had been before, and the gunboats with a small portion of the land forces were left to fight their way down the

Federal Floating Mortar Battery at Fort Pillow. There would have been no engagement at Fort Pillow had it not been for the continued annoyance inflicted upon that position by the curious little craft—one of which we see tied up to the wharf in the lower picture. Secure in the knowledge that Beauregard's presence with a large force at Corinth had precluded the Federal land attack, General Villepigue awoke one morning to the sound of bursting shells which a Federal mortar boat was rapidly dropping over his ramparts. Every day thereafter, Flag-Officer Foote continued to pay compliments to Fort Pillow by sending down a mortar boat towed by a gunboat of the type seen in the picture. There was nothing for the Confederates to do but take to their bomb-proofs, so long as the Federal gunners continued the bombardment. At last General Villepigue, chafing under the damage done to his works, called urgently upon the Confederate flotilla to come up and put an end to the mortar boats. Early on the morning of May 10, 1862, the day after Flag-Officer Foote went North, leaving Captain Davis in charge of the Federal flotilla, the *Cincinnati* towed mortar No. 16 down to

GENERAL J. B. VILLEPIGUE

THE DEFENDER OF FORT PILLOW

the usual position for shelling the fort, and then tied up to the edge of the stream to protect her. The mortar fired her first shot at five o'clock. One hour and a half later the eight rams of the Confederate River Defense fleet suddenly and unexpectedly appeared bearing down upon the *Cincinnati*. The latter quickly slipped her moorings, and opened her bow guns upon the approaching vessels. One of these, the *General Bragg*, passed quickly above the Federal ironclad, turned and struck her a violent blow on the starboard quarter. After that the *Bragg* disappeared down the river, but the *General Price* and the *Sumter* continued the attack. One struck the *Cincinnati* again, but the other received a shot through her boilers from the *Benton*, and this ended her part of the fight. The wounded *Cincinnati* was helped to the shore and sunk. The other Federal ironclad had now come upon the scene and the *mêlée* became general. The *General Van Dorn* rammed the *Mound City* so severely that she was compelled to run on the Arkansas shore. After that the Confederate rams returned to Fort Pillow and the half hour's thrilling fight was over.

BOATS THAT BROUGHT ON THE BATTLE

river alone. For two weeks the fleet bombarded Fort Pillow at long range. On May 9th, Flag-Officer Foote, whose wound received at Fort Donelson had not healed, asked to be relieved, and Captain Charles H. Davis, a man of well-known skill and bravery, was appointed in his place. The day after the retirement of Foote a Confederate fleet, known as the "River Defense," under the command of Captain J. E. Montgomery, came up and offered battle. Among them was a powerful side-wheel steam ram, the *General Bragg,* which made for the *Cincinnati.* The latter opened fire, but the shots could not drive the antagonist off. Presently the onrushing vessel struck the *Cincinnati* on the starboard side and penetrated the shell-room, rendering the ironclad almost helpless. Before the wounded vessel could get away she was rammed by two other Confederate boats, the *General Price* and the *Sumter.* Meanwhile the *Carondelet* had come to the rescue of the *Cincinnati,* firing as fast as she could load. At last the *Sumter* was struck by a 50-pound Dahlgren shot from the *Carondelet* and completely disabled. Her steam-chest was penetrated and the steam instantly poured out upon all parts of her casemate. The men ran for life, some leaping into the water and some falling on the deck, victims of the scalding steam. The *General Van Dorn,* one of the most agile of the Confederate vessels, partially disabled the *Mound City* by ramming her amidships with fearful force.

The smoke of battle had enveloped the whole scene in a dense cloud. There was a lull in the firing, and when the smoke cleared away the Confederate fleet was seen drifting slowly down the stream to Fort Pillow, and the battle was over.

For two or three days after this battle long-range firing was kept up, the Union fleet lying a mile or more up the river, the Confederate vessels being huddled under the guns of Fort Pillow.

On the 4th of June, great clouds of smoke were seen to arise from the fort, and terrific explosions accompanying

THE VESSEL WITH THE ARMED PROW. THE FEDERAL RAM *VINDICATOR*

An excellent example of the steam rams as developed from the ideas of Charles Ellet, Jr., adding a new chapter to the history of naval warfare. As far back as the siege of Sebastopol, in 1854, Charles Ellet—being then in Europe—proposed a plan to the Russians to equip their blockaded fleet with rams. The plan was not adopted, and in 1855 he published a pamphlet outlining his idea and said, in proposing it to the United States Government, "I hold myself ready to carry it out in all its details whenever the day arrives that the United States is about to become engaged in a naval contest." It was not until after the appearance of the *Merrimac* at Hampton Roads and the danger to Foote's fleet on the Mississippi from Confederate rams that Ellet was given the opportunity to try his various projects and commissioned to equip several rams at Cincinnati. The project was regarded as a perilous one. Had it not been for Ellet's extraordinary personal influence he would never have been able to obtain crews for his rams, as they were entirely unarmored with the exception of the pilot-house, but Ellet had reasoned correctly that the danger from collision was immensely against the vessel struck, while the danger from shot penetrating a vital part of the approaching ram he proved was reduced to an unappreciable fraction. He contented himself, therefore, with strengthening the hulls of the river steamers which he purchased, filling the bows with solid timbers and surrounding the boilers with a double tier of oak twenty-four inches thick. At Memphis the rams had their first trial and it resulted in complete vindication of Ellet's theories. It was a vindication, however, which cost Ellet his life. He was mortally wounded in the fight at Memphis while in command of the *Queen of the West*.

told the story. The Confederates were evacuating the place and destroying their magazines before departing. The next morning the Federals clambered up the bluff to the site of the fort and found only smoking ruins. Even the earthen breastworks had been torn to pieces by the fearful powder explosions. Fort Randolph was likewise abandoned. The great river, while not yet rolling " unvexed to the sea," was now open as far as Memphis, whither the River Defense fleet had retreated, some eighty miles below Fort Pillow, and thither steered the Federal gunboats in search of their recent antagonists.

Down the glassy river the Union fleet glided on June 5th. The banners were waving. The men were as gay as if they were going to a picnic. In the evening they came within gunshot of Memphis and anchored for the night, not far from the supposed spot where, more than three hundred years before, De Soto had first cast his eyes on the rolling tide of the Mississippi.

The Federal flotilla on the Mississippi had, some days before, been reenforced by four small steam rams under the command of Colonel Charles Ellet, Jr. Ellet was not by profession a military man, but a distinguished civil engineer. He had convinced the Government of the value of the steam ram as a weapon of war, and was given a colonel's commission and authority to fit out a fleet of rams. His vessels were not armed. He cooperated with, but was not under the direction of, Flag-Officer Davis. His " flag-ship " was the *Queen of the West* and the next in importance was the *Monarch*, commanded by his younger brother, Alfred W. Ellet.

It was understood by all that a ferocious river-battle was necessary before the Federals could get control of the city on the hill. It is true that Memphis was not fortified, but it was defended by the fleet which the previous month had had its first taste of warfare at Fort Pillow and now lay at the foot of the bluffs ready to grapple with the coming foe. The vessels, eight in number, were not equal to those of the Union fleet. They

PILOT W. J. AUSLINTY

PILOT DAVID HEINER

PILOT CHARLES ROSS

HEROES OF THE WHEEL-HOUSE

THE UNARMORED CONNING TOWER

Look into these six keen eyes which knew every current and eddy, every snag and sandbar of the Mississippi. To the hands of men like these the commanders of the Federal gunboats owed the safe conduct of their vessels. No hearts more fearless nor hands more steady under fire were brought into the fighting on either side. Standing silently at the wheel, their gaze fixed on the familiar countenance of the river before them, they guided the gunboats through showers of shell. Peering into the murky night, they felt their way through shallow channels past watchful batteries whose first shot would be aimed against the frail and unprotected pilot house.

There was no more dangerous post than the pilot house of a gunboat, standing as a target for the gunners, who knew that to disable the pilot was to render the vessel helpless to drift hither and yon or to run aground to be riddled full of holes. After the Inland Fleet passed

THE TARGET OF THE SHARPSHOOTERS

from the control of the army to that of the navy the pilots of all the gunboats except Ellet's rams were brevetted acting masters or masters' mates and wore the uniform of the navy. Their services and bravery were fully recognized by the commanders, and their intimate knowledge of the river admitted them to conferences in which the most secret and difficult naval movements were planned. A river pilot knew when he could take his vessel over sandbars and inundated shallows where soundings would have turned back any navigating officer of the navy. Such valuable men were never safe. Even when passing up and down apparently peaceful reaches of the river the singing of some sharpshooters' bullet would give sudden warning that along the banks men were lying in wait for them. The mortality among the pilots during the war speaks volumes for the simple heroism of these silent men.

carried but two guns each, except one, which carried four. It was therefore a brave thing for Captain Montgomery to lay down the gage of battle to a fleet far stronger than his own. But he and his men did not falter. They moved up the swift current and opened the battle of Memphis, one of the most hotly contested naval battles ever fought in American waters.

It was the 6th of June, 1862, and one of the most charming days that Nature ever gives. As the sun rose over the eastern hills the people of the city gathered along the bluff in thousands, standing in dark silhouette against the sky, to watch the contest, and one can imagine how their emotion rose and fell as the tide of battle ebbed and flowed on the river below.

It was at 5:00 A.M. that Montgomery moved up the stream and fired the first gun. At this opening Colonel Ellet sprang forward on the hurricane deck, waved his hat, and shouted to his brother: "Round out and follow me. Now is our chance."

The *Queen* instantly moved toward the Confederate fleet; the Federal ironclads followed, but already both fleets were engaged in a brisk cannonade and the smoke was so dense that the *Queen* was soon lost to view. The daring little vessel plunged on through the waves. She was headed for the *General Lovell,* almost in the center of the Confederate line of battle. The *Queen* struck her antagonist squarely on the side and cut her almost in two. The wounded vessel groaned and lurched, and in a few minutes she sank, with many of her devoted crew, beneath the dark waters of the river.

Soon after this the *Queen* was rammed by the *General Beauregard* and a little later when the *Beauregard* and the *General Price* were making for the *Monarch,* the *Beauregard* missed her aim and struck her comrade, the *General Price,* tearing off her wheel and putting her out of service. The *Queen* fought with desperation and in the *mêlée* Colonel Ellet, her commander, received a pistol shot in the knee. He fell on the deck and, unable to rise, continued to give orders to his men while lying prone on his ship. But the *Queen* was now dis-

A SHIP THAT FOUGHT THE FEVER

Grateful, indeed, were the Federal soldiers, in their advance from Cairo down the Mississippi, when this spacious river steamer, with its roomy cabins and wide decks, about which played the cooling breezes of the Mississippi, was added to the fleet. The Confederates were still to be encountered, but a more subtle enemy had already attacked the army. Fever and dysentery had fastened upon the unacclimated Northerners both afloat and ashore, and threatened to kill off more of them than could possibly be done by the men who strove with them for the possession of the river. When Island No. 10 was abandoned by the Confederates, they sank a gunboat and six transports, which they were compelled to leave behind. General Pope soon had the transports raised and in commission on the Federal side. None of them was more highly prized than the *Red Rover*, which we see here converted into the hospital ship of the Mississippi Squadron, commanded by Lieutenant W. R. Wells. Such floating hospitals quickly came into use by both the army and the navy along the Mississippi. Out on the bosom of the river the fever-stricken men on the shady decks grasped that chance of life which would have been denied them tossing in tents on shore, where the beating sun by day and the miasma from the bottom-lands by night, coupled with imperfect drainage, made recovery almost impossible.

abled, after her crash with the *Beauregard,* and Ellet ordered that she be headed for the Arkansas shore.

The next scene in this exciting drama came when the *Beauregard,* after disabling the *Queen,* made for the *Monarch* with like design. But the *Monarch* was the more agile. She evaded the blow, and dexterously whirling about, struck the *Beauregard* on the bow with terrific force, tearing a great hole beneath the water line. The *Beauregard,* disabled also by the gunboats, began to sink and the men on her decks fluttered handkerchiefs or any white thing at hand in token of surrender.

The *Monarch,* however, had determined to add one more to her list of trophies. There was the *Little Rebel,* the Confederate flag-ship, on whose deck Captain Montgomery had stood with unfaltering courage in the midst of Federal gun-shots. The *Monarch* now turned her prow to the *Little Rebel* and put on full steam. The latter, conscious of her inability to stand before the little fighting monster, fled toward the Arkansas shore. The race was a hot one; the *Monarch* gained rapidly, but ere she could strike the *Little Rebel,* the latter ran aground in the shallow water. Her commander and her crew leaped into the water, and they swam to shore and escaped into the forest.

The *Monarch* then steamed back to the middle of the river and rounded out her day's work by doing a deed of mercy. The *Beauregard* was still above water, but was settling rapidly, and her faithful crew, knowing that they had done all they could for the cause for which they fought, were still waving their white flags. The *Monarch* rescued them and towed the sinking *Beauregard* to shallow water, where she sank to her boiler deck.

Four of the Confederate gunboats had now been destroyed and the remaining four turned down the river and made a desperate effort to escape. But the Union fleet closed in on them and three of them turned to the Arkansas shore in the hope that the crews might make their escape. In the lead was the *General*

A RANGER OF THE RIVER

This little "tinclad" is typical of the so-called Mosquito Fleet, officially known as "Light Drafts," which rendered a magnificent minor service in the river operations of the navy. Up narrow tributaries and in and out of tortuous and shallow bayous, impassable for the larger gunboats, these dauntless fighting craft pushed their way, capturing Confederate vessels twice their size, or boldly engaging the infantry and even the field-batteries of the enemy, which were always eagerly pressing the shores to annoy the invading fleet. To Flag-Officer Davis, during his command on the Mississippi, the Federals owed the idea of these light-draft stern-wheel vessels, most of which were ordinary river steamers purchased and altered to suit the purposes of the navy. Covered to a height of eleven feet above the water line with railroad iron a half to three-quarters of an inch thick, and with their boilers still further protected, they were able to stand up to the fire of even moderate-sized guns. Many a gun in the Confederate fleets and forts was silenced by the well-directed fire of the two light bow-rifles with which some of the tinclads were equipped.

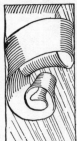

M. Jeff. Thompson. In a few minutes she had reached the goal and her officers and men leaped from the deck and ran for the protection of the woods. A moment later a shell exploded on her deck, set her on fire and she was burned to the water's edge. Closely following the *Jeff. Thompson* were the *Bragg* and the *Sumter,* and the crews of both escaped in like manner to the swamps and forests of Arkansas. Of all the eight Confederate gunboats the *General Van Dorn* alone evaded her pursuers and made her escape down the river.

The battle of Memphis, one of the fiercest of its kind on record, lasted but an hour and a quarter. The Confederate killed and wounded were never accurately reported. On the Union side there were four wounded, and with one the wound proved fatal—Colonel Ellet. His shattered knee refused to heal, and two weeks later, in the arms of his wife and daughter, the famous engineer breathed his last. His body was carried to Philadelphia and laid to rest at Laurel Hill, after being given a state funeral at Independence Hall.

The view of the battle of Memphis from the bluffs, on which the whole population of the city had gathered, was one of indescribable grandeur. Every house in the city and for miles around quivered with the explosions of burning powder. At times the smoke of the battle was so dense that scarcely a vessel could be seen by the spectators on the hill; but a continuous roar of artillery arose from the hidden surface of the river, while the impingement of the vessels crashing together sounded like a titanic battle of the elements.

There were a few Union sympathisers among the onlookers, but the great majority of them were Confederates, and when they saw their ships go down they broke into wails and lamentations. Sorrowfully they witnessed, before noon of that day, the Stars and Bars lowered from the City Hall and replaced by the Stars and Stripes, which floated over Memphis to the end of the war.

FIGHTING WESTERNERS—THE SECOND WISCONSIN CAVALRY

GENERAL C. C. WASHBURN (ORGANIZER OF THE SECOND WISCONSIN CAVALRY) AND STAFF

Wisconsin sent ninety thousand of her sons into the struggle, and her infantry and cavalry won records "East" and also in the minor, but by no means inglorious, operations west of the Mississippi. In Missouri and Arkansas they protected the inhabitants from outlaw bands and resisted the raids of the Confederates, helping the Union forces on the other side finally to gain possession of the river.

SHERMAN AND HIS OFFICERS—MEMPHIS, 1862

This photograph was taken during the summer of 1862, after Grant had made General Sherman commander of the Third Division of the Army of Tennessee, and shows the coming great marshal at Memphis, grouped with his staff and other officers. In the party are: Captain John T. Taylor; Major J. H. Hammond; Captain Lewis M. Dayton; Colonel Ezra Taylor; Captain J. Condit Smith; Captain James W. Shirk, U. S. N.; Colonel T. K. Smith; Major W. H. Hartshorn; Colonel W. H. H. Taylor; Major W. D. Sanger, and Captain James C. McCoy. Sherman had little to do at Memphis during the summer and autumn of 1862. On December 20th he left the city for the Yazoo River to take part in Grant's first movement against Vicksburg.

THE CITY ONLY A SIEGE COULD TAKE—VICKSBURG, MISSISSIPPI

The evacuation of Fort Pillow and Fort Randolph and the capture of New Orleans by Farragut left Vicksburg the main point on the Mississippi strongly defended by the Confederates, after the spring of 1862. The Federal government was most anxious for its possession. It is eight hundred miles from Memphis to New Orleans; and Vicksburg, about half way between the two, is the strongest natural position on the river. The batteries which the Confederate engineers placed on the bluffs were too high above the stream for the guns of the Federal fleet to reach them. The little Mississippi city remained the chief hope of the Confederates in holding its eastern and western territory together. With Vicksburg lost, the Confederacy would be definitely parted.

On June 28, 1862, Farragut, who had arrived with war vessels and a mortar fleet about ten days before, started to run the Vicksburg batteries with twelve ships, covered by the guns of the mortar flotilla. All but three got past with a loss of fifteen killed and thirty wounded. Above the town Farragut found some of the Ellet rams, and on the 1st of July Flag-Officer Davis and the river gunboats arrived. The Federal forces of the upper and lower Mississippi had joined hands. But Farragut was convinced that Vicksburg could not be taken without help of the army. Therefore orders on July 20th to return down the river were very welcome. Davis returned to Helena. Vicksburg's danger of Federal capture was reduced to a nullity, for the time being.

On July 24th the fleet under Farragut and the troops that had occupied the position on the river bank opposite Vicksburg under the command of General Thomas Williams went down the river, Farragut proceeding to New Orleans and Williams once more to Baton Rouge. The latter had withdrawn from his work of cutting the canal in front of Vicksburg, and a few days after his arrival at Baton Rouge the Confederate General Van Dorn sent General J. C. Breckinridge to seize the post. On the morning of August 5, 1862, the Federal forces were attacked. Williams, who had with him only about twenty-five hundred men, soon found that a much larger force was opposed to him, Breckinridge having between five and six thousand men. The brunt of the early morning attack fell upon the Indiana and Michigan troops, who slowly fell back before the fierce rushes of the bravely led men in gray. At once, Williams ordered Connecticut, Massachusetts, and Wisconsin regiments to go to their relief, sending at the same time two sections of artillery to his right wing. The Federal gunboats *Katahdin* and *Kineo* opened fire on Breckinridge's lines

THE FEDERAL DEFENDER OF
BATON ROUGE

at a signal from General Williams, wh indicated their position. For almost tw hours the battle raged fiercely, the firing be ing at short range and the fighting in som cases hand-to-hand. The Twenty-firs Indiana regiment having lost all its fiel officers, General Williams placed himself a its head, exposing himself repeatedly, an refusing all pleadings to go to the rea As he was bravely leading his men, he wa killed almost instantly by a bullet tha passed through his chest; and the Feder forces, concentrating, fell back on the out skirts of the town. The Confederates, wh had also suffered heavily, fell back als retreating to their camp. The action wa a drawn fight, but in the loss of the brav veteran of the Mexican War who had le them the land forces of the lower Missi sippi sustained a severe blow. Gener Williams' body was sent to New Orlean on an artillery transport which was sun in collision with the *Oneida* off Donaldson ville, Louisiana, a few days after the battle. Baton Roug was abandoned by the Federals on August 20th. Breckinridg had previously retired to Port Hudson.

Copyright by Review of Reviews

THE ARTILLERY TRANSPORT THAT WAS SUNK OFF DONALDSONVILLE, LOUISIANA, WITH GENERAL
WILLIAMS' BODY ON BOARD.—AUGUST, 1862

PART III

THE STRUGGLE FOR RICHMOND

YORKTOWN: UP THE PENINSULA

GUNS MARKED "GEN. MAGRUDER, YORKTOWN"
IN THE POSITIONS WHERE THEY DEFIED
McCLELLAN'S ARMY A MONTH

THE SUPERFLUOUS SIEGE

The Mortar Battery that Never Fired a Shot.   By his much heralded Peninsula Campaign, McClellan ha
planned to end the war in a few days.   He landed with his Army of the Potomac at Fortress Monroe, i
April, 1862, intending to sweep up the peninsula between the York and James rivers, seize Richmond a
one stroke, and scatter the routed Confederate army into the Southwest.   At Yorktown, he was oppose
by a line of fortifications that sheltered a force much inferior in strength to his own.   For a whole mont
McClellan devoted all the energies of his entire army to a systematic siege.   Its useless elaboration is we
illustrated by Battery No. 4, one of fifteen batteries planted to the south and southeast of Yorktown.   Th
ten monster 13-inch siege mortars, the complement of No. 4, had just been placed in position and were almo
ready for action.   It was planned to have them drop shells on the Confederate works, a mile and a ha
distant.   Just a day before this could be done, Yorktown was evacuated, May 4, 1862.

THE ELABORATE DEFENSES

dvanced Section, Three Mortars of Union Battery, No. 4. Looking due north and showing the same three
ortars pictured in the preceding views. The photograph shows (1) the stockade built above the excava-
ns as a protection from attack by Confederate infantry; (2) the ammunition that would have been used
e next day if the Confederates had not evacuated, and (3) the temporary bridge crossing the narrow
anch that runs into a northern arm of Wormley's Creek at this point. By this bridge communication
s held with the batteries to the west. The heavy stockade was intended to forestall any attempt of the
nfederate infantry to rush the battery. The mortars shown in this photograph are 13-inch sea-coast
ortars and exceeded in weight any guns previously placed in siege batteries. The first of these mortars
s landed at daybreak on April 27th and the whole battery was ready to open bombardment in a week's time.

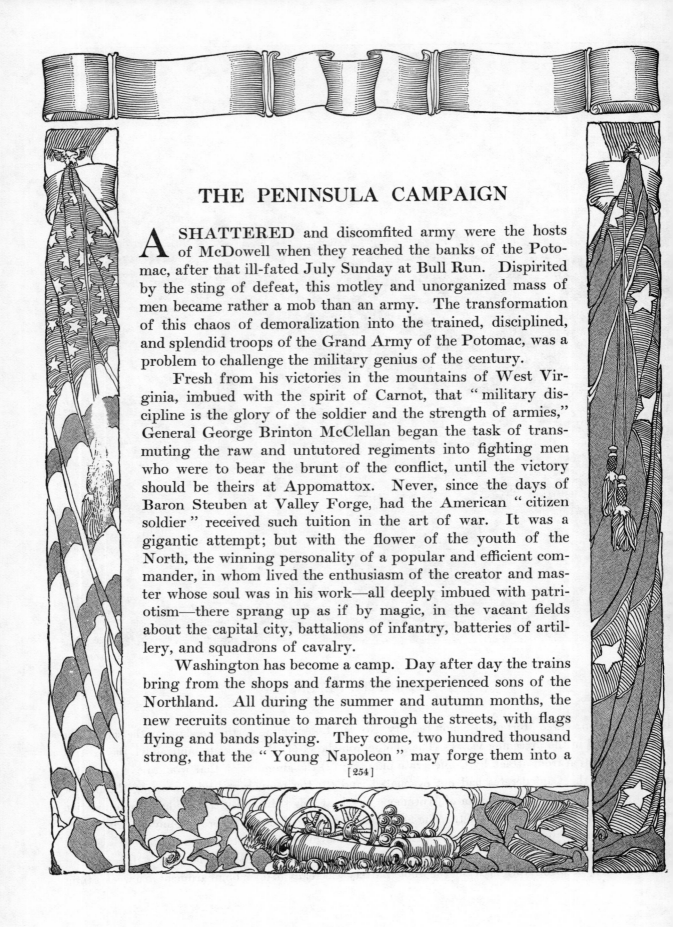

THE PENINSULA CAMPAIGN

A SHATTERED and discomfited army were the hosts of McDowell when they reached the banks of the Potomac, after that ill-fated July Sunday at Bull Run. Dispirited by the sting of defeat, this motley and unorganized mass of men became rather a mob than an army. The transformation of this chaos of demoralization into the trained, disciplined, and splendid troops of the Grand Army of the Potomac, was a problem to challenge the military genius of the century.

Fresh from his victories in the mountains of West Virginia, imbued with the spirit of Carnot, that "military discipline is the glory of the soldier and the strength of armies," General George Brinton McClellan began the task of transmuting the raw and untutored regiments into fighting men who were to bear the brunt of the conflict, until the victory should be theirs at Appomattox. Never, since the days of Baron Steuben at Valley Forge, had the American "citizen soldier" received such tuition in the art of war. It was a gigantic attempt; but with the flower of the youth of the North, the winning personality of a popular and efficient commander, in whom lived the enthusiasm of the creator and master whose soul was in his work—all deeply imbued with patriotism—there sprang up as if by magic, in the vacant fields about the capital city, battalions of infantry, batteries of artillery, and squadrons of cavalry.

Washington has become a camp. Day after day the trains bring from the shops and farms the inexperienced sons of the Northland. All during the summer and autumn months, the new recruits continue to march through the streets, with flags flying and bands playing. They come, two hundred thousand strong, that the "Young Napoleon" may forge them into a

HOW PICK AND SHOVEL SERVED

Rear Section, Seven Mortars, of Union Battery No. 4.   In order to make it impossible for Confederate sharpshooters to pick off the gunners, the batteries were placed in elaborate excavations.   At No. 4 the entire bank of Wormley's Creek was dug away.   General McClellan personally planned the location of some of these batteries for the purpose of silencing the Confederate artillery fire.

WASTED TRANSPORTATION

Both Sections of Union Battery No. 4.   The heavy barge at the landing transported the ten huge mortars, with their ammunition, all the way from Fortress Monroe up the York River and Wormley's Creek to the position of the battery.   There they were laboriously set up, and, without firing a shot, were as laboriously removed.   On the day of the evacuation the six batteries equipped were in condition to throw one hundred and seventy-five tons of metal daily into the Confederate defenses around Yorktown.

weapon, which later in the hands of the "Hammerer" will beat down the veterans of Lee before Richmond.

The autumn days come and go. The frosty nights have come. The increasing army continues its drill within the defenses. There are no indications of the forces moving. As if by instinct the men begin the construction of log huts for shelter from the cold of the coming winter.

"All's quiet along the Potomac." The winter months wear on and Public Opinion is growing restless. "Why does not the army move?" Across the country, thirty miles away, at Manassas, is the Confederate army, flushed with its July victory, under the command of General Joseph E. Johnston.

It was the 8th of March, 1862. As the Union army looked toward Manassas, down along the horizon line, clouds of smoke were seen ascending. It was from the burning huts. The Confederates were abandoning Manassas. Johnston was evacuating his camp. The next day orders came for the Army of the Potomac to move. Through the morning mists was heard the bustle of activity. Across the Long Bridge the troops took up the line of march, the old structure shaking under the tread of the passing hosts. Filled with the spirit of action, the men were jubilant at the prospect. But this buoyancy was of short duration. There was the Virginia mud, yellow and sticky, into which the feet of man and horse sank till it was almost impossible to extricate them. Throughout the day the muddy march continued. At night the bivouac was made in the oozy slime, and not till the day after, near evening, were the deserted fortifications of Manassas reached. McClellan was putting his army to a test.

Next morning the two days' return march to Washington began. The rain fell in sheets and it was a wet and bedraggled army that sought the defenses of the capital.

The strategic eye of the commander had detected two routes to the coveted capital of the Confederacy. One lost many of its possibilities by the Confederate retreat from

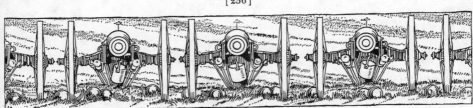

"LITTLE MAC" PREPARING FOR THE CAMPAIGN—A ROYAL AIDE

A picture taken in the fall of 1861, when McClellan was at the headquarters of General George W. Morell (who stands at the extreme left), commanding a brigade in Fitz John Porter's Division. Morell was then stationed on the defenses of Washington at Minor's Hill in Virginia, and General McClellan was engaged in transforming the raw recruits in the camps near the national capital into the finished soldiers of the Army of the Potomac. "Little Mac," as they called him, was at this time at the height of his popularity. He appears in the center between two of his favorite aides-de-camp—Lieut.-Cols. A. V. Colburn and N. B. Sweitzer—whom he usually selected, he writes, "when hard riding is required." Farther to the right stand two distinguished visitors—the Prince de Joinville, son of King Louis Phillippe of France, and his nephew, the Count de Paris, who wears the uniform of McClellan's staff, on which he was to serve through-out the Peninsula Campaign (see page 115). He afterwards wrote a valuable "History of the Cival War."

Manassas. The other was determined on. Soon the Potomac will swarm with every description of water craft. It is
to be the prelude to another drama on the military stage. On
the placid river there come canal-boats, flat-bottoms, barges,
three-decked steamers, and transatlantic packets.

On shore, the cities of tents are being deserted. The army
is massing toward the piers of Alexandria. It is a glorious
day of awakening spring, this 17th of March, 1862. From the
heights above Alexandria a beautiful spectacle is seen. Armed
men cover the hillside and the plain; columns of soldiers, with
guns flashing in the sunlight, march and countermarch; thousands of horsemen with shining arms fill the meadows to the
right; to the left are many batteries; beyond these, a long line
of marching men stretch from the hills to the streets of Alexandria; regimental bands play familiar tunes, and flags and
banners are waving over all. It is a magnificent pageant—a
far different scene from that, three years hence, when many of
these depleted, war-worn regiments, with tattered flags, will
pass in grand review through the avenues of the capital.

Here upon this assortment of transports, without confusion and with the precision of a well-oiled machine, one hundred and twenty-one thousand men, with all the equipment for
war, including fourteen thousand horses and mules, forty-four
batteries, wagons, pontoon bridges, and boats are loaded. It
comprises a fleet of four hundred vessels. On board men are
swarming like ants; they unmoor from the landings and lazily
float down the river. The unfinished dome of the Capitol fades
away in the distance. The men gather in little knots and can
but conjecture as to their destination.

Swinton tells us that it was an undertaking which " for
economy and celerity of movement is without a parallel on
record." This vast army with its entire equipage was transferred in about two weeks a distance of two hundred miles
without the loss of a man, from the scene of its preparation at
Washington to the Flanders of the Civil War.

McCLELLAN'S HEADQUARTERS BEFORE YORKTOWN

amp Winfield Scott, near Wormley's Creek. General McClellan was a stickler for neatness. His headquarters were models of
ilitary order. The guard always wore white gloves, even in the active campaign. Here we see the general's chargers with their
rooms, the waiting orderlies and the sentry standing stiffly at support arms. At the left is the guardhouse with stacked muskets.

THE TENTED MEADOW

verlooking the camp from near McClellan's headquarters. Little hardships had these troops seen as yet. Everything was new and
esh, the horses well fed and fat, the men happy and well sheltered in comfortable tents.

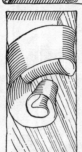

The army had already been divided into four corps, commanded, respectively, by Generals McDowell, Sumner, Heintzelman, and Keyes, but at the last moment McDowell had been detached by President Lincoln. The van was led by General Hamilton's division of the Third Corps. On the afternoon of the second day the first transports entered Chesapeake Bay. In the shadowy distance, low against the sky-line, could be descried the faint outlines of the Virginia shore. The vessels passed toward Hampton Roads where a short time before had occurred the duel of the ironclads, the *Monitor* and *Merrimac*. To the right was Old Point Comfort, at whose apex stood the frowning walls of Fortress Monroe.

The first troops landed in a terrible storm of thunder and lightning. The sea became rough; great billows were breaking on the beach; cables broke, allowing vessels to grate against each other or drift helplessly from the docks. The landing was made in an unpitying storm. Shelter was unavailable, and there was no abatement of the gale with the night.

Then came the order to march. At the command the men gathered, and in the darkness, with the incessant rain beating in their faces, with but the lightning's flash to guide them, they crossed the bridge toward Hampton. Here, in an open field, with neither tents nor fire, with water standing in pools, preparations for the night were made. The following morning some pitched their tents under the guns of Fortress Monroe while others found tenting places amid the charred ruins of the once aristocratic village of Hampton. But the cold, dreary rains were unceasing. Transport after transport continued to unload its human freight. Day after day the men stood shivering about their tents. Wet and cheerless, but patient, they awaited the coming of their magnetic chief.

General McClellan reached Fortress Monroe on April 2d. The Confederate capital was yet seventy miles away, on the northern side of the James. The route of approach lay along the narrow neck of land between the James and the York.

NATURE'S AID TO THE DEFENDERS

Confederate magazines at the southeastern end of Yorktown. Tons of powder, shot and shell could be carried from this fastness in perfect safety to the guns on the heights, behind which the Confederate artillerymen stood and so long successfully defied the besiegers.

WHENCE THE DEFENSE WAS DIRECTED

Headquarters of General Magruder in Yorktown. This pre-Revolutionary dwelling was on the main street, and here the young commander planned so cleverly the disposition of his 15,000 men—not nearly enough to man the defenses of the city—that McClellan, with nearly 100,000, was held in check.

This peninsula, marshy and thickly wooded, is from seven to fifteen miles in width, cut by smaller streams into which the tides roll. The task before the army was not an easy one.

Again the splendidly equipped and matchlessly trained Army of the Potomac was ready to move. Out from the camp at Hampton, from under the gun-bristling fort, the advance was made in two divisions along the mud-filled roads of the Peninsula. The troops marched with the precision of veterans. It was a bright April day, but the progress made was slow. Under the weight of unaccustomed burdens in the toilsome march, the men soon fell out of line and began to straggle. The warm sun and the wearisome tramp prompted many to lighten their burdens by throwing away some of their apparel. Soon the entire route was lined with an endless and reckless profusion of overcoats, blankets, parade-coats, and shoes. " Contraband " negroes were reaping a rich harvest, gathering up the discarded articles. Less than five miles was covered this first day. That night the rain came again and the soldiers who had thrown away their clothing found it a night of suffering. The morning march began in the rain. By the time Big Bethel was reached the water was coming down in torrents. The roads were cut till they were veritable rivers of mud. Along this wretched way stumbled and plodded horse and man.

Saturday afternoon, April 5th, the Federal advance guard on the right, consisting of Porter's division of Heintzelman's Third Corps, suddenly came to a river. It was the Warwick, a sluggish stream, nearly cutting the Peninsula from Yorktown to the James, a distance of thirteen and a half miles. Beyond the river was a line of trenches and forts, defended by a Confederate army. General Magruder had been stationed on the Peninsula with about eight thousand men. At the approach of McClellan reenforcements were hastened to him. The Union right wing was in front of Yorktown, the left at Lee's Mills. Now for the first time in the campaign the Union army found its way disputed. A flash of fire blazed

THE COSTLIEST RAMPART EVER BUILT

Confederate Breastworks to the South and Southeast of Yorktown, Reenforced with Cotton. This device was used once before, in the War of 1812, by the defenders of New Orleans. Before the end of the Civil War, cotton was worth $1.00 a pound, gold. It is safe to say that no fortification was ever built of material so expensive. These cotton bales were used to protect the gunners serving the 8-inch Columbiad at the parapet. The gun in the center, though of archaic pattern, was deemed worth wrecking by the Confederates when they evacuated the position to fall back upon Richmond.

FORTIFICATIONS OF TWO WARS

Earthworks of the Revolution Used in the Civil War. The ditch, dug by Cornwallis in 1781, was deepened by Magruder in 1862. The higher earthworks to the left are also of Revolutionary origin. The sand-bag ramparts were added by the Confederates as further protection for guns and gunners, and as coverings to the magazines, one of which shows at the left of the picture.

from the rifle-pits. It was returned with equal force and here on the historic soil of Yorktown men of North and South stood opposed, where eighty-one years before their fathers had stood together in the making of the Nation.

The defense confronting the Army of the Potomac was a strong one. Dams, protected by batteries and rifle-trenches, had been built in the river. Yorktown itself was fortified by a line of continuous earthworks, while across the York was Gloucester, also strongly fortified and garrisoned. The force defending the line comprised eleven thousand men, soon to be augmented by the army of General Johnston, who was assigned to the chief command on the Peninsula.

At Lee's Mills General Smith, of Keyes' corps, sent to make a reconnaissance by General McClellan, detected a seeming weak spot in the fortifications. Here would be the logical point to break the Confederate line. General Smith was ordered to send his men across the river. Accordingly four companies of "Green Mountain Boys," under cover of a heavy artillery fire from a battery of eighteen guns, plunged into the Warwick. The water reached above the waist-line, but they waded across the stream, emerging on the other side, and charged the Confederate rifle-pits. Eight additional companies came to their support. For one hour the Union troops held the trenches. The Confederates, after being driven to a redoubt, received reenforcements, reformed, and made a counter-charge. The Vermont soldiers were driven back by a galling fire, many being killed or wounded in recrossing the stream. The attempt to force the line could not succeed, since the condition of the roads and the low, boggy land rendered it impossible to use light artillery. It could not be brought close enough to do effective work.

Preparation for a protracted siege was now begun. Streams were bridged; corduroy roads constructed; a depot of supplies established. Facing the Confederate works, a parallel line extending from before Yorktown to the Warwick, a

RAMPARTS THAT BAFFLED McCLELLAN. (Hasty fortifications of the Confederates at Yorktown.) It was against such fortifications as these, which Magruder had hastily reenforced with sand-bags, that McClellan spent a month preparing his heavy batteries. Magruder had far too few soldiers to man his long line of defenses properly, and his position could have been taken by a single determined attack. This rampart was occupied by the Confederate general, D. H. Hill, who had been the first to enter Yorktown in order to prepare it for siege. He was the last to leave it on the night of May 3, 1862.

WRECKED ORDNANCE. (Gun exploded by the Confederates on General Hill's rampart, Yorktown.) Although the Confederates abandoned 200 pieces of ordnance at Yorktown, they were able to render most of them useless before leaving. Hill succeeded in terrorizing the Federals with grape-shot, and some of this was left behind. After the evacuation the ramparts were overrun by Union trophy seekers. The soldier resting his hands upon his musket is one of the Zouaves whose bright and novel uniforms were so conspicuous early in the war. This spot was directly on the line of the British fortification of 1781.

ANOTHER VOICELESS GUN. (Confederate ramparts southeast of Yorktown.) A 32-pounder Navy gun which had been burst, wrecking its embrasure. The Federal soldier seated on the sand-bags is on guard-duty to prevent camp-followers from looting the vacant fort.

THE MISSING RIFLE. (Extensive sand-bag fortifications of the Confederates at Yorktown.) The shells and carriage were left behind by the Confederates, but the rifled gun to which they belonged was taken along in the retreat. Such pieces as they could not remove they spiked.

Copyright by Patriot Pub. Co.

GUNS THE UNION LOST AND RECOVERED. (A two-gun Confederate battery in the entrenchments south of Yorktown.) The near gun is a 32-pounder navy; the far one, a 24-pounder siege-piece. More than 3,000 pieces of naval ordnance fell into the hands of the Confederates early in the war, through the ill-advised and hasty abandonment of Norfolk Navy Yard by the Federals. Many of these guns did service at Yorktown and subsequently on the James River against the Union.

THE CONFEDERATE COMMAND OF THE RIVER. (Battery Magruder, Yorktown.) Looking north up the river, four of the five 8-inch Columbiads composing this section of the battery are visible. The grape-shot and spherical shells, which had been gathered in quantities to prevent the Federal fleet from passing up the river, were abandoned on the hasty retreat of the Confederates, the guns being spiked. The vessels in the river are transport ships, with the exception of the frigate just off shore.

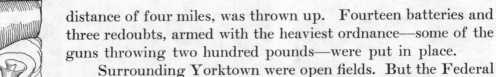

distance of four miles, was thrown up. Fourteen batteries and three redoubts, armed with the heaviest ordnance—some of the guns throwing two hundred pounds—were put in place.

Surrounding Yorktown were open fields. But the Federal troops could not remain there because of the shells from the batteries. The siege lasted less than thirty days and it rained on twenty of them. Violent thunderstorms rapidly succeeded one another. The Northern soldier, whether digging trenches, on the picket line, or standing guard, had to endure the fury of these storms. At night his bed might be in a pool of water. Sickness became prevalent, thousands were in the hospitals and many graves were dug in the marshy lowlands.

At last all was in readiness for the attack. The weather had cleared. The bombardment of Yorktown was about to begin. The shells were in position. Batteries capable of throwing sixty shells a minute were ready to belch forth.

Saturday morning, May 3d, Battery No. 1, opposite Yorktown, began its cannonading. The army waited in intense expectation of the grand spectacle. On Sunday, it was surmised, the great guns would play upon the works and ere the set of sun the victorious arms of the North would enter the historic town and unfurl the Stars and Stripes where the Father of his Country had placed them four-score years before.

Early Sunday morning a bright light from behind the Confederate works was seen by the Union pickets. A desultory cannonading had continued during the night and toward morning the firing was at times intense. The Sabbath dawned fair and warm, but no Southerners were to be seen. The Union men in the rifle-pits crept up to the very lines where but yesterday glinted the Confederate guns. The works had been abandoned. Under the cover of night the defenses had been evacuated, with masterly skill, as at Manassas. The troops were even now in full retreat toward Williamsburg.

Soon the Federals were in hot pursuit. General Stoneman with cavalry and horse artillery followed along the Wil-

AN UNPRECEDENTED SIEGE BATTERY

Federal Battery No. 1 Before Yorktown.—Never before had so heavy a siege battery been mounted. It was placed half a mile farther down the York River than Battery No. 4. From its six Parrott guns, five 100-pounders and one 200-pounder, it could at a single firing drop 700 pounds of shot and shell upon the fortifications and landing at Yorktown, two miles away. It opened up on May 1, 1862, with such telling effect that the evacuation of the town was greatly hastened, occurring two days later. These Parrott guns were in many cases failures. The reinforcement of the breach was not properly placed to stand the heavy charges and many burst, killing the artillerymen and wrecking everything in close vicinity. The life of these guns was short.

THE PRIDE OF UNION BATTERY NUMBER ONE

A 200-pounder Parrott Gun.—This, at the time, mammoth piece of ordnance stood in the center of Battery No. 1, which was located on the west bank of the York River at the mouth of Wormley's Creek. The range of the battery was upstream toward Yorktown, and this huge Parrott gun in the very center of the battery was much relied upon by the Federals to do heavy damage. Here we see how carefully McClellan's engineers did their work. The wickerwork bastions were reinforced by tiers of sand bags. Well-constructed wooden stands were made for the gunners to facilitate the loading and swabbing. This battery was near the Farenholdt House.

liamsburg road, which was littered with the debris of a re-treating army. Six miles from Williamsburg the pursuing cavalrymen came to a sudden halt. The rear guard of the Confederates had been overtaken. On the brow of the hill, in full view, was a Southern cavalry regiment, belonging to the famous brigade of J. E. B. Stuart. A quick passage of arms resulted. The advancing force pressed close but the resistance was stubborn. Stuart's men were covering the retreat of the main column toward the entrenchments of Williamsburg, which were reached by four o'clock.

Night came upon the marching troops, who all the day had been trudging the flooded roads of the Peninsula. The rain had fallen in torrents during the greater part of March. The cavalry prepared to bivouac in the rain-soaked fields in front of the Confederate works. All during the evening and even into the night the forces of Sumner and Hooker, floundering in the mud, were arriving on the scene of the next day's battle. It was a drenched and bedraggled army that slept on its arms that night.

Early in the morning the troops were again in motion. The approach to Williamsburg is along a narrow ridge, from either side of which flow the tributaries of the York and the James. At the junction of two roads stood the main defense of the fortified town. It was Fort Magruder with its bastioned front. To its right and left were a dozen redoubts for the placing of field artillery. In front of its half-mile of earthen wall ran a ditch full of water. In front of this and to the right was an open field, made so by the felling of trees, and beyond were the woods in which the army had bivouacked.

It was scarcely day when the attacking Confederate force emerged into the edge of the timber-strewn field. At once there burst from the wooded cover a vigorous fire. It was answered by the Confederate infantry and every gun in reach. The Federal troops, creeping through the slashes, steadily advanced. Heavy shot crashed amid the fallen timber,

SILENT AFTER TWO DAYS' WORK

Union Battery No. 1, Two Miles Below Yorktown.—This section of the Parrott guns was in the peach orchard of the Farenholdt House. Never had so heavy a battery been set up before in siege work. McClellan hoped by it to silence the "impregnable" water batteries of the Confederates by dropping shot and shell upon Yorktown wharf and within the defenses on the bluff. After two days of action it was rendered useless by the evacuation of Yorktown, and had to be transported up the river after the change of the base. The Farenholdt mansion, a handsome old Colonial structure, was just in the rear of this battery, and from its roof the work of the shells could be clearly observed. The good shots were cheered and the men stationed here were in holiday mood—no Confederate fire could reach them.

THE SCENE OF YORKTOWN'S ONLY SURRENDER

Moore's House, about a Mile Southeast of the Town.—Near here, in 1781, Cornwallis laid down his arms to Washington and in this house the terms of the surrender which established the independence of America were drawn up. The damage to the house is the effect of the Revolutionary guns and not those of McClellan. The guns of Battery No. 1 fired their heavy shells over this house. Near here also many of the Continentals were buried, and across their graves and the old camp of Cornwallis's beleagured troops the messengers of destruction hurtled through the air. The Federal fleet was anchored near where the Comte de Grasse's ships lay at the time of the surrender.

plowing the earth as it struck or, rebounding, tore through the branches of the wood in the rear. Slowly the Federals made their way across the field, targets for the Confederate sharpshooter. Two Union batteries, those of Webber and Bramhall, advanced to within seven hundred yards of the fort and began to play upon its walls.

Meanwhile there was seen emerging from a little ravine on the Union left a swarm of Confederates who opened at once a terrific fire. Giving their characteristic yell, they charged upon the Federals, pushing them back until the edge of the wood was again reached. There the Northerners halted, making a stand. Fresh troops came to their relief but they were insufficient. It seemed as if the Federals must give way. Both armies fought tenaciously. Neither would yield. The contest grew desperate. The Union brigades were being shattered. The last charges were made with ammunition taken from the cartridge boxes of fallen comrades.

Meanwhile "Fighting Phil" Kearny was hastening with his regiments over the bottomless roads of the Peninsula. They came most opportunely, and took the places of Hooker's tired and hungry men, who retreated in good order, leaving on the tree-strewn field seventeen hundred of their comrades, who had gone down before the Confederate fire.

On the York River side there had been no fighting during the early part of the day. But about noon, General Hancock, "the Superb," took his men near the river's bank and occupied two Confederate redoubts. Planting his batteries in these new positions, he began throwing shells into Fort Magruder. This new move of the Federals at once attracted the attention of the Confederates, and General Jubal A. Early, with the Fifth and Twenty-third North Carolina and the Twenty-fourth and Thirty-eighth Virginia regiments, was sent to intercept Hancock's movements. At the bank of a small stream, the Carolina regiments under General D. H. Hill halted to form in line. The intrepid Early did not wait,

THE DOOR TO YORKTOWN

Sallyport in the Center of the Southwestern Line of Entrenchments.—This commanded the road leading past Yorktown to Williamsburg, upon which the Confederates fell back as McClellan advanced after the evacuation. This view looks into the town and toward the river. The advancing Federals entered the city from the other side. The inhabitants, who had first hidden in their homes, flocked to the street corners as regiment after regiment swept into the town with colors flying and bands playing. Out through this gate the detachment marched in pursuit of the retreating Confederates, who made a strong stand at Williamsburg.

THE TOWN McCLELLAN THOUGHT WORTH A SIEGE

Near the Center of Yorktown.—Far from being the almost impregnable fortified city which McClellan appeared to think it, Yorktown was but a small village, to which the occupation by Cornwallis in 1781 had given an exaggerated strategic importance. It consisted chiefly of a single street, seen in the picture. Here a group of residents had gathered after the evacuation curious for a sight of the entering Union troops. A most remarkable thing to be noticed is the unharmed condition of most of the houses. The casualties among noncombatants were almost nothing. The food supply at this time was plentiful, the South as a whole had not begun to feel the pinch of hunger that it endured so bravely and so unflinchingly during the dark days of '64.

but riding at the head of the Twenty-fourth Virginia, rushed into the attack. Up across the field the column swept. On the crest of the hill stood Hancock's men—sixteen hundred strong—waiting for the charge. In front of his soldiers, with drawn sword, stood the man who later would display a similar courage on the field of Gettysburg. On came the Southerners' rush. The sword of Hancock gleamed in the light. Quick and decisive came the order to charge, and the trained soldiers, with the coolness of veterans, hurled themselves upon the Confederate column. Down by the stream, the gallant McRae of the Fifth North Carolina, seeing what was happening, dashed forward to take part in the fight. The Northern musketry fire sang in the afternoon air. So close did the opposing columns come to each other that the bayonets were used with deadly effect. The slaughter of the Fifth North Carolina regiment was appalling. The lines of the South began to waver, then broke and fled down the hill, leaving over five hundred men on the bloody field.

Now the sound of battle began to grow fainter in front of Fort Magruder. The Confederates were falling back behind its protecting walls. The Federal troops, wet and weary and hungry, slept on the field with their fallen comrades, and Hancock held undisputed sway during the starless night.

But it was not too dark for Longstreet's command to retreat once more in the direction of Richmond. It was a perilous road through the flat, swampy lowlands, with rain falling at every step of the way as they hastened toward the Chickahominy. The Union troops, too, had reason to remember this night as one of greatest suffering.

The next morning dawned in all the beauty of early May. The dead lay half buried in the mud. Many of the wounded had not yet been taken to the hospitals. But Williamsburg, the ancient capital of the Old Dominion, soon echoed with the tread of the hostile army as it swept through its quaint streets to the sound of martial music.

THE GUNS THAT DID NOT TAKE THE TOWN

Federal Ordnance Ready for Transportation from Yorktown.—The artillery thus parked at the rear of the lower wharf was by no means all that McClellan deemed necessary to overcome the resistance at Yorktown. In the center are the Parrott guns. In the background, at the upper wharf, are the transports ready for the embarkation of the troops. The little mortars in the foreground were known as coehorns. They could be lifted by half a dozen men and transported by hand to any part of the entrenchments. Their range was only a few hundred yards, but with small charges they could quite accurately drop shells at almost a stone's throw. During the siege of Petersburg they were used by both armies. Here we see troops and artillery ready for the forward move. The Louisiana Tigers had been encamped here before McClellan's army took possession.

LOADING THE TRANSPORTS

The Lower Wharf at Yorktown.—The steamer *Robert Morris* ready to depart, waiting for the embarkation of that portion of the Army of the Potomac which went up the York River to the mouth of the Pamunkey from Yorktown, May 6th, after the evacuation. Already the dismantling of both the Confederate and the Federal forts had begun. One sees gun-carriages, mortars, and tons of shot and shell, ready to be taken up the river for the operations against Richmond.

"ON TO RICHMOND!" NEAR CUMBERLAND, VIRGINIA, MAY, 1862. With Confederate opposition at Yorktown and Williamsburg broken down, the Army of the Potomac was now ready for the final rush upon Richmond. The gathering of the Union army of forty thousand men at White House, near Cumberland, was felt to be the beginning of the expected victorious advance. That part of the army not at York-town and Williamsburg was moved up the Peninsula as fast as the conditions of the road would permit. After the affair at Williamsburg the troops there joined the main army before the advance to the Chickahominy. Here we see but part of that camp—the first to be established on a large scale, in the Peninsula campaign—looking north at the bend of the Pamunkey.

THE FAR–STRETCHING ENCAMPMENT. (Cumberland Landing.) Three quarters of a mile from the landing, looking north toward the river. The distance is obscured by the haze of smoke from thousands of camp-fires. Every bit of dried wood had been collected and consumed, and standing timber was felled in all directions.

WHERE SUPPLIES WERE LANDED AT CUMBERLAND. The south bank of the Pamunkey, looking northwest across the lower camp. In this bend of the river was gathered the nondescript fleet of transports, steamers, barges, and schooners that conveyed Federal army supplies up to this point from Fortress Monroe, via York River.

HEADQUARTERS UNDER CANVAS. (Cumberland, May, 1862.) A photograph from a tree-top. Although a long distance from home, McClellan's army presented in the early days of its march up the Peninsula much of the panoply of war. The camera caught a cluster of officers' tents, probably the headquarters of a division or corps.

ON THE BANKS OF THE PAMUNKEY. (Looking south from Cumberland Landing.) The ground here slopes down directly to the river. The supplies for the camps farther up the river were hauled along a well traveled road which bisected this stretch of encampment. This road, called New Kent Road, was the main highway of the region and led to Richmond.

[274]

A VISTA OF THE FEDERAL CAMP. The Army of the Potomac waiting for the expected victorious advance on the Confederate capital. Yorktown had been evacuated on May 4th and Williamsburg abandoned on May 5th to the Union forces. During the week following, the divisions of Franklin, Sedgwick, Porter, and Richardson, after some opposition, gathered on the banks of the Pamunkey, the southern branch of the York River. Thence they marched toward White House, which —after communication with the divisions that had been fighting at Williamsburg, was established—became headquarters for the whole army. This panoramic view shows a part of the encampment.

IDLE DAYS AT CUMBERLAND. The farm-lands occupied by the impatient, waiting army were soon stripped of fences for firewood. The men sat idly about, discussing the situation. Everyone expected to be in Richmond before the end of June, and no one dreamed that the great campaign would come to nothing.

WAITING FOR ORDERS TO MOVE. (Cumberland, May, 1862.) During the ten days of inaction the soldiers rested after their heavy labors on the elaborate fortifications before Yorktown. The Confederate general, Magruder, had completely deceived McClellan as to the number of men under his command. The siege delayed the army a month.

THE CITY OF TENTS. The Army of the Potomac encamped in readiness for the forward movement on Richmond. These comfortable canvas houses were transported by the army wagons. The Confederates had no such complete shelter during the spring of 1862, which was remarkable for the inclemency of the weather.

HEADQUARTERS OF GENERAL McCLELLAN. (White House on the Pamunkey.) This house, the residence of W. H. F. Lee, son of General R. E. Lee, looked east over the river, which flows south at this point. It was burned in June, 1862, when the Federal army base was changed to the James River by order of General McClellan.

In May, 1862, the news spread throughout Richmond that a Federal fleet of ironclads, led by the dread *Monitor*, was advancing up the James River. Panic at once seized upon the Confederate capital. The Government archives were shipped to Columbia, South Carolina, and every preparation was made to evacuate the city should the expedition against it succeed in passing up the James. Meanwhile the Confederate forces were working at Drewry's Bluff to establish a battery that would command the river. Earthworks were thrown up and guns were hastily gotten into position seven miles below Richmond. Sailing vessels were sunk in the channel; torpedoes were anchored and every possible obstruction opposed to the approaching ironclads. When the *Monitor* and the *Galena* arrived they did not attempt to run the gantlet, and Richmond breathed freely again. These works ultimately formed Fort Darling.

THE FORT THAT STOPPED A PANIC

In the foreground of the picture we see what a mass of missiles were hurled into the fort, at the heads of the doughty defenders of Richmond. The *Monitor*, the *Galena*, and the gunboats—when Fort Darling opened on them to dispute the passage of the river, May 15, 1862—responded with a rain of projectiles in an effort to silence the Confederate battery and make it possible to proceed up the James. The fort was not silenced, and the gunboats, thoroughly convinced of its strength, did not again seriously attempt to pass it. Fort Darling held the water approach to Richmond until the fall of Petersburg made it necessary for the Confederates to evacuate their capital. This picture was taken in April, 1865, after the fort had been abandoned, and while it was occupied by the First Connecticut Heavy Artillery. The cabin seen in the picture was the quarters of the regimental chaplain.

THE SHOWER OF SHOT AND SHELL

PART III
THE STRUGGLE FOR RICHMOND

———

FAIR
OAKS

———

A HAVEN FOR THE WOUNDED—THE "SEVEN PINES" FARM-HOUSE SERVING AS A HOSPITAL
FOR HOOKER'S DIVISION, SHORTLY AFTER THE BATTLE OF MAY 30–JUNE 1, 1862

BRIDGING THE MORASS

From the necessity of getting an army across such barriers as this Chickahominy morass arise the most difficult problems of the army engineer. Here is shown Woodbury's Bridge, across the Chickahominy, named after its builder, which was flanked on either side by bottom lands, in some places forming a swamp stretching nearly a mile back from the stream the stagnant air, shrouded in a pall of mist, and accompanied by an immense orchestra of double-bass bullfrogs, the soldiers worked for weeks constructing causeways and bridges for the advance of the army toward Richmond, in 1862. The cutting of dams above, and the heavy rains, several times swept away the half-finished constructions, likewise

A VICTORY OVER SWAMP AND FLOOD

Here we see the Fifth New Hampshire Infantry, reenforced by details from the Sixty-fourth New York and from the Irish Brigade, at work in the swamp strengthening the upper bridge across the Chickahominy so as to enable Sumner's troops to cross. The bridge had been completed on the night of May 29, 1862, and Colonel Cross, of the Fifth New Hampshire, was the first man to ride over it. The heavy rains on the night of May 30th had so loosened the supports that when Sumner led his troops across on the afternoon of May 31st only the weight of the cautiously marching column kept the logs in place. Sumner named it the Grapevine Bridge because of its tortuous course. It enabled his troops to turn the tide at Fair Oaks and ward off Federal defeat on the first day. After they had crossed much of the Grapevine Bridge was submerged by the rising flood of the Chickahominy.

THE GUNS THAT GOT THERE.

Mud, according to Napoleon, is the fifth important element in war. Here we see the guns of Pettit's Battery, Company B, First New York Artillery, which had just conquered in a contest with mud. On the night of May 30th the swollen Chickahominy had swept away most of the recently constructed bridges. Some of the Federal Artillery had man-aged to get across, but the soil was so water-soaked that it was almost impossible to move the guns which were needed for the battle of the two following days. During the night of May 31st Pettit's command dragged their guns through the mud up from the river to Richardson's division on the right of the Federal line near the railroad; caisson and gun carriage had sunk to the very hubs, as their condition shows. Of all the artillery that had been ordered up these were the only guns able to answer at the dawn of June 1st.

THE BELATED BATTERIES

Regulars Who Arrived Too Late at Fair Oaks. One can well imagine the feelings of the men and officers of these companies of the United States Artillery—Companies C, G, B and L of the reserve, who on the 31st of May could hear the battle raging on the south side of the flooded Chickahominy. The presence of regular troops in the early part of the war always steadied the volunteers. No men were so eager to bring their guns into action as these cannoneers. In the lower picture, to the left, we see part of Captain Robertson's batteries, Companies B and L, drawn up in a cornfield. Before the battle of Fair Oaks he had been attached to General Stoneman's cavalry column operating most of the time in the vicinity of New

Bridge, where the Artillery Reserve camp was at length established. To the right we see Batteries C and G (Gibson's) of the Third United States Artillery ready for action which was not renewed. McClellan's fatal pause had just begun, and here the artillery men so much needed during the two days' fighting are standing idly by, where they had been robbed by the river of the anticipated chance to distinguish themselves and with no further compensation for their disappointment than the diversion of having their pictures taken. Weeks of waiting were to follow before these batteries were to be again needed to do their share in holding back Lee's forces during their advance in the Seven Days' battles. Robertson's guns were in the thick of it at Gaines' Mill and the captain was complimented by General Porter for that day's work.

GIBSON'S BATTERY—ARTILLERY RESERVE

CAPTAIN GIBSON AND OFFICERS OF THE BATTERY THAT BORE HIS NAME

ROBERTSON'S BATTERY—ARTILLERY RESERVE

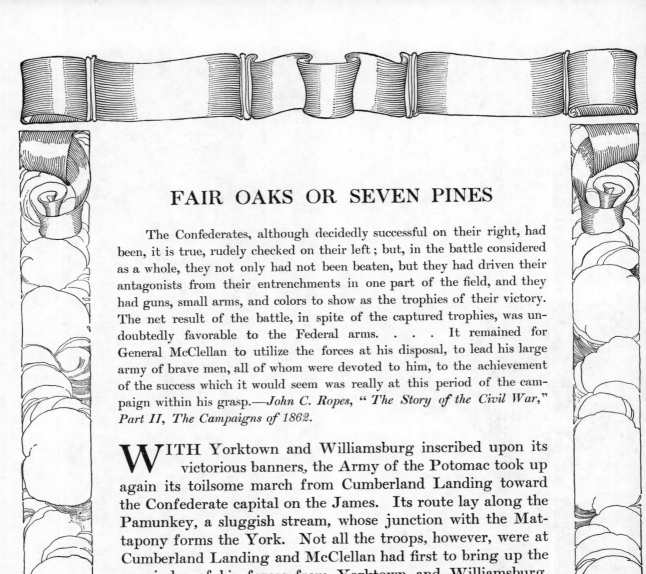

FAIR OAKS OR SEVEN PINES

The Confederates, although decidedly successful on their right, had been, it is true, rudely checked on their left; but, in the battle considered as a whole, they not only had not been beaten, but they had driven their antagonists from their entrenchments in one part of the field, and they had guns, small arms, and colors to show as the trophies of their victory. The net result of the battle, in spite of the captured trophies, was undoubtedly favorable to the Federal arms. . . . It remained for General McClellan to utilize the forces at his disposal, to lead his large army of brave men, all of whom were devoted to him, to the achievement of the success which it would seem was really at this period of the campaign within his grasp.—*John C. Ropes, " The Story of the Civil War," Part II, The Campaigns of 1862.*

WITH Yorktown and Williamsburg inscribed upon its victorious banners, the Army of the Potomac took up again its toilsome march from Cumberland Landing toward the Confederate capital on the James. Its route lay along the Pamunkey, a sluggish stream, whose junction with the Mattapony forms the York. Not all the troops, however, were at Cumberland Landing and McClellan had first to bring up the remainder of his forces from Yorktown and Williamsburg. Some came by water up the York, some by land. The march was a picturesque one, through a magnificent country arrayed in all the gorgeousness of a Virginia spring, with its meadows of green set between the wooded hills. Dotted here and there could be seen the mansions of planters, with their slave quarters in the rear. The progress was necessarily slow, for the roads were next to impassable and the rains still continued at intervals.

It was the 16th of May, 1862, when the advanced corps reached White House, the ancestral home of the Lees. On

TWO KEEPERS OF THE GOAL

The North expected General McClellan to possess himself of this citadel of the Confederacy in June, 1862, and it seemed likely the expectation would be realized. In the upper picture we get a near view of the State House at Richmond, part of which was occupied as a Capitol by the Confederate Congress during the war. In this building were stored the records and archives of the Confederate Government, many of which were

THE GOAL—THE CONFEDERATE CAPITOL

lost during the hasty retreat of President Davis and his cabinet at the evacuation of Richmond, April, 1865. Below, we see the city of Richmond from afar, with the Capitol standing out boldly on the hill. McClellan was not destined to reach this coveted goal, and it would not have meant the fall of the Confederacy had he then done so. When Lincoln entered the building in 1865, the Confederacy had been beaten as much by the blockade as by the operations of Grant and Sherman with vastly superior forces.

Copyright by Patriot Pub. Co.

THE SPIRES OF RICHMOND

Here are the portraits of the two military leaders who were conspicuous in the Confederate attack upon McClellan's camp at Fair Oaks. General D. H. Hill did most of the fierce fighting which drove back the Federals on the first day, and only the timely arrival of Sumner's troops enabled the Federals to hold their ground. Had they failed they would have been driven into the morasses of the Chickahominy, retreat across which would have been difficult as the bridges were partly submerged by the swollen stream. After General Johnston was wounded, General G. W. Smith was in command during the second day's fighting.

GENERAL G. W. SMITH, C. S. A.

GENERAL D. H. HILL, C. S. A.

every side were fields of wheat, and, were it not for the presence of one hundred thousand men, there was the promise of a full harvest. It was here that General McClellan took up his headquarters, a distance of twenty-four miles from Richmond.

In the Confederate capital a panic had seized the people. As the retreating army of Johnston sought the environs of Richmond and news of the invading hosts was brought in, fear took possession of the inhabitants and many wild rumors were afloat as to the probable capture of the city. But it was not a fear that Johnston would not fight. The strategic policy of the Southern general had been to delay the advance of the Northern army. Fortunately for him, the rainy weather proved a powerful ally. The time had now come when he should change his position from the defensive to the offensive. The Army of Northern Virginia had been brought to bay, and it now turned to beat off the invaders and save its capital.

On the historic Peninsula lay two of the greatest and most splendid armies that had ever confronted each other on the field of battle. The engagement, now imminent, was to be the first in that series of contests, between the Army of the Potomac and the Army of Northern Virginia, ending three years thereafter, at Appomattox, when the war-worn veterans of gray should lay down their arms, in honor, to the war-worn veterans of blue.

The Union advance was retarded by the condition of the weather and the roads. Between McClellan's position at White House and the waiting Confederate army lay the Chickahominy, an erratic and sluggish stream, that spreads itself out in wooded swamps and flows around many islands, forming a valley from half a mile to a mile wide, bordered by low bluffs. In dry weather it is but a mere brook, but a moderate shower will cause it to rise quickly and to offer formidable opposition to any army seeking its passage. The valley is covered with trees whose tops reach to the level of

FROM CAPTAIN TO BREVET MAJOR-GENERAL

hn C. Tidball, Who Won His Spurs on the Peninsula. There is hardly a despatch that concerns the doings of the artillery in the ninsula Campaign that does not mention the name of the gallant officer we see here leaning against his mud-spattered gun. Tidball's ttery was the first to try for the position of honor on the artillery firing line and the last to retire. He was a graduate of West int, class of '48, and like all West Pointers, was imbued with the slogan and motto of that cradle of soldiers, "Duty, Valor, Patriot- n." He was appointed captain in '61 and given command of four rifled 10-pounder Parrotts and two 12-pounder smooth- res. Through the heavy roads he kept his guns well to the fore throughout all of the Peninsula Campaign. For his participation the skirmish at New Bridge he was thrice mentioned in despatches. But previous to this he had been reported for gallantry at ackburn's Ford in the first battle of Bull Run, his guns being the last of Barry's battery to limber up and retire in order. It was the 23d of May that Tidball's guns swept the Confederate troops from New Bridge on the banks of the Chickahominy. His fir- was so accurate and his men so well drilled that the discharge of his guns was spoken of as being so rapid as to be almost con- uous. At Gaines' Mill Tidball and his guns won laurels. The artillery had begun the battle at about 11 o'clock, and it s their fight until nearly 3 o'clock in the afternoon of June 27th, when the fighting became general. The batteries were well in nt and occupied a dangerous position, but despite the vigor of the attack the guns stayed where they were. General Sykes reported the artillery this day: "The enemy's attack was frustrated mainly through the services of Captain Reade and Captain Tidball." lball emerged from the action with a brevet of major. He was brevetted lieut.-colonel for gallantry at Antietam on September h. At Gettysburg he commanded a brigade of horse artillery which he led in the Wilderness campaign, also, and was brevetted gadier-general on August 1, 1864, brevetted major-general for gallant and meritorious services at Fort Stedman and Fort Sedgwick the Petersburg campaign, and confirmed as a brigadier-general at the end of the war.

the adjacent highlands, thus forming a screen from either side. The bridges crossing it had all been destroyed by the retreating army except the one at Mechanicsville, and it was not an easy task that awaited the forces of McClellan as they made their way across the spongy soil.

The van of the Union army reached the Chickahominy on May 20th. The bridge was gone but the men under General Naglee forded the little river, reaching the plateau beyond, and made a bold reconnaissance before the Confederate lines. In the meantime, newly constructed bridges were beginning to span the Chickahominy, and the Federal army soon was crossing to the south bank of the river.

General McClellan had been promised reenforcements from the north. General McDowell with forty thousand men had started from Fredericksburg to join him north of the Chickahominy. For this reason, General McClellan had thrown the right wing of his army on the north of the river while his left would rest on the south side of the stream. This position of his army did not escape the eagle eye of the Confederate general, Joseph E. Johnston, who believed the time had now come to give battle, and perhaps destroy the small portion of the Union forces south of the river.

Meanwhile, General " Stonewall " Jackson, in the Shenandoah, was making threatening movements in the direction of Washington, and McDowell's orders to unite with McClellan were recalled.

The roads in and about Richmond radiate from that city like the spokes of a wheel. One of these is the Williamsburg stage-road, crossing the Chickahominy at Bottom's Bridge, only eleven miles from Richmond. It was along this road that the Federal corps of Keyes and Heintzelman had made their way. Their orders were " to go prepared for battle at a moment's notice " and " to bear in mind that the Army of the Potomac has never been checked."

Parallel to this road, and about a mile to the northward,

THE ADVANCE THAT BECAME A RETREAT

Here, almost within sight of the goal (Richmond), we see McClellan's soldiers preparing the way for the passage of the army and its supplies. The soil along the Chickahominy was so marshy that in order to move the supply trains and artillery from the base at White House and across the river to the army, corduroy approaches to the bridges had to be built. It was well that the men got this early practice in road-building. Thanks to the work kept up, McClellan was able to unite the divided wings of the army almost at will.

"REGULARS" NEAR FAIR OAKS—OFFICERS OF McCLELLAN'S HORSE ARTILLERY BRIGADE

These trained soldiers lived up to the promise in their firm-set features. Major Hays and five of his Lieutenants and Captains here—Pennington, Tidball, Hains, Robertson and Barlow—had, by '65, become general officers. From left to right (standing) are Edm. Pendleton, A. C. M. Pennington, Henry Benson, H. M. Gibson, J. M. Wilson, J. C. Tidball, W. N. Dennison; (sitting) P. C. Hains, H. C. Gibson, Wm. Hays, J. M. Robertson, J. W. Barlow; (on ground) R. H. Chapin, Robert Clarke, A. C. Vincent.

runs the Richmond and York River Railroad. Seven miles from Richmond another highway intersects the one from Williamsburg, known as the Nine Mile road. At the point of this intersection once grew a clump of seven pines, hence the name of " Seven Pines," often given to the battle fought on this spot. A thousand yards beyond the pines were two farmhouses in a grove of oaks. This was Fair Oaks Farm. Where the Nine Mile road crossed the railroad was Fair Oaks Station.

Southeast of Seven Pines was White Oak Swamp. Casey's division of Keyes' corps was stationed at Fair Oaks Farm. A fifth of a mile in front lay his picket line, extending crescent shape, from the swamp to the Chickahominy. Couch's division of the same corps was at Seven Pines, with his right wing extending along the Nine Mile road to Fair Oaks Station. Heintzelman's corps lay to the rear; Kearney's division guarded the railroad at Savage's Station and Hooker's the approaches to the White Oak Swamp. This formed three lines of defense. It was a well-wooded region and at this time was in many places no more than a bog. No sooner had these positions been taken, than trees were cut to form abatis, rifle-pits were hastily dug, and redoubts for placing artillery were constructed. The picket line lay along a dense growth of woods. Through an opening in the trees, the Confederate army could be seen in force on the other side of the clearing.

The plans of the Confederate general were well matured. On Friday, May 30th, he gave orders that his army should be ready to move at daybreak.

That night the " windows of heaven seemed to have been opened " and the " fountains of the deep broken up." The storm fell like a deluge. It was the most violent storm that had swept over that region for a generation. Throughout the night the tempest raged The thunderbolts rolled without cessation. The sky was white with the electric flashes. The earth was thoroughly drenched. The lowlands became a

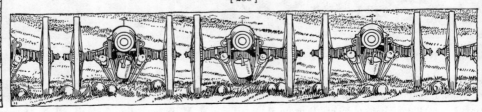

CUSTER AND HIS CLASSMATE—NOW A CONFEDERATE PRISONER

Friends and even relatives who had been enlisted on opposite sides in the great Civil War met each other during its vicissitudes upon the battle-field. Here, caught by the camera, is one of the many instances. On the left sits Lieutenant J. B. Washington, C. S. A., who was an aide to General Johnston at Fair Oaks. Beside him sits Lieutenant George A. Custer, of the Fifth U. S. Cavalry, aide on McClellan's staff, later famous cavalry general and Indian fighter. Both men were West Point graduates and had attended the military academy together. On the morning of May 31, 1862, at Fair Oaks, Lieutenant Washington was captured by some of General Casey's pickets. Later in the day his former classmate ran across him and a dramatic meeting was thus recorded by the camera.

morass. From mud-soaked beds the soldiers arose the next morning to battle.

Owing to the storm the Confederates did not move so early as intended. However, some of the troops were in readiness by eight o'clock. Hour after hour the forces of Longstreet and Hill awaited the sound of the signal-gun that would tell them General Huger was in his position to march. Still they waited. It was near noon before General Hill, weary of waiting, advanced to the front, preceded by a line of skirmishers, along the Williamsburg road. The Union pickets were lying at the edge of the forest. The soldiers in the pits had been under arms for several hours awaiting the attack. Suddenly there burst through the woods the soldiers of the South. A shower of bullets fell beneath the trees and the Union pickets gave way. On and on came the lines of gray in close columns. In front of the abatis had been planted a battery of four guns. General Naglee with four regiments, the Fifty-sixth and One hundredth New York and Eleventh Maine and One hundred and fourth Pennsylvania, had gone forward, and in the open field met the attacking army. The contest was a stubborn one. Naglee's men charged with their bayonets and pressed the gray lines back again to the edge of the woods. Here they were met by a furious fire of musketry and quickly gave way, seeking the cover of the rifle-pits at Fair Oaks Farm. The Confederate infantrymen came rushing on.

But again they were held in check. In this position, for nearly three hours the Federals waged an unequal combat against three times their number. Then, suddenly a galling fire plowed in on them from the left. It came from Rains' brigade, which had executed a flank movement. At the same time the brigade of Rodes rushed toward them. The Federals saw the hopelessness of the situation. The officers at the batteries tried to spike their guns but were killed in the attempt. Hastily falling back, five guns were left to be turned on them

THE SLAUGHTER FIELD AT FAIR OAKS

THE UNFINISHED REDOUBT

ver this ground the fiercest fighting of the two days' battle took place, on May 31, 1862. Some 400 soldiers ere buried here, where they fell, and their hastily dug graves appear plainly in the picture. In the redoubt seen st beyond the two houses was the center of the Federal line of battle, equi-distant, about a mile and a half, from both Seven Pines and Fair Oaks. The entrenchments near these farm dwellings were begun on May 28th by Casey's Division, 4th Corps. There was not time to finish them before the Confederate attack opened the battle, and the artillery of Casey's Division was hurriedly placed in position behind the incomplete works.

In the smaller picture we see the inside of the redoubt at the left background of the picture above. The scene is just before the battle and picks and shovels were still busy throwing up the embankments to strengthen this center of the Federal defense. Casey's artillery was being hurriedly brought up. In the background General Sickles' Brigade appears drawn up in line of battle. When the Confederates first advanced Casey's artillery did telling work, handsomely repelling the attack early in the afternoon of May 31st. Later in the day Confederate sharpshooters from vantage points in neighboring trees began to pick off the officers and the gunners and the redoubt had to be relinquished. The abandoned guns were turned against the retreating Federals.

THE "REDHOT BATTERY"

In the afternoon of May 31st, at Fair Oaks, the Confederates were driving the Federal soldiers through the woods in disorder when this battery (McCarthy's) together with Miller's battery opened up with so continuous and severe a fire that the Federals were able to make a stand and hold their own for the rest of the day. The guns grew so hot from constant firing that it was only with the greatest care that they could be swabbed and loaded. These earthworks were thrown up for McCarthy's Battery, Company C, 1st Pennsylvania Artillery, near Savage's Station. The soldiers nicknamed it the "Redhot Battery."

in their retreat. This move was not too soon. In another minute they would have been entirely surrounded and captured. The gray lines pressed on. The next stand would be made at Seven Pines, where Couch was stationed. The forces here had been weakened by sending relief to Casey. The situation of the Federals was growing critical. At the same time General Longstreet sent reenforcements to General Hill. Couch was forced out of his position toward the right in the direction of Fair Oaks Station and was thus separated from the main body of the army, then in action.

The Confederates pushed strongly against the Federal center. Heintzelman came to the rescue. The fight waged was a gallant one. For an hour and a half the lines of blue and gray surged back and forth. The Federals were gradually giving way. The left wing, alone, next to the White Oak Swamp, was holding its own.

At the same time over at Fair Oaks Station whither Couch had been forced, were new developments. He was about to strike the Confederate army on its left flank, but just when the guns were being trained, there burst across the road the troops of General G. W. Smith, who up to this time had been inactive. These men were fresh for the fight, superior in number, and soon overpowered the Northerners. It looked for a time as if the whole Union army south of the Chickahominy was doomed.

Over at Seven Pines the center of McClellan's army was about to be routed. Now it was that General Heintzelman personally collected about eighteen hundred men, the fragments of the broken regiments, and took a decided stand at the edge of the timber. He was determined not to give way. But this alone would not nor did not save the day. To the right of this new line of battle, there was a rise of ground. From here the woods abruptly sloped to the rear. If this elevation were once secured by the Confederates, all would be lost and rout would be inevitable. The quick eye of General

A VETERAN OF THREE WARS

General Silas Casey at Fair Oaks. Three years before General Lee had left West Point, Silas Casey had been graduated. He was fifty-four years old when the war began. Active service in two exacting campaigns had aged him in appearance, but not in efficiency. He had been with General Worth at Florida in the Seminole War and under Scott at Mexico and had fought the Indians on the Pacific Coast. At Fair Oaks the old veteran's division, after fighting bravely through the woods, was driven back, for it received the whole brunt of the first Confederate attack. The bravely advancing Confederates had gained possession of his camp before supports could reach him.

GENERAL SILAS· CASEY

TWO LEADERS OF THE FOREFRONT

In the center of this group sits General Naglee. At Fair Oaks his troops had rushed to arms in the dark gloom of that cloudy day, the 31st of May. The woods before his forces were filled with sharpshooters, and back of them, massing on his front, came overpowering numbers. Fighting stubbornly, contesting every inch, General Naglee was driven back to the protection of McCarthy's battery near Savage's Station. Twice during the action had Naglee placed himself personally at the head of his men in the firing line. General Stoneman is handing a note to an orderly. Before the battle of Fair Oaks, he had conducted the successful raids against the railroad. At Hanover Court House Stoneman's riders were opposed to those of the great Stuart.

GENERAL NAGLEE AND THE CAVALRY GENERAL STONEMAN AT FAIR OAKS

Keyes took in the situation. He was stationed on the left; to reach the hill would necessitate taking his men between the battle-lines. The distance was nearly eight hundred yards. Calling on a single regiment to follow he made a dash for the position. The Southern troops, divining his intention, poured a deadly volley into his ranks and likewise attempted to reach this key to the situation. The Federals gained the spot just in time. The new line was formed as a heavy mass of Confederates came upon them. The tremendous Union fire was too much for the assaulting columns, which were checked. They had forced the Federal troops back from their entrenchments a distance of two miles, but they never got farther than these woods. The river fog now came up as the evening fell and the Southern troops spent the night in the captured camps, sleeping on their arms. The Federals fell back toward the river to an entrenched camp.

Meanwhile at Fair Oaks Station the day was saved, too, in the nick of time, for the Federals. On the north side of the Chickahominy were stationed the two divisions of Sedgwick and Richardson, under command of General Sumner. Scarcely had the battle opened when McClellan at his headquarters, six miles away, heard the roar and rattle of artillery. He was sick at the time, but he ordered General Sumner to be in readiness. At this time there were four bridges across the river—two of them were Bottom's Bridge and the railroad bridge. To go by either of these would consume too much time in case of an emergency. General Sumner had himself constructed two more bridges, lying between the others. The heavy flood of the preceding night, which was still rising, had swept one of these partially away. In order to save time, he put his men under arms and marched them to the end of the upper bridge and there waited throughout the greater part of the afternoon for orders to cross. Before them rolled a muddy and swollen stream, above whose flood was built a rude and unstable structure. From the other side

Not long after this picture was taken, the names of most of these men were mentioned in despatches. Against Major D. H. Van Valkenburgh, the gallant soldier leaning on his saber, his arm thrust into his coat, was written, "killed in action at Fair Oaks." He helped to make the name of the First New York Light Artillery a proud one; and next to him stands Major Luther Kieffer. Perhaps the youngest, who is standing next, is Adjutant Rumsey, who by firing his guns so continuously helped save the wing of the Second Army Corps. He was wounded but recovered. Next to him, looking straight at the camera, is Lieut.-Colonel Henry E. Turner; and standing nearest to the tent is Major C. S. Wainright, who won his spurs at Williamsburg, and again proved the metal he was made of at Fair Oaks. Seated in the camp chair is Colonel Guilford T. Bailey, who later died beside his guns. It rained during the days that preceded Fair Oaks. It was the treacherous River Chickahominy that helped to baffle the

FIGHTING OFFICERS OF THE FIRST NEW YORK LIGHT ARTILLERY

well-laid plans of the Federal commander. Well did the Confederate leaders know that with the downpour then falling the stream would rise. Not immediately, but within the next few hours it would gain strength until at last it became a sweeping torrent. All this proved true; only a part of McClellan's army had crossed the river when the Confederates moved to attack, May 31st. Let the Prince de Joinville, who was a spectator, describe the guns that helped to save the day. "They are not those rifled cannon, the objects of extravagant admiration of late, good for cool firing and long range; these are the true guns for a fight—12-pound howitzers (Napoleons), the old pattern, throwing round projectiles or heavy charges of grape and canister. The simple and rapid discharging of these pieces makes terrible havoc in the opposing ranks. In vain Johnston sends against this battery his best troops—those of South Carolina, the Hampton legion among others, in vain he rushes on it himself; nothing can shake the line!"

TWENTY-POUND PARROTT RIFLED GUNS OF THE FIRST NEW YORK

could be distinctly heard the roar of battle. The fate of the day and of the Army of the Potomac rested upon these men at the end of the bridge.

The possibility of crossing was doubted by everyone, including the general himself. The bridge had been built of logs, held together and kept from drifting by the stumps of trees. Over the river proper it was suspended by ropes attached to trees, felled across the stream.

At last the long-expected order to advance came. The men stepped upon the floating bridge. It swayed to and fro as the solid column passed over it. Beneath the men was the angry flood which would engulf all if the bridge should fall. Gradually the weight pressed it down between the solid stumps and it was made secure till the army had crossed. Had the passage been delayed another hour the flood would have rendered it impassable.

Guided by the roar of battle the troops hurried on. The artillery was left behind in the mud of the Chickahominy. The steady, rolling fire of musketry and the boom of cannon told of deadly work in front. It was nearly six o'clock before Sedgwick's column deployed into line in the rear of Fair Oaks Station. They came not too soon. Just now there was a lull in the battle. The Confederates were gathering themselves for a vigorous assault on their opponents' flaming front. Their lines were re-forming. General Joseph E. Johnston himself had immediate command. President Jefferson Davis had come out from his capital to witness the contest. Rapidly the Confederates moved forward. A heavy fusillade poured from their batteries and muskets. Great rents were made in the line of blue. It did not waver. The openings were quickly filled and a scorching fire was sent into the approaching columns. Again and again the charge was repeated only to be repulsed. Then came the order to fix bayonets. Five regiments—Thirty-fourth and Eighty-second New York, Fifteenth and Twentieth Massachusetts and Seventh Michigan

SUMNER IN THE FIELD—A GENERAL FULL OF YEARS AND HONORS.

Not many men distinguished in the war could look back upon forty-two years of actual service at the outbreak of hostilities. But such was the case with General Edwin V. Sumner. He stands above in the Peninsula Campaign, at St. Peter's church, near New Kent Court House, Virginia, not far from White House Landing. In this sacred edifice George Washington had worshiped. When this picture was taken Sumner was one year past the age when generals of the present day are deemed too old for service. Commanding the Second Army Corps in the Peninsula Campaign, he was twice wounded; and again, leading his men at Antietam, once more he was struck. He fought again at Fredericksburg, but died from the effects of his wounds in March, 1863. The group above from the left, includes Maj. A. M. Clark, Volunteer A. D. C.; Lieut.-Col. J. H. Taylor, A. G.; Capt. F. N. Clarke, Chief of Artillery; General Sumner; Lieut.-Col. J. F. Hammond, Medical Director; Captain Pease, Minnesota Volunteers, Chief Commissary; Capt. Gabriel Grant.

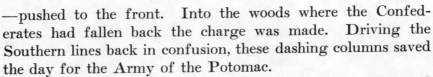

—pushed to the front. Into the woods where the Confederates had fallen back the charge was made. Driving the Southern lines back in confusion, these dashing columns saved the day for the Army of the Potomac.

Night was now settling over the wooded field. Here and there flashes of light could be seen among the oaks, indicating a diligent search for the wounded. General Johnston ordered his troops to sleep on the field. A few minutes later he was struck by a rifle-ball and almost immediately a shell hit him, throwing him from his horse, and he was borne off the field. The first day of the battle was over.

The disability of the Southern commander made it possible for the promotion of a new leader upon whom the fortunes of the Army of Northern Virginia would soon rest. This was General Robert E. Lee; although the immediate command for the next day's contest fell upon General G. W. Smith. Early Sunday morning the battle was again in progress. The command of Smith, near Fair Oaks Station, advanced down the railroad, attacking Richardson, whose lines were north of it and were using the embankment as a fortification. Longstreet's men were south of the railroad. The firing was heavy all along this line, the opposing forces being not more than fifty yards from each other. For an hour and a half the musketry fire was intensely heavy. It was, indeed, a continuous roar. The line of gray could not withstand the galling fire and for the first time that day fell back. But the Union line had been broken, too. A brief lull ensued. Both sides were gathering themselves for another onslaught. It was then that there were heard loud shouts from the east of the railroad.

There, coming through the woods, was a large body of Federal troops. They were the men of Hooker. They formed a magnificent body of soldiers and seemed eager for the fray. Turning in on the Williamsburg road they rapidly deployed to the right and the left. In front of them was an open field, with a thick wood on the other side. The Confederates had

AIMING THE GUNS AT FAIR OAKS.

Here we see the beginning of the lull in the fighting of the second day at Fair Oaks, which it has been asserted led to a fatal delay and the ruin of McClellan's Peninsula Campaign. The first day's battle at Fair Oaks, May 31, 1862, was decidedly a Federal reverse which would have developed into a rout had not Sumner, crossing his troops on the perilous Grapevine Bridge, come up in time to rally the retreating men. Here we see some of them within the entrenchments at Fair Oaks Station on the Richmond & York River Railroad. The order will soon come to cease firing at the end of the second day's fighting, the result of which was to drive the Confederates back to Richmond. McClellan did not pursue. The heavy rainstorm on the night of May 30th had made the movement of artillery extremely difficult, and McClellan waited to complete the bridges and build entrenchments before advancing. This delay gave the Confederates time to reorganize their forces and place them under the new commander, Robert E. Lee, who while McClellan lay inactive effected a junction with "Stonewall" Jackson. Then during the Seven Days' Battles Lee steadily drove McClellan from his position, within four or five miles of Richmond, to a new position on the James River. From this secure and advantageous water base McClellan planned a new line of advance upon the Confederate Capital. In the smaller picture we see the interior of the works at Fair Oaks Station, which were named Fort Sumner in honor of the General who brought up his Second Corps and saved the day. The camp of the Second Corps is seen beyond the fortifications to the right.

FORT SUMNER, NEAR FAIR OAKS

posted themselves in this forest and were waiting for their antagonists. The Federals marched upon the field in double-quick time; their movements became a run, and they began firing as they dashed forward. They were met by a withering fire of field artillery and a wide gap being opened in their ranks. It immediately filled. They reached the edge of the woods and as they entered its leafy shadows the tide of battle rolled in with them. The front line was lost to view in the forest, except for an occasional gleam of arms from among the trees. The din and the clash and roar of battle were heard for miles. Bayonets were brought into use. It was almost a hand-to-hand combat in the heavy forest and tangled slashings. The sound of battle gradually subsided, then ceased except for the intermittent reports of small arms, and the second day's fight was over.

The Confederate forces withdrew toward Richmond. The Federal troops could now occupy without molestation the positions they held the previous morning. The forest paths were strewn with the dead and the dying. Many of the wounded were compelled to lie under the scorching sun for hours before help reached them. Every farmhouse became an improvised hospital where the suffering soldiers lay. Many were placed upon cars and taken across the Chickahominy. The dead horses were burned. The dead soldiers, blue and gray, found sometimes lying within a few feet of each other, were buried on the field of battle. The two giants had met in their first great combat and were even now beginning to gird up their loins for a desperate struggle before the capital of the Confederacy.

PART III
THE STRUGGLE FOR RICHMOND

———

IN THE
SHENANDOAH
VALLEY

———

JUNE, 1862—McCLELLAN'S MEN DRILLING WITHIN FIVE MILES OF RICHMOND,
IGNORANT OF JACKSON'S MOVEMENTS FROM THE VALLEY, SO SOON TO RESULT
IN THEIR REPULSE—RICHARDSON'S ENTRENCHMENTS SOUTH OF FORT SUMNER

MEN JACKSON COULD AFFORD TO LOSE

These two hundred Confederate soldiers captured the day after "Stonewall" Jackson's victory at Front Royal, were an insignificant
reprisal for the damage done to the Federal cause by that dashing and fearless Confederate leader. When Richmond was threatened
both by land and water in May, 1862, Johnston sent Jackson to create a diversion and alarm the Federal capital. Rushing down
the Valley of the Shenandoah, his forces threatened to cut off and overwhelm those of General Banks, who immediately began a retreat. It became a race between the two armies down the Valley toward Winchester and Harper's Ferry. Forced marches, sometimes
as long as thirty-five miles a day, were the portion of both during the four weeks in which Jackson led his forces after the retreating

CONFEDERATE PRISONERS CAPTURED IN THE SHENANDOAH

Federals, engaging them in six actions and two battles, in all of which he came off victorious. Just after these prisoners were taken, Banks was driven back to the Potomac. Once more a panic spread through the North, and both the troops of Banks and McDowell were held in the vicinity of Washington for its defense. But Jackson's purpose was accomplished. He had held Banks in the Shenandoah Valley until McClellan's Peninsula Campaign was well advanced. Then again by forced marches his men disappeared up the Valley to join Lee in teaching the overconfident Union administration that Richmond was not to be won without long and costly fighting. But a year later the Confederacy lost this astonishing military genius.

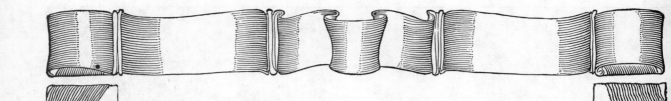

THE SHENANDOAH VALLEY

Always mystify, mislead, and surprise the enemy, if possible, and when you strike and overcome him, never let up in the pursuit so long as your men have strength to follow. . . . The other rule is, never fight against heavy odds, if by any possible maneuvering you can hurl your own force on only a part, and that the weakest part, of your enemy and crush it. Such tactics will win every time, and a small army may thus destroy a large one in detail.—"Stonewall" Jackson.

THE main move of the Union army, for 1862, was to be McClellan's advance up the Peninsula toward Richmond. Everything had been most carefully planned by the brilliant strategist. With the assistance of McDowell's corps, he expected in all confidence to be in the Confederate capital before the spring had closed. But, comprehensively as he had worked the scheme out, he had neglected a factor in the problem which was destined in the end to bring the whole campaign to naught. This was the presence of "Stonewall" Jackson in the Valley of Virginia.

The strategic value to the Confederacy of this broad, sheltered avenue into Maryland and Pennsylvania was great. Along the northeasterly roads the gray legions could march in perfect safety upon the rear of Washington so long as the eastern gaps could be held. No wonder that the Federal authorities, however much concerned with other problems of the war, never removed a vigilant eye from the Valley.

Jackson had taken possession of Winchester, near the foot of the Valley, in November, 1861. He then had about ten thousand men. The Confederate army dwindled greatly during the winter. At the beginning of March there were but forty-five hundred men. With Banks and his forty thousand now on Virginia soil at the foot of the Valley, and Fremont's

"STONEWALL" JACKSON
AT WINCHESTER
1862

It is the great good fortune of American hero-lovers that they can gaze here upon the features of Thomas Jonathan Jackson precisely as that brilliant Lieutenant-General of the Confederate States Army appeared during his masterly "Valley Campaign" of 1862. Few photographers dared to approach this man, whose silence and modesty were as deep as his mastery of warfare. Jackson lived much to himself. Indeed, his plans were rarely known even to his immediate subordinates, and herein lay the secret of those swift and deadly surprises that raised him to first rank among the world's military figures. Jackson's ability and efficiency won the utter confidence of his ragged troops; and their marvelous forced marches, their contempt for privations if under his guidance, put into his hands a living weapon such as no other leader in the mighty conflict had ever wielded.

army approaching the head, why should the Federal commander even think about this insignificant fragment of his foe? But the records of war have shown that a small force, guided by a master mind, sometimes accomplishes more in effective results than ten times the number under a less active and able commander.

The presence of Banks compelled Jackson to withdraw to Woodstock, fifty miles south of Winchester. If McClellan ever experienced any anxiety as to affairs in the Valley, it seems to have left him now, for he ordered Banks to Manassas on March 16th to cover Washington, leaving General Shields and his division of seven thousand men to hold the Valley. When Jackson heard of the withdrawal, he resolved that, cut off as he was from taking part in the defense of Richmond, he would do what he could to prevent any aggrandizement of McClellan's forces.

Shields hastened to his station at Winchester, and Jackson, on the 23d of March, massed his troops at Kernstown, about three miles south of the former place. Deceived as to the strength of his adversary, he led his weary men to an attack on Shields' right flank about three o'clock in the afternoon. He carried the ridge where the Federals were posted, but the energy of his troops was spent, and they had to give way to the reserves of the Union army after three hours of stubborn contest. The Federal ranks were diminished by six hundred; the Confederate force by more than seven hundred. Kernstown was a Union victory; yet never in history did victory bring such ultimate disaster upon the victors.

At Washington the alarm was intense over Jackson's audacious attack. Williams' division of Banks' troops was halted on its way to Manassas and sent back to Winchester. Mr. Lincoln transferred Blenker's division, nine thousand strong, to Fremont. These things were done at once, but they were by no means the most momentous consequence of Kernstown. The President began to fear that Jackson's goal was

McDOWELL AND McCLELLAN—TWO UNION LEADERS WHOSE
PLANS "STONEWALL" JACKSON FOILED

In General McClellan's plan for the Peninsula Campaign of 1862, General McDowell, with the First Army
Corps of 37,000 men, was assigned a most important part, that of joining him before Richmond.   Lincoln had
reluctantly consented to the plan, fearing sufficient protection was not provided for Washington.   By the
battle of Kernstown, March 23d, in the Valley of Virginia, Jackson, though defeated, so alarmed the Administration that McDowell was ordered to remain at Manassas to protect the capital.   The reverse at Kernstown was therefore a real triumph for Jackson, but with his small force he had to keep up the game of holding
McDowell, Banks, and Frémont from reënforcing McClellan.   If he failed, 80,000 troops might move up to
Richmond from the west while McClellan was approaching from the North.   But Jackson, on May 23d and
25th, surprised Banks' forces at Front Royal and Winchester, forcing a retreat to the Potomac.   At the news
of this event McDowell was ordered not to join McClellan in front of Richmond.

Washington. After consulting six of his generals he became
convinced that McClellan had not arranged proper protection
for the city. Therefore, McDowell and his corps of thirty-
seven thousand men were ordered to remain at Manassas.
The Valley grew to greater importance in the Federal eyes.
Banks was made entirely independent of McClellan and the
defense of this region became his sole task. McClellan, to his
great chagrin, saw his force depleted by forty-six thousand
men. There were now four Union generals in the East operating independently one of the other.

General Ewell with eight thousand troops on the upper
Rappahannock and General Johnson with two brigades were
now ordered to cooperate with Jackson. These reenforcements were badly needed. Schenck and Milroy, of Fremont's
corps, began to threaten Johnson. Banks, with twenty thousand, was near Harrisonburg.

The Confederate leader left General Ewell to watch
Banks while he made a dash for Milroy and Schenck. He
fought them at McDowell on May 8th and they fled precipitately to rejoin Fremont. The swift-acting Jackson now darted
at Banks, who had fortified himself at Strasburg. Jackson
stopped long enough to be joined by Ewell. He did not attack
Strasburg, but stole across the Massanutten Mountain unknown to Banks, and made for Front Royal, where a strong
Union detachment was stationed under Colonel Kenly. Early
on the afternoon of May 23d, Ewell rushed from the forest.
Kenly and his men fled before them toward Winchester. A
large number were captured by the cavalry before they had
gotten more than four miles away.

Banks at Strasburg realized that Jackson was approaching from the rear, the thing he had least expected and had
made no provision for. His fortifications protected his front
alone. There was nothing to be done but retreat to Winchester. Even that was prevented by the remarkable speed
of Jackson's men, who could march as much as thirty-five

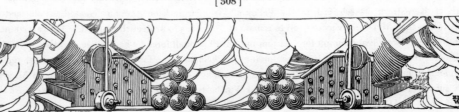

THE GERMAN DIVISION SENT AGAINST JACKSON

Blenker's division, composed of three brigades of German volunteers, was detached from the Army of the Potomac in March, 1862, to assist Frémont in his operations against Jackson. The German troops were but poorly equipped, many of them carrying old-pattern Belgian and Austrian muskets. When they united with Frémont he was obliged to rearm them with Springfield rifles from his own stores. When the combined forces met Jackson and Ewell at Cross Keys, five of Blenker's regiments were sent forward to the first attack. In the picture Brigadier-General Louis Blenker is standing, with his hand on his belt, before the door. At his left is Prince Felix Salm-Salm, a Prussian military officer, who joined the Federal army as a colonel of volunteers. At the right of Blenker is General Stahel, who led the advance of the Federal left at Cross Keys.

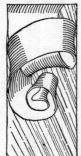

miles a day. On May 24th, the Confederates overtook and struck the receding Union flank near Newtown, inflicting heavy loss and taking many prisoners. Altogether, three thousand of Banks' men fell into Jackson's hands.

This exploit was most opportune for the Southern arms. It caused the final ruin of McClellan's hopes. Banks received one more attack from Ewell's division the next day as he passed through Winchester on his way to the shelter of the Potomac. He crossed at Williamsport late the same evening and wrote the President that his losses, though serious enough, might have been far worse "considering the very great disparity of forces engaged, and the long-matured plans of the enemy, which aimed at nothing less than entire capture of our force." Mr. Lincoln now rescinded his resolution to send McDowell to McClellan. Instead, he transferred twenty thousand of the former's men to Fremont and informed McClellan that he was not, after all, to have the aid of McDowell's forty thousand men.

Fremont was coming from the west; Shields lay in the other direction, but Jackson was not the man to be trapped. He managed to hold Fremont while he marched his main force quickly up the Valley. At Port Republic he drove Carroll's brigade of Shields' division away and took possession of a bridge which Colonel Carroll had neglected to burn. Fremont in pursuit was defeated by Ewell at Cross Keys. Jackson immediately put his force of twelve thousand over the Shenandoah at Port Republic and burned the bridge. Safe from the immediate attack by Fremont, he fell upon Tyler and Carroll, who had not more than three thousand men between them. The Federals made a brave stand, but after many hours' fighting were compelled to retreat. Jackson emerged through Swift Run Gap on the 17th of June, to assist in turning the Union right on the Peninsula, and Banks and Shields, baffled and checkmated at every move, finally withdrew from the Valley.

PART III
THE STRUGGLE FOR RICHMOND

THE
SEVEN DAYS'
BATTLES

VIEW ON THE JAMES, THE RIVER TO WHICH McCLELLAN DECIDED TO
SWING HIS BASE ON THE FIRST OF THE SEVEN DAYS, JUNE 26, 1862—NOT
SIX WEEKS BEFORE, THE GUN SHOWN HAD HELPED TO REPEL THE UNION
GUNBOATS THAT ENDEAVORED TO OPEN McCLELLAN'S WAY TO RICHMOND

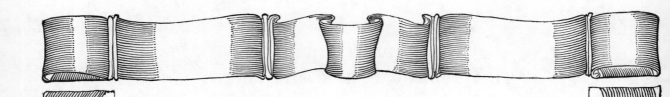

THE SEVEN DAYS' BATTLES

McClellan's one hope, one purpose, was to march his army out of the swamps and escape from the ceaseless Confederate assaults to a point on James River where the resistless fire of the gunboats might protect his men from further attack and give them a chance to rest. To that end, he retreated night and day, standing at bay now and then as the hunted stag does, and fighting desperately for the poor privilege of running away.

And the splendid fighting of his men was a tribute to the skill and genius with which he had created an effective army out of what he had described as "regiments cowering upon the banks of the Potomac, some perfectly raw, others dispirited by recent defeat, others going home." Out of a demoralized and disorganized mass reenforced by utterly untrained civilians, McClellan had within a few months created an army capable of stubbornly contesting every inch of ground even while effecting a retreat the very thought of which might well have disorganized an army. —*George Cary Eggleston, in " The History of the Confederate War."*

GENERAL LEE was determined that the operations in front of Richmond should not degenerate into a siege, and that the Army of Northern Virginia should no longer be on the defensive. To this end, early in the summer of 1862, he proceeded to increase his fighting force so as to make it more nearly equal in number to that of his antagonist. Every man who could be spared from other sections of the South was called to Richmond. Numerous earthworks soon made their appearance along the roads and in the fields about the Confederate capital, giving the city the appearance of a fortified camp. The new commander in an address to the troops said that the army had made its last retreat.

Meanwhile, with the spires of Richmond in view, the Army of the Potomac was acclimating itself to a Virginia summer. The whole face of the country for weeks had been a

JOHNSTON AND LEE—A PHOTOGRAPH OF 1869.

These men look enough alike to be brothers. They were so in arms, at West Point, in Mexico and throughout the war. General Joseph E. Johnston (on the left), who had led the Confederate forces since Bull Run, was wounded at Fair Oaks. That wound gave Robert E. Lee (on the right) his opportunity to act as leader. After Fair Oaks, Johnston retired from the command of the army defending Richmond. The new commander immediately grasped the possibilities of the situation which confronted him. The promptness and completeness with which he blighted McClellan's high hopes of reaching Richmond showed at one stroke that the Confederacy had found its great general. It was only through much sifting that the North at last picked military leaders that could rival him in the field.

veritable bog. Now that the sweltering heat of June was coming on, the malarious swamps were fountains of disease. The polluted waters of the sluggish streams soon began to tell on the health of the men. Malaria and typhoid were prevalent; the hospitals were crowded, and the death rate was appalling.

Such conditions were not inspiring to either general or army. McClellan was still hoping for substantial reenforcements. McDowell, with his forty thousand men, had been promised him, but he was doomed to disappointment from that source. Yet in the existing state of affairs he dared not be inactive. South of the Chickahominy, the army was almost secure from surprise, owing to well-protected rifle-pits flanked by marshy thickets or covered with felled trees. But the Federal forces were still divided by the fickle stream, and this was a constant source of anxiety to the commander. He proceeded to transfer all of his men to the Richmond side of the river, excepting the corps of Franklin and Fitz John Porter. About the middle of June, General McCall with a force of eleven thousand men joined the Federal army north of the Chickahominy, bringing the entire fighting strength to about one hundred and five thousand. So long as there remained the slightest hope of additional soldiers, it was impossible to withdraw all of the army from the York side of the Peninsula, and it remained divided.

That was a brilliant initial stroke of the Confederate general when he sent his famous cavalry leader, J. E. B. Stuart, with about twelve hundred Virginia troopers, to encircle the army of McClellan. Veiling his intentions with the utmost secrecy, Stuart started June 12, 1862, in the direction of Fredericksburg as if to reenforce " Stonewall " Jackson. The first night he bivouacked in the pine woods of Hanover. No fires were kindled, and when the morning dawned, his men swung upon their mounts without the customary bugle-call of " Boots and Saddles." Turning to the east, he surprised and captured a Federal picket; swinging around a corner of the road, he

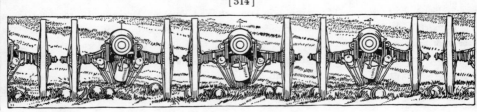

THE FLEET THAT FED THE ARMY

THE ABANDONED BASE

White House, Virginia, June 27, 1862.—Up the James and the Pamunkey to White House Landing came the steam and sailing vessels den with supplies for McClellan's second attempt to reach Richmond. Tons of ammunition and thousands of rations were sent forard from here to the army on the Chickahominy in June, 1862. A short month was enough to cause McClellan to again change his lans, and the army base was moved to the James River. The Richmond and York Railroad was lit up by burning cars along its urse to the Chickahominy. Little was left to the Confederates save the charred ruins of the White House itself.

suddenly came upon a squadron of Union cavalry. The Confederate yell rent the air and a swift, bold charge by the Southern troopers swept the foe on.

They had not traveled far when they came again to a force drawn up in columns of fours, ready to dispute the passage of the road. This time the Federals were about to make the charge. A squadron of the Confederates moved forward to meet them. Some Union skirmishers in their effort to get to the main body of their troops swept into the advancing Confederates and carried the front ranks of the squadron with them. These isolated Confederates found themselves in an extremely perilous position, being gradually forced into the Federal main body. Before they could extricate themselves, nearly every one in the unfortunate front rank was shot or cut down.

The Southern cavalrymen swept on and presently found themselves nearing the York River Railroad—McClellan's supply line. As they approached Tunstall's Station they charged down upon it, with their characteristic yell, completely surprising a company of Federal infantry stationed there. These at once surrendered. Telegraph wires were cut and a tree felled across the track to obstruct the road. This had hardly been done before the shriek of a locomotive was heard. A train bearing Union troops came thundering along, approaching the station. The engineer, taking in the situation at a glance, put on a full head of steam and made a rush for the obstruction, which was easily brushed aside. As the train went through a cut the Confederates fired upon it, wounding and killing some of the Federal soldiers in the cars.

Riding all through a moonlit night, the raiders reached Sycamore Ford of the Chickahominy at break of day. As usual this erratic stream was overflowing its banks. They started to ford it, but finding that it would be a long and wearisome task, a bridge was hastily improvised at another place where the passage was made with more celerity. Now,

ELLERSON'S MILL—WHERE HILL ASSAULTED.

ot until after nightfall of June 26, 1862, did the Confederates of General A. P. Hill's division cease their assaults upon this
sition where General McCall's men were strongly entrenched. Time after time the Confederates charged over the ground we see
re at Ellerson's Mill, near Mechanicsville. Till 9 o'clock at night they continued to pour volleys at the position, and then at last
thdrew. The victory was of little use to the Federals, for Jackson on the morrow, having executed one of the flanking night
arches at which he was an adept, fell upon the Federal rear at Gaines' Mill.

THE WASTE OF WAR

lroad trains loaded with tons of food and ammunition were run deliberately at full speed off the embankment shown in the left
ground. They plunged headlong into the waters of the Pamunkey. This was the readiest means that McClellan could devise
keeping his immense quantity of stores out of the hands of the Confederates in his hasty change of base from White House to the
es after Gaines' Mill. This was the bridge of the Richmond and York River Railroad, and was destroyed June 28, 1862, to
der the railroad useless to the Confederates.

on the south bank of the river, haste was made for the confines of Richmond, where, at dawn of the following day, the troopers dropped from their saddles, a weary but happy body of cavalry.

Lee thus obtained exact and detailed information of the position of McClellan's army, and he laid out his campaign accordingly. Meanwhile his own forces in and about Richmond were steadily increasing. He was planning for an army of nearly one hundred thousand and he now demonstrated his ability as a strategist. Word had been despatched to Jackson in the Shenandoah to bring his troops to fall upon the right wing of McClellan's army. At the same time Lee sent General Whiting north to make a feint of joining Jackson and moving upon Washington. The ruse proved eminently successful. The authorities at Washington were frightened, and McClellan received no more reenforcements. Jackson now began a hide-and-seek game among the mountains, and managed to have rumors spread of his army being in several places at the same time, while skilfully veiling his actual movements.

It was not until the 25th of June that McClellan had definite knowledge of Jackson's whereabouts. He was then located at Ashland, north of the Chickahominy, within striking distance of the Army of the Potomac. McClellan was surprised but he was not unprepared. Seven days before he had arranged for a new base of supplies on the James, which would now prove useful if he were driven south of the Chickahominy.

On the very day he heard of Jackson's arrival at Ashland, McClellan was pushing his men forward to begin his siege of Richmond—that variety of warfare which his engineering soul loved so well. His advance guard was within four miles of the Confederate capital. His strong fortifications were bristling upon every vantage point, and his fond hope was that within a few days, at most, his efficient artillery, for which the Army of the Potomac was famous, would be

[318]

THE BRIDGE THAT STOOD

The force under General McCall was stationed by McClellan on June 19, 1862, to observe the Meadow and Mechanicsville bridges over the Chickahominy which had only partially been destroyed. On the afternoon of June 26th, General A. P. Hill crossed at Meadow Bridge, driving the Union skirmish-line back to Beaver Dam Creek. The divisions of D. H. Hill and Longstreet had been waiting at Mechanicsville Bridge (shown in this photograph) since 8 A.M. for A. P. Hill to open the way for them to cross. They passed over in time to bear a decisive part in the Confederate attack at Gaines' Mill on the 27th.

DOING DOUBLE DUTY

Here are some of McClellan's staff-officers during the strenuous period of the Seven Days' Battles. One commonly supposes that a general's staff has little to do but wear gold lace and transmit orders. But it is their duty to multiply the eyes and ears and thinking power of the leader. Without them he could not direct the movements of his army. There were so few regular officers of ripe experience that members of the staff were invariably made regimental commanders, and frequently were compelled to divide their time between leading their troops into action and reporting to and consulting with their superior.

belching forth its sheets of fire and lead into the beleagured city. In front of the Union encampment, near Fair Oaks, was a thick entanglement of scrubby pines, vines, and ragged bushes, full of ponds and marshes. This strip of woodland was less than five hundred yards wide. Beyond it was an open field half a mile in width. The Union soldiers pressed through the thicket to see what was on the other side and met the Confederate pickets among the trees. The advancing column drove them back. Upon emerging into the open, the Federal troops found it filled with rifle-pits, earthworks, and redoubts. At once they were met with a steady and incessant fire, which continued from eight in the morning until five in the afternoon. At times the contest almost reached the magnitude of a battle, and in the end the Union forces occupied the former position of their antagonists. This passage of arms, sometimes called the affair of Oak Grove or the Second Battle of Fair Oaks, was the prelude to the Seven Days' Battles.

The following day, June 26th, had been set by General "Stonewall" Jackson as the date on which he would join Lee, and together they would fall upon the right wing of the Army of the Potomac. The Federals north of the Chickahominy were under the direct command of General Fitz John Porter. Defensive preparations had been made on an extensive scale. Field works, heavily armed with artillery, and rifle-pits, well manned, covered the roads and open fields and were often concealed by timber from the eye of the opposing army. The extreme right of the Union line lay near Mechanicsville on the upper Chickahominy. A tributary of this stream from the north was Beaver Dam Creek, upon whose left bank was a steep bluff, commanding the valley to the west. This naturally strong position, now well defended, was almost impregnable to an attack from the front.

Before sunrise of the appointed day the Confederate forces were at the Chickahominy bridges, awaiting the arrival of Jackson. To reach these some of the regiments had

THE RETROGRADE CROSSING

LOWER BRIDGE ON THE CHICKAHOMINY

Woodbury's Bridge on the Chickahominy. Little did General D. F. Woodbury's engineers suspect, when they built this bridge, early in June, 1862, as a means of communication between the divided wings of McClellan's army on the Chickahominy that it would be of incalculable service during battle. When the right wing, under General Fitz John Porter, was engaged on the field of Gaines' Mill against almost the entire army of Lee, across this bridge the division of General Slocum marched from its position in the trenches in front of Richmond on the south bank of the river to the support of Porter's men. The battle lasted until nightfall and then the Federal troops moved across this bridge and rejoined the main forces of the Federal army. Woodbury's engineers built several bridges across the Chickahominy, but among them all the bridge named for their commander proved to be, perhaps, the most serviceable.

marched the greater part of the night. For once Jackson was behind time. The morning hours came and went. Noon passed and Jackson had not arrived. At three o'clock, General A. P. Hill, growing impatient, decided to put his troops in motion. Crossing at Meadow Bridge, he marched his men along the north side of the Chickahominy, and at Mechanicsville was joined by the commands of Longstreet and D. H. Hill. Driving the Union outposts to cover, the Confederates swept across the low approach to Beaver Dam Creek. A murderous fire from the batteries on the cliff poured into their ranks. Gallantly the attacking columns withstood the deluge of leaden hail and drew near the creek. A few of the more aggressive reached the opposite bank but their repulse was severe.

Later in the afternoon relief was sent to Hill, who again attempted to force the Union position at Ellerson's Mill, where the slope of the west bank came close to the borders of the little stream. From across the open fields, in full view of the defenders of the cliff, the Confederates moved down the slope. They were in range of the Federal batteries, but the fire was reserved. Every artilleryman was at his post ready to fire at the word; the soldiers were in the rifle-pits sighting along the glittering barrels of their muskets with fingers on the triggers. As the approaching columns reached the stream they turned with the road that ran parallel to the bank.

From every waiting field-piece the shells came screaming through the air. Volley after volley of musketry was poured into the flanks of the marching Southerners. The hillside was soon covered with the victims of the gallant charge. Twilight fell upon the warring troops and there were no signs of a cessation of the unequal combat. Night fell, and still from the heights the lurid flames burst in a display of glorious pyrotechnics. It was nine o'clock when Hill finally drew back his shattered regiments, to await the coming of the morning. The Forty-fourth Georgia regiment suffered most in the fight;

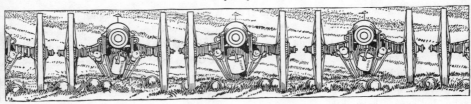

THE FIGHT FOR THE WAGON TRAINS

Three times General Magruder led the Confederates against this position on June 29, 1862, and was as many times repulsed in his attempt to seize the supplies which McClellan was shifting to his new position. Here we see the peaceful morning of that day. Allen's farmhouse in the foreground stands just back from the Williamsburg Road, along which the Federal wagon trains were attempting to move toward Savage's Station. The corps of Sumner and Heintzelman are camped in the background. At dusk of the same day, after Magruder's attacks, the camp was hastily broken and the troops, to avoid being cut off, were marching swiftly and silently toward Savage's Station, leaving behind large quantities of supplies which fell into the hands of the eager Confederates.

three hundred and thirty-five being the dreadful toll, in dead and wounded, paid for its efforts to break down the Union position. Dropping back to the rear this ill-fated regiment attempted to re-form its broken ranks, but its officers were all among those who had fallen. Both armies now prepared for another day and a renewal of the conflict.

The action at Beaver Dam Creek convinced McClellan that Jackson was really approaching with a large force, and he decided to begin his change of base from the Pamunkey to the James, leaving Porter and the Fifth Corps still on the left bank of the Chickahominy, to prevent Jackson's fresh troops from interrupting this great movement. It was, indeed, a gigantic undertaking, for it involved marching an army of a hundred thousand men, including cavalry and artillery, across the marshy peninsula. A train of five thousand heavily loaded wagons and many siege-guns had to be transported; nearly three thousand cattle on the hoof had to be driven. From White House the supplies could be shipped by the York River Railroad as far as Savage's Station. Thence to the James, a distance of seventeen miles, they had to be carried overland along a road intersected by many others from which a watchful opponent might easily attack. General Casey's troops, guarding the supplies at White House, were transferred by way of the York and the James to Harrison's Landing on the latter river. The transports were loaded with all the material they could carry. The rest was burned, or put in cars. These cars, with locomotives attached, were then run into the river.

On the night of June 26th, McCall's Federal division, at Beaver Dam Creek, was directed to fall back to the bridges across the Chickahominy near Gaines' Mill and there make a stand, for the purpose of holding the Confederate army. During the night the wagon trains and heavy guns were quietly moved across the river. Just before daylight the operation of removing the troops began. The Confederates were

A VAIN RIDE TO SAFETY

During the retreat after Gaines' Mill, McClellan's army was straining every nerve to extricate itself and present a strong front to Lee before he could strike a telling blow at its untenable position. Wagon trains were struggling across the almost impassable White Oak Swamp, while the troops were striving to hold Savage's Station to protect the movement. Thither on flat cars were sent the wounded as we see them in the picture. The rear guard of the Army of the Potomac had hastily provided such field hospital facilities as they could. We see the camp near the railroad with the passing wagon trains in the lower picture. But attention to these wounded men was, perforce, secondary to the necessity of holding the position. Their hopes of relief from their suffering were to be blighted. Lee was about to fall upon the Federal rear guard at Savage's Station. Instead of to a haven of refuge, these men were being railroaded toward the field of carnage, where they must of necessity be left by their retreating companions.

THE STAND AT SAVAGE'S STATION

Here we see part of the encampment to hold which the divisions of Richardson, Sedgwick, Smith, and Franklin fought valiantly when Magruder and the Confederates fell upon them, June 29, 1862. Along the Richmond & York River Railroad, seen in the picture, the Confederates rolled a heavy rifled gun, mounted on car-wheels. They turned its deadly fire steadily upon the defenders. The Federals fought fiercely and managed to hold their ground till nightfall, when hundreds of their bravest soldiers lay on the field and had to be left alone with their wounded comrades who had arrived on the flat cars.

equally alert, for about the same time they opened a heavy fire on the retreating columns. This march of five miles was a continuous skirmish; but the Union forces, ably and skilfully handled, succeeded in reaching their new position on the Chickahominy heights.

The morning of the new day was becoming hot and sultry as the men of the Fifth Corps made ready for action in their new position. The selection of this ground had been well made; it occupied a series of heights fronted on the west by a sickle-shaped stream. The battle-lines followed the course of this creek, in the arc of a circle curving outward in the direction of the approaching army. The land beyond the creek was an open country, through which Powhite Creek meandered sluggishly, and beyond this a wood densely tangled with undergrowth. Around the Union position were also many patches of wooded land affording cover for the troops and screening the reserves from view.

Porter had learned from deserters and others that Jackson's forces, united to those of Longstreet and the two Hills, were advancing with grim determination to annihilate the Army of the Potomac. He had less than eighteen thousand men to oppose the fifty thousand Confederates. To protect the Federals, trees had been felled along a small portion of their front, out of which barriers protected with rails and knapsacks were erected. Porter had considerable artillery, but only a small part of it could be used. It was two o'clock, on June 27th, when General A. P. Hill swung his division into line for the attack. He was unsupported by the other divisions, which had not yet arrived, but his columns moved rapidly toward the Union front. The assault was terrific, but twenty-six guns threw a hail-storm of lead into his ranks. Under the cover of this magnificent execution of artillery, the infantry sent messages of death to the approaching lines of gray.

The Confederate front recoiled from the incessant outpour of grape, canister, and shell. The heavy cloud of battle

[326]

A GRIM CAPTURE

The Second and Sixth Corps of the Federal Army repelled a desperate attack of General Magruder at Savage Station on June 29th. The next day they disappeared, plunging into the depths of White Oak Swamp, leaving only the brave medical officers behind, doing what they could to relieve the sufferings of the men that had to be abandoned. Here we see them at work upon the wounded, who have been gathered from the field. Nothing but the strict arrest of the stern sergeant Death can save these men from capture, and when the Confederates occupied Savage's Station on the morning of June 30th, twenty-five hundred sick and wounded men and their medical attendants became prisoners of war. The Confederate hospital facilities were already taxed to their full capacity in caring for Lee's wounded, and most of these men were confronted on that day with the prospect of lingering for months in the military prisons of the South. The brave soldiers lying helpless here were wounded at Gaines' Mill on June 27th and removed to the great field-hospital established at Savage's Station. The photograph was taken just before Sumner and Franklin withdrew the rear-guard of their columns on the morning of June 30th.

smoke rose lazily through the air, twisting itself among the trees and settling over the forest like a pall. The tremendous momentum of the repulse threw the Confederates into great confusion. Men were separated from their companies and for a time it seemed as if a rout were imminent. The Federals, pushing out from under the protection of their great guns, now became the assailants. The Southerners were being driven back. Many had left the field in disorder. Others threw themselves on the ground to escape the withering fire, while some tenaciously held their places. This lasted for two hours. General Slocum arrived with his division of Franklin's corps, and his arrival increased the ardor of the victorious Federals.

It was then that Lee ordered a general attack upon the entire Union front. Reenforcements were brought to take the place of the shattered regiments. The engagement began with a sharp artillery fire from the Confederate guns. Then the troops moved forward, once more to assault the Union position. In the face of a heavy fire they rushed across the sedgy lowland, pressed up the hillside at fearful sacrifice and pushed against the Union front. It was a death grapple for the mastery of the field. General Lee, sitting on his horse on an eminence where he could observe the progress of the battle, saw, coming down the road, General Hood, of Jackson's corps, who was bringing his brigade into the fight. Riding forward to meet him, Lee directed that he should try to break the line. Hood, disposing his men for the attack, sent them forward, but, reserving the Fourth Texas for his immediate command, he marched it into an open field, halted, and addressed it, giving instructions that no man should fire until ordered and that all should keep together in line.

The forward march was sounded, and the intrepid Hood, leading his men, started for the Union breastworks eight hundred yards away. They moved at a rapid pace across the open, under a continually increasing shower of shot and shell. At every step the ranks grew thinner and thinner. As they

THE TANGLED RETREAT

Through this well-nigh impassable morass of White Oak Swamp, across a single long bridge, McClellan's wagon trains were being hurried the last days of June, 1862. On the morning of the 30th, the rear-guard of the army was hastily tramping after them, and by ten o'clock had safely crossed and destroyed the bridge. They had escaped in the nick of time, for at noon "Stonewall" Jackson opened fire upon Richardson's division and a terrific artillery battle ensued for the possession of this, the single crossing by which it was possible to attack McClellan's rear. The Federal batteries were compelled to retire but Jackson's crossing was prevented on that day by the infantry.

reached the crest of a small ridge, one hundred and fifty yards from the Union line, the batteries in front and on the flank sent a storm of shell and canister plowing into their already depleted files. They quickened their pace as they passed down the slope and across the creek. Not a shot had they fired and amid the sulphurous atmosphere of battle, with the wing of death hovering over all, they fixed bayonets and dashed up the hill into the Federal line. With a shout they plunged through the felled timber and over the breastworks. The Union line had been pierced and was giving way. It was falling back toward the Chickahominy bridges, and the retreat was threatening to develop into a general rout. The twilight was closing in and the day was all but lost to the Army of the Potomac. Now a great shout was heard from the direction of the bridge; and, pushing through the stragglers at the river bank were seen the brigades of French and Meagher, detached from Sumner's corps, coming to the rescue. General Meagher, in his shirt sleeves, was leading his men up the bluff and confronted the Confederate battle line. This put a stop to the pursuit and as night was at hand the Southern soldiers withdrew. The battle of Gaines' Mill, or the Chickahominy, was over.

When Lee came to the banks of the little river the next morning he found his opponent had crossed over and destroyed the bridges. The Army of the Potomac was once more united. During the day the Federal wagon trains were safely passed over White Oak Swamp and then moved on toward the James River. Lee did not at first divine McClellan's intention. He still believed that the Federal general would retreat down the Peninsula, and hesitated therefore to cross the Chickahominy and give up the command of the lower bridges. But now on the 29th the signs of the movement to the James were unmistakable. Early on that morning Longstreet and A. P. Hill were ordered to recross the Chickahominy by the New Bridge and Huger and Magruder were sent in hot pursuit of the Federal forces. It was the brave Sumner who covered the

MAJOR MEYERS AND LIEUTENANTS STRYKER AND NORTON, 10TH PENN. RESERVES

THREE GROUPS

OF McCLELLAN'S

FIGHTING OFFICERS

COLONEL A. V. COLBURN, COLONEL D. B. SACKETT, AND GENERAL JOHN SEDGWICK

PHOTOGRAPHED

THE MONTH AFTER

THE SEVEN DAYS' BATTLES

COLONEL JAMES H. CHILDS AND OFFICERS, FOURTH PENNSYLVANIA CAVALRY

march of the retreating army, and as he stood in the open field near Savage's Station he looked out over the plain and saw with satisfaction the last of the ambulances and wagons making their way toward the new haven on the James.

In the morning of that same day he had already held at bay the forces of Magruder at Allen's Farm. On his way from Fair Oaks, which he left at daylight, he had halted his men at what is known as the "Peach Orchard," and from nine o'clock till eleven had resisted a spirited fire of musketry and artillery. And now as the grim warrior, on this Sunday afternoon in June, turned his eyes toward the Chickahominy he saw a great cloud of dust rising on the horizon. It was raised by the troops of General Magruder who was pressing close behind the Army of the Potomac. The Southern field-guns were placed in position. A contrivance, consisting of a heavy gun mounted on a railroad car and called the "Land Merrimac," was pushed into position and opened fire upon the Union forces. The battle began with a fine play of artillery. For an hour not a musket was fired. The army of blue remained motionless. Then the mass of gray moved across the field and from the Union guns the long tongues of flame darted into the ranks before them. The charge was met with vigor and soon the battle raged over the entire field. Both sides stood their ground till darkness again closed the contest, and nearly eight hundred brave men had fallen in this Sabbath evening's battle. Before midnight Sumner had withdrawn his men and was following after the wagon trains.

The Confederates were pursuing McClellan's army in two columns, Jackson closely following Sumner, while Longstreet was trying to cut off the Union forces by a flank movement. On the last day of June, at high noon, Jackson reached the White Oak Swamp. But the bridge was gone. He attempted to ford the passage, but the Union troops were there to prevent it. While Jackson was trying to force his way across the stream, there came to him the sound of a desperate battle being

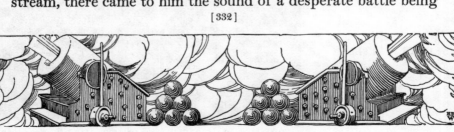

HEROES OF MALVERN HILL

Brigadier-General J. H. Martindale (seated) and his staff, July 1, 1862. Fitz John Porter's Fifth Corps and Couch's division, Fourth Corps, bore the brunt of battle at Malvern Hill where the troops of McClellan withstood the terrific attacks of Lee's combined and superior forces. Fiery "Prince John" Magruder hurled column after column against the left of the Federal line, but every charge was met and repulsed through the long hot summer afternoon. Martindale's brigade of the Fifth Corps was early called into action, and its commander, by the gallant fighting of his troops, won the brevet of Major-General.

THE NAVY LENDS A HAND

Officers of the *Monitor* at Malvern Hill. Glad indeed were the men of the Army of the Potomac as they emerged from their perilous march across White Oak Swamp to hear the firing of the gunboats on the James. It told them the Confederates had not yet preempted the occupation of Malvern Hill, which General Fitz John Porter's Corps was holding. Before the battle opened McClellan went aboard the *Galena* to consult with Commodore John Rodgers about a suitable base on the James. The gunboats of the fleet supported the flanks of the army during the battle and are said to have silenced one of the Confederate batteries.

fought not more than two miles away, but he was powerless to give aid.

Longstreet and A. P. Hill had come upon the Federal regiments at Glendale, near the intersection of the Charles City road, guarding the right flank of the retreat. It was Longstreet who, about half-past two, made one of his characteristic onslaughts on that part of the Union army led by General McCall. It was repulsed with heavy loss. Again and again attacks were made. Each brigade seemed to act on its own behalf. They hammered here, there, and everywhere. Repulsed at one place they charged at another. The Eleventh Alabama, rushing out from behind a dense wood, charged across the open field in the face of the Union batteries. The men had to run a distance of six hundred yards. A heavy and destructive fire poured into their lines, but on they came, trailing their guns. The batteries let loose grape and canister, while volley after volley of musketry sent its death-dealing messages among the Southerners. But nothing except death itself could check their impetuous charge. When two hundred yards away they raised the Confederate yell and rushed for Randol's battery.

Pausing for an instant they deliver a volley and attempt to seize the guns. Bayonets are crossed and men engage in a hand-to-hand struggle. The contending masses rush together, asking and giving no quarter and struggling like so many tigers. Darkness is closing on the fearful scene, yet the fighting continues with unabated ferocity. There are the shouts of command, the clash and the fury of the battle, the sulphurous smoke, the flashes of fire streaking through the air, the yells of defiance, the thrust, the parry, the thud of the clubbed musket, the hiss of the bullet, the spouting blood, the death-cry, and beneath all lie the bodies of America's sons, some in blue and some in gray.

While Lee and his army were held in check by the events of June 30th at White Oak Swamp and the other battle at

Again we see the transports and supply schooners at anchor—this time at Harrison's Landing on the James River. In about a month, McClellan had changed the position of his army twice, shifting his base from the Pamunkey to the James. The position he held on Malvern Hill was abandoned after the victory of July 1, 1862, and the army marched to a new base farther down the James, where the heavy losses of men and supplies during the

THE SECOND ARMY BASE

Seven Days could be made up without danger and delay. Harrison's Landing was the point selected, and here the army recuperated, wondering what would be the next step. Below we see the historic mansion which did service as General Porter's headquarters, one of McClellan's most efficient commanders. For his services during the Seven Days he was made Major-General of Volunteers. McClellan was his lifelong friend.

WESTOVER HOUSE: HEADQUARTERS OF GENERAL FITZ JOHN PORTER, HARRISON'S LANDING

Glendale or Nelson's Farm, the last of the wagon trains had arrived safely at Malvern Hill. The contest had hardly closed and the smoke had scarcely lifted from the blood-soaked field, when the Union forces were again in motion toward the James. By noon on July 1st the last division reached the position where McClellan decided to turn again upon his assailants. He had not long to wait, for the Confederate columns, led by Longstreet, were close on his trail, and a march of a few miles brought them to the Union outposts. They found the Army of the Potomac admirably situated to give defensive battle. Malvern Hill, a plateau, a mile and a half long and half as broad, with its top almost bare of woods, commanded a view of the country over which the Confederate army must approach. Along the western face of this plateau there are deep ravines falling abruptly in the direction of the James River; on the north and east is a gentle slope to the plain beneath, bordered by a thick forest. Around the summit of the hill, General Mc-Clellan had placed tier after tier of batteries, arranged like an amphitheater. Surmounting these on the crest were massed seven of his heaviest siege-guns. His army surrounded this hill, its left flank being protected by the gunboats on the river.

The morning and early afternoon were occupied with many Confederate attacks, sometimes formidable in their nature, but Lee planned for no general move until he could bring up a force that he considered sufficient to attack the strong Federal position. The Confederate orders were to advance when the signal, a yell, cheer, or shout from the men of Armistead's brigade, was given.

Late in the afternoon General D. H. Hill heard some shouting, followed by a roar of musketry. No other general seems to have heard it, for Hill made his attack alone. It was gallantly done, but no army could have withstood the galling fire of the batteries of the Army of the Potomac as they were massed upon Malvern Hill. All during the evening, brigade after brigade tried to force the Union lines. The gunners

ON DARING DUTY

Lieut.-Colonel Albert V. Colburn, a favorite Aide-de-Camp of General McClellan's.—Here is the bold soldier of the Green Mountain State who bore despatches about the fields of battle during the Seven Days. It was he who was sent galloping across the difficult and dangerous country to make sure that Franklin's division was retreating from White Oak Swamp, and then to carry orders to Sumner to fall back on Malvern Hill. Such were the tasks that constantly fell to the lot of the despatch bearer. Necessarily a man of quick and accurate judgment, perilous chances confronted him in his efforts to keep the movements of widely separated divisions in concert with the plans of the commander. The loss of his life might mean the loss of a battle; the failure to arrive in the nick of time with despatches might mean disaster for the army. Only the coolest headed of the officers could be trusted with this vital work in the field.

stood coolly and manfully by their batteries. The Confederates were not able to make concerted efforts, but the battle waxed hot nevertheless. They were forced to breast one of the most devastating storms of lead and canister to which an assaulting army has ever been subjected. The round shot and grape cut through the branches of the trees and the battle-field was soon in a cloud of smoke. Column after column of Southern soldiers rushed up to the death-dealing cannon, only to be mowed down. The thinned and ragged lines, with a valor born of desperation, rallied again and again to the charge, but to no avail. The batteries on the heights still hurled their missiles of death. The field below was covered with the dead and wounded of the Southland.

The gunboats in the river made the battle scene more awe-inspiring with their thunderous cannonading. Their heavy shells shrieked through the forest, and great limbs were torn from the trees as they hurtled by in their outburst of fury.

Night was falling. The combatants were no longer distinguishable except by the sheets of flame. It was nine o'clock before the guns ceased their fire, and only an occasional shot rang out over the bloody field of Malvern Hill.

The courageous though defeated Confederate, looking up the next day through the drenching rain to where had stood the embrasured wall with its grim batteries and lines of blue, that spoke death to so many of his companions-in-arms, saw only deserted ramparts. The Union army had retreated in the darkness of the night. But this time no foe harassed its march. Unmolested, it sought its new camp at Harrison's Landing, where it remained until August 3d, when, as President Lincoln had been convinced of the impracticability of operating from the James River as a base, orders were issued by General Halleck for the withdrawal of the Army of the Potomac from the Peninsula.

The net military result of the Seven Days was a disappointment to the South. Although thankful that the siege of

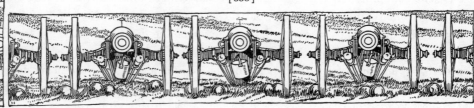

AVERELL—THE COLONEL WHO BLUFFED AN ARMY.

Colonel W. W. Averell and Staff.—This intrepid officer of the Third Pennsylvania Cavalry held the Federal position on Malvern Hill on the morning of July 2, 1862, with only a small guard, while McClellan completed the withdrawal of his army to Harrison's Landing. It was his duty to watch the movements of the Confederates and hold them back from any attempt to fall upon the retreating trains and troops. A dense fog in the early morning shut off the forces of A. P. Hill and Longstreet from his view. He had not a single fieldpiece with which to resist attack. When the mist cleared away, he kept up a great activity with his cavalry horses, making the Confederates believe that artillery was being brought up. With apparent reluctance he agreed to a truce of two hours in which the Confederates might bury the dead they left on the hillside the day before. Later, with an increased show of unwillingness, he extended the truce for another two hours. Just before they expired, Frank's Battery arrived to his support, with the news that the Army of the Potomac was safe. Colonel Averell rejoined it without the loss of a man.

Richmond had been raised, the Southern public believed that McClellan should not have been allowed to reach the James River with his army intact.

"That army," Eggleston states, "splendidly organized, superbly equipped, and strengthened rather than weakened in morale, lay securely at rest on the James River, within easy striking distance of Richmond. There was no knowing at what moment McClellan might hurl it again upon Richmond or upon that commanding key to Richmond—the Petersburg position. In the hands of a capable commander McClellan's army would at this time have been a more serious menace than ever to the Confederate capital, for it now had an absolutely secure and unassailable base of operations, while its fighting quality had been improved rather than impaired by its seven days of battling."

General Lee's own official comment on the military problem involved and the difficulties encountered was: "Under ordinary circumstances the Federal army should have been destroyed. Its escape was due to the causes already stated. Prominent among these is the want of correct and timely information. This fact, attributable chiefly to the character of the country, enabled General McClellan skilfully to conceal his retreat and to add much to the obstructions with which nature had beset the way of our pursuing columns; but regret that more was not accomplished gives way to gratitude to the Sovereign Ruler of the Universe for the results achieved."

Whatever the outcome of the Seven Days' Battle another year was to demonstrate beyond question that the wounding of General Johnston at Fair Oaks had left the Confederate army with an even abler commander. On such a field as Chancellorsville was to be shown the brilliancy of Lee as leader, and his skilful maneuvers leading to the invasion of the North. And the succeeding volume will tell, on the other hand, how strong and compact a fighting force had been forged from the raw militia and volunteers of the North.

OFFICERS OF THE THIRD PENNSYLVANIA CAVALRY

AFTER THE SEVEN DAYS

Within a week of the occupation of Harrison's Landing, McClellan's position had become so strong that the Federal commander no longer anticipated an attack by the Confederate forces. General Lee saw that his opponent was flanked on each side by a creek and that approach to his front was commanded by the guns in the entrenchments and those of the Federal navy in the river. Lee therefore deemed it inexpedient to attack, especially as his troops were in poor condition owing to the incessant marching and fighting of the Seven Days. Rest was what both armies needed most, and on July 8th the Confederate forces returned to the vicinity of Richmond. McClellan scoured the country before he was satisfied of the Confederate withdrawal. The Third and Fourth Pennsylvania cavalry made a reconnaisance to Charles City Court House and beyond, and General Averell reported on July 11th that there were no Southern troops south of the lower Chickahominy. His scouting expeditions extended in the direction of Richmond and up the Chickahominy.

CHARLES CITY COURT HOUSE, VIRGINIA, JULY, 1862

GEN. W. H. C. WHITING

WHERE JACKSON'S MEN SCORED

From this old ruin, Gaines' Mill, the momentous battle of June 27, 1862, took its name, and on the ridge known as Turkey Hill, a mile to the southeast, the men of the First Maryland Confederate regiment won glory for themselves and their cause. "Stonewall" Jackson's corps at the end of a rapid march had arrived in the middle of the afternoon. After a brief rest, it was hurled against the Federal center on Turkey Hill. A battery defending the position poured a rapid fire upon the ranks of the attackers. The Confederates wavered, broke, and "regiment after regiment rushed back in utter disorder." General Winder was then ordered to send his brigade forward and he found, as he

COL. BRADLEY T. JOHNSON

headed by Colonel Bradley T. Johnson. The new line swept forward. The Federal battery on Turkey Hill, which Johnson was ordered to take, limbered up and fled. The Union troops were finally driven from their lost position. Meanwhile on Jackson's extreme right General Whiting's division was making what proved to be the fiercest charge of the Seven Days' Battles. The Southern troops came on with tremendous impetus, scattering some of their own regiments that were retreating in disorder. The Texan brigades of Hood and Law bore the brunt of the desperate and vain effort of the Federals to drive Whiting back. Finally General Hood and the Fourth Texas broke the line in the

THE COW BELL

THE STEADY MEN AT GAINES' MILL

Officers of a stalwart Irish regiment which gloriously distinguished itself at Gaines' Mill, the third battle in its career. We see them here at Camp Cass on Arlington Heights, where they had been waiting all winter near Washington for a sight of active service. This regiment was organized as the Ninth Massachusetts Infantry in April, 1861. It was not till almost a year later that, joining McClellan's forces on the Peninsula, it jumped immediately into the thick of things at Hanover Court House and Mechanicsville. Battles came fast and furious during the Seven Days' struggle, and, with Morell's division of the Fifth Corps, this regiment with marvelous steadiness sustained the fierce assault of "Stonewall" Jackson's troops at Turkey Hill. Its total loss that day was 231, including six line officers killed. Four days later at Malvern Hill its Colonel, Thomas Cass, fell mortally wounded. The regiment was commanded thenceforth by Colonel Patrick R. Guiney, and throughout the war gave abundant evidence of the valor of the Irish soldier.

BUILDING WINTER QUARTERS

VI

ENGAGEMENTS OF THE CIVIL WAR

ENGAGEMENTS OF THE CIVIL WAR

WITH LOSSES ON BOTH SIDES

DECEMBER, 1860—AUGUST, 1862

CHRONOLOGICAL summary and record of historical events, and of important engagements between the Union and the Confederate armies, in the Civil War in the United States, showing troops participating, losses and casualties, collated and compiled by George L. Kilmer from the official records of the Union and Confederate armies filed in the United States War Department. Minor engagements are omitted; also some concerning which statistics, especially Confederate, are not available.

PRELIMINARY EVENTS FROM THE SECESSION OF SOUTH CAROLINA TO THE BOMBARDMENT OF FORT SUMTER.

DECEMBER, 1860.

20.—Ordinance of Secession adopted by South Carolina.

JANUARY, 1861.

9.—U. S. Steamer *Star of the West* fired upon in Charleston harbor by South Carolina troops.
Mississippi seceded.
10.—Florida seceded.
11.—Alabama seceded.
19.—Georgia seceded.
26.—Louisiana seceded.

FEBRUARY, 1861.

1.—Texas seceded.
4.—" Confederate States of America " provisionally organized at Montgomery, Ala.
9.—Jefferson Davis elected provisional President of the Confederate States of America.
18.—Jefferson Davis inaugurated President of the Confederate States at Montgomery, Ala.

MARCH, 1861.

4.—Abraham Lincoln inaugurated President of the United States at Washington.

APRIL, 1861.

12 and 13.—Bombardment of Fort Sumter, S. C. *Union* 1st U. S. Art. *Confed.* S. C. Art. No casualties.
14.—Evacuation of Fort Sumter, S. C., by U. S. Losses: *Union* 1 killed, 5 wounded by premature explosion of cannon in firing a salute to the United States flag.
17.—Virginia adopted the ordinance of secession, subject to popular vote.
19.—Riots in Baltimore, Md. *Union* 6th Mass., 27th Pa. *Baltimoreans*, Citizens of Baltimore. Losses: *Union* 4 killed, 36 wounded. Citizens, 12 killed.
23.—Co. A 8th U. S. Infantry captured at San Antonio, Tex., by a company of organized citizen volunteers.

MAY, 1861.

6.—Arkansas seceded.
10.—Camp Jackson, Mo., occupied by Mo. militia, seized by *Union* 1st, 3d, and 4th Mo. Reserve Corps, 3d Mo. Vols. 639 militiamen taken prisoners.
11.—St. Louis, Mo. Collision of *Union* 5th Mo., U. S. Reserves, with citizens of St. Louis. Losses: *Union* 4 killed. *Citizens* 27 killed.
20.—North Carolina seceded.
24.—Col. E. Elmer Ellsworth, 11th N. Y. Vols., killed by a civilian while removing a Southern flag from the roof of the Marshall House, Alexandria, Va.

THE
THREATENED
FORT

ort Pickens, guard-
g the entrance to
ensacola Bay, 1861.
ever was a perilous
osition more gallant-
held than was Fort
ckens by Lieutenant
J. Slemmer and his
tle garrison from
nuary to May, 1861.
large force of Con-
derates were con-
antly menacing the
rt. Slemmer discov-
ed a plot to betray
e fort into the hands
a thousand of them

on the night of April
11th. Attempts to
seize the fort by Con-
federates gathered in
force for the purpose
were held off only by
the timely arrival of
gunboats with reën-
forcements from the
North. All the efforts
to take Fort Pickens
failed and it remained
in the hands of the
Federals throughout
the war. In the lower
picture we see one of
the powerful Confed-
erate batteries at Fort
McRee, which fired on
Pickens from across
the channel.

Engagements of the Civil War

JUNE, 1861.

1.—Fairfax C. H., Va. *Union,* Co. B 2d U. S. Cav. *Confed.,* Va. Vols. Losses: *Union* 1 killed, 4 wounded. *Confed.* 1 killed, 14 wounded.

3.—Philippi, W. Va. *Union,* 1st W. Va., 14th and 16th Ohio, 7th and 9th Ind. *Confed.,* Va. Vols. Losses: Union 2 wounded. *Confed.* 15 killed, wounded (*).

10.—Big Bethel, Va. *Union,* 1st, 2d, 3d, 5th, and 7th N. Y., 4th Mass. Detachment of 2d U. S. Artil. *Confed.,* 1st N. C., Randolph's Battery, Va. Infantry and Cavalry. Losses: *Union* 16 killed, 34 wounded. *Confed.* 1 killed, 7 wounded.

13.—Romney, W. Va. *Union,* 11th Ind. *Confed.,* Va. Vols. Losses: *Union* 1 wounded. *Confed.* 2 killed, 1 wounded.

17.—Vienna, Va. *Union,* 1st Ohio. *Confed.,* 1st S. C. Losses: *Union* 5 killed, 6 wounded. *Confed.* 6 killed.

—Booneville, Mo. *Union,* 2d Mo. (three months') Volunteers, Detachments 1st, Totten's Battery Mo. Light Artil. *Confed.,* Mo. Militia. Losses: Union 3 killed, 8 wounded. *Confed.* (*).

—Edwards Ferry, Md. *Union,* 1st Pa. *Confed.,* Va. Vols. Losses: *Union* 1 killed, 4 wounded. *Confed.* 15 killed.

26.—Patterson Creek or Kelley's Island, Va. *Union,* 11th Ind. *Confed.,* Va. Vols. Losses: *Union* 1 killed, 1 wounded. *Confed.* 7 killed, 2 wounded.

27.—Mathias Point, Va. *Union,* Gunboats *Pawnee* and *Freeborn. Confed.,* Va. Vols. Losses: *Union* 1 killed, 4 wounded.

JULY, 1861.

2.—Falling Waters, Md., also called Haynesville or Martinsburg, Md. *Union,* 1st Wis., 11th Pa. *Confed.,* Va. Vols. Losses: *Union* 8 killed, 15 wounded. *Confed.* 31 killed, 50 wounded.

5.—Carthage or Dry Forks, Mo. *Union,* 3d and 5th Mo., one battery of Mo. Artil. *Confed.,* Mo. State Guard. Losses: *Union* 13 killed, 31 wounded. *Confed.* 30 killed, 125 wounded, 45 prisoners.

—Newport News, Va. *Union,* 1 Co. 9th N. Y. *Confed.,* Stanard's Va. Battery, La. Battalion, Crescent Rifles, Collins'

Cav. Troop. Losses: *Union* 6 wounded. *Confed.* 2 killed, 1 wounded.

6.—Middle Creek Fork or Buckhannon, W. Va. *Union,* One Co. 3d Ohio. *Confed.,* 25th Va. Losses: *Union* 1 killed, 6 wounded. *Confed.* 7 killed.

7.—Great Falls, Md. Losses: *Union* 2 killed. *Confed.* 12 killed.

10.—Laurel Hill or Bealington, W. Va. *Union,* 14th Ohio, 9th Ind. *Confed.,* 20th Va. Losses: *Union* 2 killed, 6 wounded.

10.—Monroe Station, Mo. Losses: *Union* 3 killed. *Confed.* 4 killed, 20 wounded, 75 prisoners.

11.—Rich Mountain, W. Va. *Union,* 8th, 10th, and 13th Ind., 19th Ohio. *Confed.,* Gen. Jno. C. Pegram's command. Losses: *Union* 11 killed, 35 wounded. *Confed.* 60 killed, 140 wounded, 100 prisoners.

13.—Carrick's Ford, W. Va. *Union,* Gen. Geo. B. McClellan's command. *Confed.,* Gen. R. E. Lee's command. Losses: *Union* 13 killed, 40 wounded. *Confed.* 20 killed, 10 wounded, 50 prisoners. *Confed.* Gen. R. S. Garnett killed.

16.—Millsville or Wentzville, Mo. Losses: *Union* 7 killed, 1 wounded. *Confed.* 7 killed.

17.—Fulton, Mo. Losses: *Union* 1 killed, 15 wounded.

—Scarey Creek, W. Va. Losses: *Union* 9 killed, 38 wounded.

—Martinsburg, Mo. Losses: *Union* 1 killed, 1 wounded.

18.—Blackburn's Ford, Va. *Union,* 1st Mass., 2d and 3d Mich., 12th N. Y., Detachment of 2d U. S. Cav., Battery E 3d U. S. Artil. *Confed.,* 5th, 11th N. C., 2d, 3d, 7th S. C., 1st, 7th, 11th, 17th, 24th Va., 7th La., 13th Miss. Losses: *Union* 19 killed, 38 wounded. *Confed.* 15 killed, 53 wounded.

21.—Bull Run or Manassas, Va. *Union,* 2d Me., 2d N. H., 2d Vt., 1st, 4th, and 5th Mass., 1st and 2d R. I., 1st, 2d, and 3d Conn., 8th, 11th, 12th, 13th, 16th, 18th, 27th, 29th, 31st, 32d, 35th, 38th, and 39th N. Y., 2d, 8th, 14th, 69th, 71st, and 79th N. Y. Militia, 27th Pa., 1st, 2d, and 3d Mich., 1st and 2d Minn., 2d Wis., 1st and 2d Ohio, Detachments of 2d, 3d, and 8th U. S. Regulars, Battalion of Marines, Batteries D, E, G, and M, 2d

* No record found.

[348]

MAJOR ROBERT ANDERSON AND FAMILY

This Federal major of artillery was summoned on April 11, 1861, to surrender Fort Sumter and the property of the government whose uniform he wore. At half-past four the following morning the boom of the first gun from Fort Johnson in Charleston Harbor notified the breathless, waiting world that war was on. The flag had been fired on, and hundreds of thousands of lives were to be sacrificed ere the echoes of the great guns died away at the end of four years into the sobs of a nation whose best and bravest, North and South, had strewn the many battlefields. No wonder that the attention of the civilized world was focussed on the man who provoked the first blow in the greatest conflict the world has ever known. He was the man who handled the situation at the breaking point. To him the North looked to preserve the Federal property in Charleston Harbor, and the honor of the National flag. The action of the South depended upon his decision. He played the part of a true soldier, and two days after the first shot was fired he led his little garrison of the First United States Artillery out of Sumter with the honors of war.

Engagements of the Civil War

U. S. Artil., Battery E, 3d Artil., Battery D, 5th Artil., 2d R. I. Battery, Detachments of 1st and 2d Dragoons. *Confed.,* 6th, 7th, 8th La., 7th, 8th Ga., 1st Ark., 2d, 3d Tenn., 2d, 3d, 4th, 5th, 7th, 8th S. C., Hampton's Legion, 5th, 6th, 11th N. C., 1st Md., 2d, 11th, 13th, 17th, 18th Miss., 4th, 5th, 6th Ala., 1st, 2d, 4th, 5th, 7th, 8th, 10th, 11th, 13th, 17th, 18th, 19th, 24th, 27th, 28th, 33d, 49th Va., 1st, 30th Va. Cavalry, Harrison's Battalion. Losses: *Union* 481 killed, 1,011 wounded, 1,210 missing and captured. *Confed.* 387 killed, 1,582 wounded, 13 missing. *Confed.* Brig.-Gens. Bee and Bartow killed.

22.—Forsyth, Mo. Losses: *Union* 3 wounded. *Confed.* 5 killed, 10 wounded.

24.—Blue Mills, Mo. Losses: *Union* 1 killed, 12 wounded.

26.—Lane's Prairie, near Rolla, Mo. Losses: *Union* 3 wounded. *Confed.* 1 killed, 3 wounded.

27.—Fort Fillmore and San Augustine Springs, N. Mex. 7th U. S. Inft. and 3d U. S. Mounted Rifles, in all 400 men, captured by Confederates commanded by Col. John R. Baylor.

AUGUST, 1861.

2.—Dug Springs, Mo. *Union,* Steele's Battalion, 2d U. S. Infantry, Stanley's Cav. Troop, Totten's Battery. *Confed.,* Rains' Mo. State Guard. Losses: *Union* 4 killed, 37 wounded. *Confed.* 40 killed, 41 wounded.

5.—Athens, Mo. *Union,* Home Guards, 21st Mo. Vol. *Confed.* (*). Losses: *Union* 3 killed, 8 wounded. *Confed.* 14 killed, 14 wounded.
—Point of Rocks, Md. *Union,* 28th N. Y. *Confed.* (*) Losses: *Confed.* 3 killed, 2 wounded.

7.—Hampton, Va. *Union,* 20th N. Y. Losses: *Confed.* 3 killed, 6 wounded.

8.—Lovettsville, Va. *Union,* 19th N. Y. Losses: *Confed.* 1 killed, 5 wounded.

10.—Wilson's Creek, Mo., also called Springfield and Oak Hill. *Union,* 6th and 10th Mo. Cav., 2d Kan. Mounted Vols., one Co. of 1st U. S. Cav., 1st Ia., 1st Kan., 1st, 2d, 3d, and 5th Mo., Detachments of 1st and 2d U. S. Regulars, Mo. Home Guards, 1st Mo. Light Artil., Battery

F 2d U. S. Artil. *Confed.,* 1st, 3d, 4th, 5th Mo. State Guard, Graves' Infantry, Bledsoe's Battery, Cawthorn's Brigade, Kelly's Infantry, Brown's Cavalry, Burbridge's Infantry, 1st Cavalry, Hughes', Thornton's, Wingo's, Foster's Infantry, Rives', Campbell's Cavalry, 3d, 4th, 5th Ark., 1st Cavalry, Woodruff's, Reid's Battery, 1st, 2d Mounted Riflemen, South Kansas-Texas Mounted Regiment, 3d La. Losses: *Union* 223 killed, 721 wounded, 291 missing. *Confed.* 265 killed, 800 wounded, 30 missing. *Union* Brig.-Gen. Nathaniel Lyon killed.
—Potosi, Mo. *Union,* Mo. Home Guards. Losses: *Union* 1 killed. *Confed.* 2 killed, 3 wounded.

17.—Brunswick, Mo. *Union,* 5th Mo. Reserves. Losses: *Union* 1 killed, 7 wounded.

19.—Charleston or Bird's Point, Mo. Losses: *Union* 1 killed, 6 wounded. *Confed.* 40 killed.

20.—Hawk's Nest, W. Va. Losses: *Union* 3 wounded. *Confed.* 1 killed, 3 wounded.

26.—Cross Lanes or Summerville, W. Va. Losses: *Union* 5 killed, 40 wounded, 200 captured.

27.—Ball's Cross Roads, Va. Losses: Union 1 killed, 2 wounded.

28 and 29.—Fort Hatteras, N. C. *Union,* 9th, 20th, and 89th N. Y. and Naval force. *Confed.* North Carolina troops under Col. W. F. Martin. Losses: *Union* 1 killed, 2 wounded. *Confed.* 5 killed, 51 wounded, 715 prisoners.

31.—Munson's Hill, Va. Losses: *Union* 2 killed, 2 wounded.

SEPTEMBER, 1861.

1.—Bennett's Mills, Mo. Losses: *Union* 1 killed, 8 wounded.

2.—Dallas, Mo. Losses: *Union* 2 killed.
—Dry Wood or Ft. Scott, Mo. Losses: *Union* 4 killed, 9 wounded.

10.—Carnifex Ferry, W. Va. *Union,* 9th, 10th, 12th, 13th, 28th, and 47th Ohio. *Confed.,* Gen. J. B. Floyd's command. Losses: *Union* 17 killed, 141 wounded. *Confed.* (*).

11.—Lewinsville, Va. *Union,* 19th Ind., 3d Vt., 79th N. Y., 1st U. S. Chasseurs, Griffin's Battery, detachment of Cavalry. *Confed.,* 13th Va., Rosser's Bat-

* No record found.

THE LAST LETTER

COLONEL EPHRAIM ELMER ELLSWORTH

ne of the First to Fall. The shooting of this young patriot profoundly shocked and stirred the Federals at the opening of the ar. Colonel Ellsworth had organized a Zouave regiment in Chicago, and in April, 1861, he organized another from the Fire De- rtment in New York City. Colonel Ellsworth, on May 24, 1861, led his Fire Zouaves to Alexandria, Virginia, seized the city, and with s own hands pulled down a Southern flag floating over the Marshall House. Descending the stairs with the flag in his hand, he ied, "Behold my trophy!" "Behold mine!" came the reply from the proprietor of the hotel, James T. Jackson, as he emptied shotgun into Ellsworth's breast. Jackson was immediately shot dead by Private Brownell.

MARSHALL HOUSE, ALEXANDRIA, VIRGINIA, 1861

tery, detachments of Cavalry. Losses: *Union* 6 killed, 8 wounded.

12 and 13.—Cheat Mountain, W. Va. *Union,* 13th, 14th, 15th, and 17th Ind., 3d, 6th, 24th, and 25th Ohio, 2d W. Va. *Confed.,* Va. Vols. commanded by Gen. W. W. Loring. Losses: *Union* 9 killed, 12 wounded, 60 missing. *Confed.* (*).

12 to 20.—Lexington, Mo. *Union,* 23d Ill., 8th, 25th, and 27th Mo., 13th and 14th Mo. Home Guards, Berry's and Van Horne's Mo. Cav., 1st Ill. Cav. *Confed.,* Parsons' and Rains' Divisions, Bledsoe's, Churchill's, Guibor's, Kelly's, Kneisley's and Clark's batteries. Losses: *Union* 42 killed, 108 wounded, 1,624 missing and captured. *Confed.* 25 killed, 75 wounded.

13.—Booneville, Mo. *Union,* Mo. Home Guards. *Confed.,* Gen. Price's Mo. State Guard. Losses: *Union* 1 killed, 4 wounded. *Confed.* 12 killed, 30 wounded.

14.—Confederate Privateer *Judah* destroyed near Pensacola, Fla., by the U. S. Flagship *Colorado.* Losses: *Union* 3 killed, 15 wounded.

15.—Pritchard's Mills, Md., or Darnestown, Md. *Union,* detachments 13th Mass., 28th Pa., 9th N. Y. Battery. *Confed.** Losses: *Union* 1 killed, 3 wounded. *Confed.* (estimate) 18 killed, 25 wounded.

17.—Morristown, Mo. *Union,* 5th, 6th, 9th Kan. Cav., 1st Kan. Battery. *Confed.** Losses: *Union* 2 killed, 6 wounded. *Confed.* 7 killed.
　—Blue Mills, Mo. *Union,* 3d Ia. *Confed.,* Mo. State Guard. Losses: *Union* 11 killed, 39 wounded. *Confed.* 12 killed, 63 wounded.

19.—Barboursville, Ky. *Union,* Ky. Home Guards. *Confed.,* Gen. F. K. Zollicoffer's brigade. Losses: *Union* 1 killed, 1 wounded. *Confed.* 2 killed, 3 wounded.

23.—Romney or Hanging Rock, W. Va. *Union,* 4th and 8th Ohio. *Confed.,* 77th and 114th Va., 1 battery Art. Losses: *Union* 3 killed, 50 wounded. *Confed.* 35 killed.

25.—Kanawha Gap, W. Va. *Union,* 1st Ky., 34th Ohio. *Confed.** Losses: *Union* 4 killed, 9 wounded. *Confed.* 20 killed, 50 wounded.

25 and 27.—Alamosa, near Ft. Craig, N. Mex. *Union,* Capt. Mink's Cavalry. *Confed.,* Capt. Coopwood's Tex. Scouts. Losses: *Union.* Confed.* 2 killed, 8 wounded.

OCTOBER, 1861.

3.—Greenbrier, W. Va. *Union,* 24th, 25th, and 32d Ohio, 7th, 9th, 13th, 14th, 15th, and 17th Ind., Battery G, 4th U. S. Artil., Battery A 1st Mich. Artil. *Confed.,* Va. Vols. of Gen. W. W. Loring's command. Losses: *Union* 8 killed, 32 wounded. *Confed.* 100 killed, 75 wounded.

9.—Santa Rosa, Fla. *Union,* 6th N. Y., Co. A 1st U. S. Artil., Co. H 2d U. S. Artil., Co.'s C and E 3d U. S. Inft. *Confed.,* 9th and 10th Miss., 1st Ala., 1st Fla. and 5th Ga. Losses: *Union* 14 killed, 29 wounded. *Confed.* 17 killed, 39 wounded, 30 captured.

13.—Wet Glaze, or Monday's Hollow, Mo. *Union,* 13th Ill., 1st Mo. Battalion, Fremont Battalion, Mo. Cav. *Confed.** Losses: *Confed.* 67 killed (estimate).

14.—Underwood's Farm (12 miles from Bird's Point), Mo. *Union,* 1st Ill. Cav. *Confed.,* 1st Miss. Cav. Losses: *Union* 2 killed, 5 wounded. *Confed.* 1 killed, 2 wounded.

15.—Big River Bridge, near Potosi, Mo. *Union,* 40 men of the 38th Ill. *Confed.,* 2d, 3d Miss. Cav. Losses: *Union* 1 killed, 6 wounded, 33 captured. *Confed.* 5 killed, 4 wounded.

16.—Bolivar Heights, Va. *Union,* detachments of 28th Pa., 3d Wis. and 6th Mo. Cavalry. *Confed.,* detachments commanded by Col. Turner Ashby. Losses: *Union* 4 killed, 7 wounded.

17 to 21.—Fredericktown and Ironton, Mo. *Union,* 21st, 33d, and 38th Ill., 8th Wis., 1st Ind. Cav., Co. A 1st Mo. Light Artil. *Confed.,* Mo. State Guard. Losses: *Union* 7 killed, 41 wounded. *Confed.* 200 killed, wounded, and missing (estimate).

21.—Ball's Bluff, also called Edwards Ferry, Harrison's Landing, Leesburg, Va. *Union,* 15th, 20th Mass., 40th N. Y., 71st Pa., Battery I, 1st U. S., B, R. I. Artil. *Confed.,* 13th, 17th, 18th Miss., 8th Va., 3 co.'s Va. Cavalry. Losses: *Union* 49 killed, 158 wounded, and 714 missing.

* No record found.

A WESTERN LEADER—MAJOR-GENERAL FRANK P. BLAIR, JR., AND STAFF

One of the most interesting characters in Missouri at the outbreak of the war was Frank P. Blair, Jr., of St. Louis, a Member of Congress. When Governor Jackson refused to obey President Lincoln's proclamation and call out troops, Mr. Blair immediately raised a regiment of three-months men (the First Missouri Infantry) which later became the First Missouri Light Artillery. The First Missouri, under Colonel Blair, assisted Captain Lyon, U. S. A., in the capture of Camp Jackson, May 10, 1861. When, through Blair's influence, Lyon was made brigadier-general and placed in command of the Federal forces in Missouri, Governor Jackson and General Sterling Price at once ordered the militia to prepare itself for service on the Southern side, knowing that Lyon and Blair would quickly attack them. The First Missouri regiment accompanied General Lyon when he went to Booneville and dispersed over a thousand volunteers who had gathered there to enlist under the Confederacy, June 17th. This affair at Booneville practically made it impossible for Missouri to secede from the Union. Colonel Blair was promoted to brigadier-general in August, 1862, and was made major-general the following November.

(This photograph was taken when General Blair was at the head of the Seventeenth Army Corps in 1864–65. The composition of his staff was announced November 9, 1864, from Smyrna Camp Ground, Georgia. In the picture the general is seated in the armchair; on his right is Assistant Inspector-General A. Hickenlooper; on his left Assistant Adjutant-General C. Cadle, Jr. Standing are three of his aides-de-camp: from right to left, Logan Tompkins, William Henley, and G. R. Steele.)

Confed., 33 killed, 115 wounded, and 1 missing. *Union* Acting Brig.-Gen. E. D. Baker killed.

23.—West Liberty, Ky. *Union,* 2d Ohio, Konkle's Battery, Laughlin's Cavalry. *Confed.*, Capt. May's command. Losses: *Union* 2 wounded. *Confed.* 10 killed, 5 wounded.

25.—Springfield, Mo. "Zagonyi's Charge." *Union,* Fremont's Body Guard and White's Prairie Scouts. *Confed.** Losses: *Union* 18 killed, 37 wounded. *Confed.* 106 killed (estimate).

26.—Romney or Mill Creek Mills, W. Va. *Union,* 4th and 8th Ohio, 7th W. Va., Md. Volunteers, 2d Regt. of Potomac Home Guards and Ringgold (Pa.) Cav. *Confed.*, Va. Vols. commanded by Gen. J. B. Floyd. Losses: *Union* 2 killed, 15 wounded. *Confed.* 20 killed, 15 wounded, 50 captured.

—Saratoga, Ky. *Union,* 9th Ill. *Confed.*, Capt. Wilcox's Cavalry. Losses: *Union* 4 wounded. *Confed.* 8 killed, 17 wounded.

NOVEMBER, 1861.

7.—Belmont, Mo. *Union,* 22d, 27th, 30th, and 31st Ill., 7th Ia., Battery B 1st Ill. Artil., 2 companies 15th Ill. Cav. *Confed.*, 13th Ark., 11th La., 2d, 12th, 13th, 15th, 21st, 22d, 154th (Senior) Tenn. Watson's, Stewart's La. Art., Smith's Miss. Battery, Hamilton's siege Battery. Losses: *Union* 90 killed, 173 wounded, 235 missing. *Confed.* 261 killed, 427 wounded, 278 missing.

—Galveston Harbor, Tex. U. S. Frigate *Santee* burned the *Royal Yacht.* Losses: *Union* 1 killed, 8 wounded. *Confed.* 3 wounded.

—Port Royal, S. C. Capture of Fort Beauregard and Fort Walker (Confederate). *Union,* Du Pont's fleet, 17 vessels, and 3 brigades of land forces under Gen. Thomas W. Sherman. *Confed.*, 3 vessels under Flag-officer Josiah Tattnall, and 1 brigade of land forces under Gen. Thomas F. Drayton. Losses: *Union* 8 killed, 23 wounded. *Confed.* 11 killed, 48 wounded, 7 missing.

8.—Seizure of Jas. M. Mason and John Slidell, *Confed.* Commissioners to Europe on board of British steamer *Trent,* by U. S. steamer *San Jacinto.*

9.—Piketown or Ivy Mountain, Ky. *Union,* 33d Ohio and Col. Metcalf's Ky. Vols. *Confed.*, Col. J. S. Williams' command. Losses: *Union* 6 killed, 24 wounded. *Confed.* 18 killed, 45 wounded, 200 captured.

10.—Guyandotte, W. Va. *Union,* 9th Va. Vols. *Confed.*, Jenkins' Cav. Losses: *Union* 7 killed, 20 wounded. *Confed.* 3 killed, 10 wounded.

12.—Occoquan River and Pohick Church, Va. *Union,* 2d, 3d, 5th Mich., 37th N. Y., 4th Me., 2 cos. 1st N. Y. Cav., Randolph's and Thompson's Batteries U. S. Art. *Confed.*, outposts of Gen. Beauregard's command. Losses: *Union* 3 killed, 1 wounded.

23.—Ft. Pickens, Pensacola, Fla. *Union,* Cos. C and E 3d U. S. Inft., Cos. G and I 6th N. Y., Batteries A, F, and L 1st U. S. Artil., and C, H, and K 2d U. S. Artil. *Confed.*, Gen. Braxton Bragg's command in Fort McRee and numerous shore batteries. Losses: *Union* 5 killed, 7 wounded. *Confed.* 5 killed, 93 wounded.

26.—Drainesville, Va. *Union,* 1st Pa. Cav. *Confed.*, Stuart's Va. Cav. Losses: *Union* 1 wounded. *Confed.* 2 killed, 4 captured.

DECEMBER, 1861.

3.—Salem, Mo. *Union,* 1st Battalion Mo. Cav. *Confed.*, Freeman's and Turner's Cav. Losses: *Union* 3 killed, 9 wounded. *Confed.* 16 killed, 20 wounded.

4.—Anandale, Va. *Union,* 45th N. Y. *Confed.*, Va. Cav. Losses: *Union* 1 killed, 14 missing. *Confed.* 3 killed, 2 missing.

13.—Camp Allegheny or Buffalo Mountain, W. Va. *Union* 9th and 13th Ind., 25th and 32 Ohio, 2d W. Va., *Confed.*, 12th Ga., 25th, 31st and 52d W. Va., Lee's and Miller's Art. Losses: *Union* 20 killed, 107 wounded. *Confed.* 20 killed, 98 wounded.

17.—Rowlett's Station, also called Mumfordsville or Woodsonville, Ky. *Union,* 32d Ind. *Confed.*, Col. Terry's Texas Rangers. Losses: *Union* 10 killed, 22 wounded. *Confed.* 33 killed, 50 wounded.

18.—Milford, also called Shawnee Mound, or Blackwater, Mo. *Union,* 8th Ia., 7th

* No record found.

FIRST FOOTHOLD ON THE SOUTHERN COAST.—THE FIFTIETH PENNSYLVANIA

Although the 12,600 troops under Brigadier-General Thomas W. Sherman took no part in the bombardment of the forts at Port Royal in November, 1861, their work was cut out for them when the abandoned works had to be occupied and rendered adequate for the defense of the Federal naval base here established upon the Southern coast. Particularly active in these operations was the brigade of General Stevens. We see him with his staff at his headquarters, an old Colonial mansion near Hilton Head. The Fiftieth Pennsylvania in Stevens Brigade won its first laurels in the campaigning and fighting which followed upon the conquest of Port Royal.

GENERAL ISAAC I. STEVENS AND STAFF

Engagements of the Civil War

Mo., 22d Ind., 1st Ia. Cav., Detach. 4th U. S. Cav., 1st Mo. Cav., 2 Batteries of 1st Mo. Lt. Artil. *Confed.*, Rains' Division. Losses: *Union* 2 killed, 8 wounded. *Confed.* 1,300 captured.

20.—Drainesville, Va. *Union*, 1st Rifles, 6th, 9th, 10th and 12th Infty., 1st Artil., 1st Cav. Pa. Reserves. *Confed.*, 1st Ky., 10th Ala., 6th S. C., 11th Va., Cutt's Art. Losses: *Union* 7 killed, 61 wounded. *Confed.* 43 killed, 143 wounded.

28.—Sacramento, Ky. *Union*, 3d Ky. Cav. *Confed.*, Forrest's Tenn. Cav. Losses: *Union* 8 killed, 8 captured. *Confed.* 2 killed, 3 wounded.

—Mt. Zion and Hallsville, Mo. *Union*, Birge's Sharpshooters, 3d Mo. Cav. *Confed.** Losses: *Union* 5 killed, 63 wounded. *Confed.* 25 killed, 150 wounded.

JANUARY, 1862.

4.—Bath, Va. *Union*, 39th Ill. *Confed.*, Col. Loring's command. Losses: *Union* 3 killed, 3 wounded, 8 captured. *Confed.* 4 wounded.

7.—Hanging Rock Pass, Va. *Union*, parts of the 4th, 5th, 7th, 8th Ohio, 14th Ind., detachments of cavalry, Baker's and Daum's batteries. *Confed.*, Col. Monroe's Va. Vols. Losses: *Confed.* 15 killed.

8.—Charleston, Mo. *Union*, 10th Ia., 20th Ill., detachment Tenn. Cav. *Confed.** Losses: *Union* 8 killed, 16 wounded.

10.—Middle Creek, near Paintsville, Ky. *Union*, 14th, 22d Ky., 2d Va. Cav., 1st Ky. Cav., Squadron Ohio Cav. *Confed.*, 5th Ky., 29th, 54th Va., Ky. Mounted Rifles, 2 cos. dismounted Cav. Losses: *Union* 2 killed, 25 wounded. *Confed.* 11 killed, 15 wounded.

19 and 20.—Mill Springs, Ky., also called Logan's Cross Roads, Fishing Creek, Somerset and Beech Grove. *Union*, 9th Ohio, 2d Minn., 4th Ky., 10th Ind., 1st Ky. Cav. *Confed.*, 17th, 19th, 20th, 25th, 28th, 29th Tenn., 16th Ala., 15th Miss., Saunder's Cavalry, Bledsoe's Battery. Losses: *Union* 38 killed, 194 wounded. *Confed.* 190 killed, 160 wounded. *Confed.* Gen. F. K. Zollicoffer killed.

FEBRUARY, 1862.

6.—Fort Henry, Tenn. *Union*, Gunboats *Essex, Carondelet, St. Louis, Cincinnati, Conestoga, Tyler,* and *Lexington. Confed.*, 10th, 48th, 51st Tenn., 15th Ark., 4th Miss., 27th Ala., B. 1st Tenn. Art. Culbertson's and Crain's Art., Milner's and Milton's Cavalry. Losses: *Union* 40 wounded. *Confed.* 5 killed, 11 wounded.

8.—Roanoke Island, N. C. *Union*, 21st, 23d, 24th, 25th and 27th Mass., 10th Conn., 9th, 51st, and 53d N. Y., 9th N. J., 51st Pa., 4th and 5th R. I., U. S. Gunboats *Southfield, Delaware, Stars and Stripes, Louisiana, Hetzel, Commodore Perry, Underwriter, Valley City, Commodore Barney, Hunchback, Ceres, Putnam, Morse, Lockwood, Seymour, Granite, Brinker, Whitehead, Shawseen, Pickett, Pioneer, Hussar, Vidette, Chasseur. Confed.*, 2d, 7th, 8th, 17th, 19th, 26th, 27th, 28th, 31st, 33d, 35th, 37th, 46th, 59th N. C., Brem's, Latham's, Whitehurst's N. C. Art., Gunboats *Seabird, Curlew, Ellis, Beaufort, Raleigh, Fanny, Forrest.* Losses: *Union* 35 killed, 200 wounded. *Confed.* 16 killed, 39 wounded, 2,527 taken prisoners.

10.—Elizabeth City, or Cobb's Point, N. C. *Union*, Gunboats *Delaware, Underwriter, Louisiana, Seymour, Hetzel, Shawseen, Valley City, Putnam, Commodore Perry, Ceres, Morse, Whitehead,* and *Brinker. Confed.*, "Mosquito fleet" commanded by Commodore W. F. Lynch, and comprising the vessels engaged at Roanoke Island on the 8th, except the *Curlew.* Losses: *Union* 3 killed.

13.—Bloomery Gap, Va. *Union*, Gen. Lander's Brigade. *Confed.*, 31st, 67th, 89th Va. Losses: *Union* 11 killed, 5 wounded. *Confed.* 13 killed, 65 missing.

14–16.—Fort Donelson, or Dover, Tenn. *Union*, Gunboats *Carondelet, Pittsburgh, Louisville, St. Louis, Tyler,* and *Conestoga,* 17th and 25th Ky., 11th, 25th, 31st, and 44th Ind., 2d, 7th, 12th and 14th Iowa, 1st Neb., 58th and 76th Ohio, 8th and 13th Mo., 8th Wis., 8th, 9th, 11th, 12th, 17th, 18th, 20th, 28th, 29th, 30th, 31st, 41st, 45th, 46th, 48th, 49th, 57th, and 58th Ill., Batteries B and D 1st Ill.

* No record found.

[356]

THE 10-INCH COLUMBIAD AT FORT WALKER, HILTON HEAD, SOUTH CAROLINA

The Capture of the Confederate forts at Port Royal, South Carolina. On the 29th of October, 1861, there sailed from Hampton Roads the most formidable squadron ever fitted out in American waters—men-of-war commanded by Flag-Officer Samuel F. Du-Pont in the *Wabash*, and army transports with a force of twelve thousand men under General Thomas W. Sherman, bound for Port Royal Harbor, twenty miles north of the mouth of the Savannah River. On November 1st, off Hatteras, a severe gale was encountered and for a time the fleet was much scattered, but by the 4th it was again united at the bar outside Port Royal Harbor over which the *Wabash* led the way. The harbor fortifications which had been erected by the Confederates were no small affairs. Fort Walker on Hilton Head Island was two miles and a half across the entrance from Fort Beauregard. Each had at least twenty guns of different caliber. On November 7th the Federal fleet attacked in close action. The men on shore were scarcely able to reply to the terrific broadsides of the main body of the big fleet as it passed back and forth through the harbor entrance, while other vessels outside enfiladed the forts. At the third round of the ships the Confederates could be seen leaving Fort Walker and before half-past two in the afternoon Commander Rodgers had planted the Federal flag on the ramparts. Before sunset Fort Beauregard was likewise deserted. This victory placed in possession of the North one of the finest harbors of the Southern coast. In the lower picture we see the ferry over the Coosaw River, near Port Royal, showing on the opposite shore the site of the Confederate batteries seized and demolished by General I. I. Stevens, January 1, 1862.

FERRY ACROSS THE COOSAW, PORT ROYAL

Engagements of the Civil War

Art., D and E 2d Ill. Artil., four cos. Ill. Cav., Birge's Sharpshooters and six gunboats. *Confed.*, 2d, 8th Ky., 1st, 3d, 4th, 20th, 26th Miss., 27th Ala., 3d, 10th, 18th, 26th, 30th, 42d, 48th, 49th, 50th, 53d Tenn., 7th Tex., 15th Ark., 36th, 50th, 51st, 56th Va., Forrest's Cavalry, 9th Tenn. Battalion Colm's Battalion. Losses: *Union* 500 killed, 2,108 wounded, 224 missing. *Confed.* 231 killed, 1,534 wounded, 13,829 prisoners (estimated). *Union* Maj.-Gen. John A. Logan wounded.

17.—Sugar Creek, or Pea Ridge, Ark. *Union,* 1st, 6th Mo., 3d Ill. Cav. *Confed.*, Bowen's Mo. Battalion. Losses: *Union* 13 killed, 15 wounded.

21.—Ft. Craig, or Valverde, N. Mex. *Union,* 1st N. Mex. Cav., 2d Col. Cav., Detachments of 1st, 2d, and 5th N. Mex., and of 5th, 7th, and 10th U. S. Inft., Hill's and McRae's Batteries. *Confed.*, 2d, 4th, 5th, 7th Tex. Cavalry, Teel's Art. Losses: *Union* 62 killed, 140 wounded. *Confed.* 36 killed, 150 wounded.

26.—Keetsville, Mo. *Union,* 6th Mo. Cav. *Confed.*, Ross' Texas Rangers. Losses: *Union* 2 killed, 1 wounded. *Confed.* 3 killed, 1 missing.

MARCH, 1862.

1.—Pittsburg Landing, Tenn. *Union,* 32d Ill. and U. S. Gunboats *Lexington* and *Tyler.* *Confed.*, Gen. Daniel Ruggles' command. Losses: *Union* 5 killed, 5 wounded. *Confed.* 20 killed, 200 wounded.

6, 7, and 8.—Pea Ridge, Ark., including engagements at Bentonville, Leetown, and Elkhorn Tavern. *Union,* 25th, 35th, 36th, 37th, 44th, and 59th Ill., 2d, 3d, 12th, 15th, 17th, 24th, and Phelps' Mo., 8th, 18th, and 22d Ind., 4th and 9th Iowa, 3d Iowa Cav., 3d and 15th Ill. Cav., 1st, 4th, 5th, and 6th Mo. Cav., Batteries B and F 2d Mo. Light Artil., 2d Ohio Battery, 1st Ind. Battery, Battery A 2d Ill. Artil. *Confed.*, 1st, 2d Mo. State Guard, Greene's Brigade, 1st, 2d, 3d, 4th, 5th, 6th Mo., 4th, 14th, 16th, 17th, 19th, 21st, 22d Ark., 1st, 2d Ark. Mounted Rifles, 3d La., 3 Indian regiments, Wade's, Guibor's, Bledsoe's, Teel's, Clark's, MacDonald's, Hart's, Provence's, Gaines' and Good's batteries, 1st Mo. Cavalry, Shel-

by's Cavalry, 3d, 4th, 6th, 11th Tex. Cavalry. Losses: *Union* 203 killed, 972 wounded, 174 missing. *Confed.* 800 to 1,000 killed and wounded, 200 to 300 missing and captured (estimated). *Union* Brig.-Gen. Asboth and Actg. Brig.-Gen. Carr wounded. *Confed.* Brig.-Gen. B. McCulloch and Actg. Brig.-Gen. James McIntosh killed.

8.—Near Nashville, Tenn. *Union,* 4th Ohio Cav. *Confed.*, Morgan's Ky. Cav. Losses: *Union* 1 killed, 2 wounded. *Confed.* 4 killed, 2 wounded.

—Hampton Roads, Va. *Union,* 20th Ind., 7th and 11th N. Y., Gunboats *Minnesota, Congress, Zouave,* and *Cumberland. Confed.,* Ram *Virginia (Merrimac).* Losses: *Union* 261 killed, 108 wounded. *Confed.* 7 killed, 17 wounded. *Confed.* Commodore Buchanan, wounded.

9.—Hampton Roads, Va. First battle between iron-clad warships. *Union, The Monitor. Confed.,* Ram *Virginia.* Losses: *Union* Capt. J. L. Worden, wounded.

14.—Jacksborough, Big Creek Gap, Tenn. *Union,* 2d E. Tenn. *Confed.*, 1st E. Tenn. Cav. Losses: *Union* 2 wounded. *Confed.* 5 killed, 15 wounded, 15 missing.

11.—Paris, Tenn. *Union,* 1 Battalion 5th Ia. Cav., Bulliss' Mo. Art. *Confed.*, King's Mounted Rifles. Losses: *Union* 5 killed, 3 wounded. *Confed.* 10 wounded.

13–14.—New Madrid, Mo. Bombardment and capture by Gen. Jno. Pope's command. *Union,* 10th and 16th Ill., 27th, 39th, 43d, and 63d Ohio, 3d Mich. Cav., 1st U. S. Inft., Bissell's Mo. Engineers. *Confed.*, 1st Ala., 40th C. S., 46th, 55th Tenn., Heavy Art. Corps. Losses: *Union* 51 wounded. *Confed.* 100 wounded.

14.—Newberne, N. C. *Union,* 51st N. Y., 8th, 10th, and 11th Conn., 21st, 23d, 24th, 25th, and 27th Mass., 9th N. J., 51st Pa., 4th and 5th R. I. *Confed.*, 7th, 26th, 33d, 35th N. C. Losses: *Union* 91 killed, 466 wounded. *Confed.* 64 killed, 106 wounded, 413 captured.

16.—Pound Gap, Tenn. *Union,* Detachs. of 22d Ky., 40th and 42d Ohio Vols., and 1st Ohio Cav. *Confed.*, 21st Va. Losses: *Confed.* 7 killed.

18.—Salem, or Spring River, Ark. *Union,* Detachments 6th Mo., 3d Ia. Cav.

THE GARDEN OF A SOUTHERN MANSION

Here we see the garden of the manor house of John E. Seabrook on Edisto Island, off the Carolina coast. It is now in possession of the Federal troops, but the fine old house was unharmed, and the garden, although not in luxuriant bloom, gives an idea of its own beauty. In the distance are seen the slave quarters, and some of the old plantation servants have mingled with the troops when the picture was being taken. Observe the little colored boy saluting on the pedestal against which leans a Federal officer.

THE SOUTHERN NAVAL BASE OF THE BLOCKADING SQUADRON OF THE NORTH

The Transformation Wrought at Hilton Head by the Naval Engineers. Hilton Head became the base of supplies and the most important part of the blockade, for it was within a few hours' steaming of the ports of entry that the South depended upon in gaining supplies from the outer world, Savannah, Charleston, and Wilmington. After the Federal occupation it was turned into a busy place. Colliers were constantly landing and supplies of all kinds being sent out from here to the blockading vessels kept at sea.

*Confed.** Losses: *Union* 4 killed, 18 wounded. *Confed.* 100 killed, wounded, and missing (estimated).

22.—Independence or Little Santa Fé, Mo. *Union,* 2d Kan. Cav. *Confed.,* Quantrell's Irregulars. Losses: *Union* 1 killed, 2 wounded. *Confed.* 7 killed.

23.—Winchester or Kearnstown, Va. *Union,* 1st W. Va., 84th and 110th Pa., 5th, 7th, 8th, 29th, 62d, and 67th Ohio, 7th, 13th, and 14th Ind., 39th Ill., 1st Ohio Cav., 1st Mich. Cav., 1st W. Va. Artil., 1st Ohio Artil., Co. E 4th U. S. Artil. *Confed.,* 2d, 4th, 5th, 21st, 23d, 27th, 33d, 37th, 42d Va. 1st Va. (Irish) Battalion, Pleasant's, Chew's, Lanier's Va. batteries, 7th Va. Cavalry. Losses: *Union* 103 killed, 440 wounded, 24 missing. *Confed.* 80 killed 342 wounded, 269 prisoners.

26.—Humansville, Mo. *Union,* Battalion Mo. Cav. *Confed.,* Col. Frazier's command. Losses: *Union* 12 wounded. *Confed.* 15 killed, 20 wounded.

26, 27, and 28.—Apache Cañon, or Glorietta, near Santa Fé, N. Mex. *Union,* 1st and 2d Colo. Cav. *Confed.,* 2d, 4th, 5th, and 7th Tex. Cavalry, Teel's Art. Losses: *Union* 32 killed, 75 wounded, 35 missing. *Confed.* 36 killed, 60 wounded, 93 missing.

28.—Warrensburg, Mo. *Union,* 1st Ia. Cav. *Confed.,* Col. Parker's command. Losses: *Union* 1 killed, 2 wounded. *Confed.* 15 killed and wounded, 15 missing.

APRIL, 1862.

5.—Warwick and Yorktown Roads, Va. *Union,* Advance of 4th Corps, Army of Potomac, towards Yorktown. *Confed.* Gen. J. B. Magruder's command. Losses: *Union* 3 killed, 12 wounded. *Confed.* 1 killed, 10 wounded.

5-May 4.—Siege of Yorktown, Va. *Union,* Army of Potomac, Gen. Geo. B. McClellan. *Confed.,* Army commanded by Gen. Joseph E. Johnston.

6 and 7.—Shiloh or Pittsburg Landing, Tenn. *Union,* Army of Western Tennessee, commanded by Maj.-Gen. U. S. Grant, as follows: 1st Div., Maj.-Gen. J. A. McClernand; 2d Div., Maj.-Gen. C. F. Smith; 3d Div., Brig.-Gen. Lew Wallace; 4th Div., Brig.-Gen. S. A. Hurlburt; 5th Div., Brig.-Gen. W. T. Sherman; 6th Div., Brig.-Gen. B. M. Prentiss. Army of the Ohio commanded by Maj.-Gen. D. C. Buell, as follows: 2d Div., Brig.-Gen. A. McD. Cook; 4th Div., Brig.-Gen. W. Nelson; 5th Div., Brig.-Gen. T. L. Crittenden, 21st Brigade of the 6th Div., Gunboats *Tyler* and *Lexington.* *Confed.,* Army of the Mississippi, commanded by Gen. Albert Sidney Johnston, as follows: 1st Corps, Maj.-Gen. Leonidas Polk; 2d Corps, Maj.-Gen. Braxton Bragg; 3d Corps, Maj.-Gen. Wm. J. Hardee; Reserve Corps, Brig.-Gen. John C. Breckinridge; Forrest's, Wharton's and Clanton's Cavalry. Losses: *Union* 1,754 killed, 8,408 wounded, 2,885 captured. *Confed.* 1,728 killed, 8,012 wounded, 959 captured. *Union* Brig.-Gen. W. T. Sherman and W. H. L. Wallace wounded and B. M. Prentiss captured. *Confed.* Gen. A. S. Johnston and Brig.-Gen. A. H. Gladden killed; Maj.-Gen. W. S. Cheatham and Brig.-Gens. C. Clark, B. R. Johnson, and J. S. Bowen wounded.

7 and 8.—Island No. 10, Tenn., captured. *Union,* Maj.-Gen. Pope's command and the Navy, under Flag-officer Foote. *Confed.,* Brigade of Infantry and Battalion Art., commanded by Gen. J. P. McCown, 7 gunboats, under Flag-officer Hollins. Losses: *Union* 17 killed, 34 wounded, 3 missing. *Confed.* 30 killed and wounded. Captured, 2,000 to 5,000 (*Union* and *Confed.* estimates).

10 and 11.—Ft. Pulaski, Ga., Siege and capture. *Union,* 6th and 7th Conn., 3d R. I., 46th and 48th N. Y., 8th Maine, 15th U. S. Inft., Crew of U. S. S. *Wabash.* *Confed.,* 5 companies heavy art., commanded by Col. C. H. Olmstead. Losses: *Union* 1 killed. *Confed.* 4 wounded, 360 prisoners.

14.—Montevallo, Mo. *Union,* 2 cos. 1st Iowa Cav. *Confed.** Losses: *Union* 2 killed, 4 wounded. *Confed.* 22 captured.

16.—Whitemarsh or Wilmington Island, Ga. *Union,* 8th Mich., Battery of R. I. Light Artil. *Confed.,* 13th Ga. Losses: *Union* 10 killed, 35 wounded. *Confed.* 4 killed, 15 wounded.

—Lee's Mills, Va. *Union,* 3d, 4th, and 6th Vt., 3d N. Y. Battery and Battery of 5th U. S. Artil. *Confed.,* Gen. J. B. Ma-

* No record found.

THE CLOSING OF SAVANNAH, APRIL 12, 1862

This terrific punishment was inflicted upon the nearest angle of the fort by the thirty-six heavy rifled cannon and the mortars which the Federals had planted on Big Tybee Island, and by the gunboats which had found a channel enabling them to get in the rear of the fort. We get a more distant view of the angle in the lower picture. Fort Pulaski had been effectually blockaded since February, 1862, as a part of the Federal plan to establish supreme authority along the Atlantic coast from Wassaw Sound, below Savannah, north to Charleston. On April 10, 1862, General Hunter demanded the surrender of Fort Pulaski and when it was refused opened the bombardment. For two days the gallant garrison held out and then finding the fort untenable, surrendered. This enabled the Federal Government effectually to close Savannah against contraband traffic.

FORT PULASKI AT THE ENTRANCE TO SAVANNAH RIVER

gruder's division, Yorktown garrison. Losses: *Union* 35 killed, 129 wounded. *Confed.* 20 killed, 75 wounded, 50 captured.

17 to 19.—Falmouth and Fredericksburg, Va. *Union,* Gen. McDowell's Army. *Confed.,* Gen. Field's Brigade. Losses: *Union* 7 killed, 16 wounded. *Confed.* 3 killed, 8 captured.

18 to 28.—Forts Jackson and St. Philip, and the capture of New Orleans, La. *Union,* Commodore Farragut's fleet of gunboats, and mortar boats under Commander D. D. Porter. *Confed.,* Gen. Mansfield Lovell's army, fleet of gunboats. Losses: *Union* 36 killed, 193 wounded. *Confed.* 185 killed, 197 wounded, 400 captured.

19.—Camden, N. C., also called South Mills. *Union,* 9th and 89th N. Y., 21st Mass., 51st Pa., 6th N. H. *Confed.,* 3d Ga., McComas' Art., 1 co. Cavalry. Losses: *Union* 12 killed, 98 wounded. *Confed.* 6 killed, 19 wounded.

25.—Fort Macon, N. C. *Union,* U. S. Gunboats *Daylight, State of Georgia, Chippewa,* the Bark *Gemsbok,* and Gen. Parke's division. *Confed.,* Garrison commanded by Col. M. J. White. Losses: *Union* 1 killed, 11 wounded. *Confed.* 7 killed, 18 wounded, 450 captured.

26.—Neosho, Mo. *Union,* 1st Mo. Cav. *Confed.,* Stand Watie's Cherokee Regiment. Losses: *Union* 3 killed, 3 wounded. *Confed.* 2 killed, 5 wounded.

—In front of Yorktown, Va. *Union,* 3 companies 1st Mass. *Confed.** Losses: *Union* 4 killed, 12 wounded. *Confed.* 14 captured.

29.—Bridgeport, Ala. *Union,* 3d Div. Army of the Ohio. *Confed.* Leadbetter's Division. Losses: *Confed.* 72 killed and wounded, 350 captured.

—to June 10.—Siege of Corinth, Miss. *Union,* Gen. Halleck's Army. *Confed.,* Army commanded by Gen. Beauregard.

MAY, 1862.

1.—Camp Creek, W. Va. *Union,* Co. C, 23d Ohio. *Confed.,* Detachment 8th Va. Cav. Losses: *Union* 1 killed, 21 wounded. *Confed.* 1 killed, 12 wounded.

4.—Evacuation of Yorktown, Va., by Confederate Army under Gen. Joseph E. Johnston.

5.—Lebanon, Tenn. *Union,* 1st, 4th, and 5th Ky. Cav., Detachment of 7th Pa. *Confed.,* Col. J. H. Morgan's Ky. Cavalry. Losses: *Union* 6 killed, 25 wounded. *Confed.* 66 prisoners.

—Lockridge Mills or Dresden, Ky. *Union,* 5th Iowa Cav. *Confed.,* 6th Confederate Cav. Losses: *Union* 4 killed, 16 wounded, 71 missing.

—Williamsburg, Va. *Union,* 3d and 4th Corps, Army of the Potomac. *Confed.,* Gen. James Longstreet's, Gen. D. Hill's Division of Gen. Joseph E. Johnston's army, J. E. B. Stuart's Cavalry Brigade. Losses: *Union* 456 killed, 1,400 wounded, 372 missing. *Confed.* 1,000 killed, wounded, and captured.

7.—West Point or Eltham's Landing, Va. *Union,* 16th, 27th, 31st, and 32d N. Y., 95th and 96th Pa., 5th Maine, 1st Mass. Artil., Battery D 2d U. S. Artil. *Confed.,* Gen. Wade Hampton's Brigade, Gen. J. B. Hood's Texan Brigade. Losses: *Union* 49 killed, 104 wounded, 41 missing. *Confed.* 8 killed, 40 wounded.

—Somerville Heights, Va. *Union,* 13th Ind. *Confed.* Maj. Wheat's La. Battalion. Losses: *Union* 3 killed, 5 wounded, 21 missing.

8.—McDowell or Bull Pasture, Va. *Union,* 25th, 32d, 75th, and 82d Ohio, 3d W. Va., 1st W. Va. Cav., 1st Conn. Cav., 1st Ind. Battery. *Confed.,* 12th Ga., 10th, 21st, 23d, 25th, 31st, 37th, 42d, 44th, 48th, 52d, 58th, Va., 1st Va. (Irish) Battalion. Losses: *Union* 28 killed, 225 wounded, 3 missing. *Confed.* 75 killed, 424 wounded and missing.

9.—Elk River, Ala. *Union,* 1st Ky. Cav. *Confed.,* Texas Rangers. Losses: *Union* 5 killed, 7 wounded. *Confed.* 45 missing.

—Norfolk, Va. Evacuated by the Confederates.

—Farmington, Miss. *Union,* Gen. Plummer's Brigade, Army of the Mississippi. *Confed.,* Gen. Ruggles' Division. Losses: *Union* 16 killed, 148 wounded, 192 missing. *Confed.* 8 killed, 189 wounded, 110 missing.

10.—Plum Point, near Fort Pillow, Tenn. Gunboat battle. *Union,* Gunboats *Cincinnati, Carondelet, Benton, Pittsburg, St. Louis,* and *Mound City. Confed.,* eight rams of the River Defense Fleet.

* No record found.

OHIO SOLDIERS WHO FOUGHT UNDER GARFIELD FOR KENTUCKY

The Forty-second Ohio Infantry was one of the regiments that helped to settle the position of Kentucky in the issue between the States. A large Southern element was contained within its borders although it had not joined the Confederacy, and in order to obtain recruits for their army, and to control the great salt works, lead-mines, and lines of railway, the Confederate authorities sent General Humphrey Marshall with a small force into eastern Kentucky in November, 1861. General Buell promptly formed a brigade from the Army of the Ohio, put it in command of James A. Garfield, Colonel of the Forty-second Ohio, with orders to drive General Marshall from the State. This was accomplished by the engagement at Middle Creek, January 10, 1862. This photograph was taken in 1864 while the regiment was stationed at Plaquemine, Louisiana.

General John Charles Frémont (1813–1890). Already a famous explorer and scientist, the first presidential candidate of the Republican party (in 1856), Frémont, at the outbreak of the war, hastened home from Europe to take command of the newly created Western Department. He was born in Savannah, Georgia. His father was a Frenchman and his mother a Virginian, and his temperament was characterized by all the impetuosity of such an ancestry. Upon his arrival in St. Louis he found things in great confusion. The Missourians were divided in sentiment and the home guards were unwilling to reënlist. The U. S. Treasurer at St. Louis had

GENERAL FRÉMONT (ON THE RIGHT) AND
MRS. FRÉMONT

$300,000 in his hands, and Frémont called upon him for a portion of it to enable him to enlist men in the Federal cause. The Treasurer refused, but upon Frémont's threatening to take $100,000 without further ceremony, the funds were turned over. With about four thousand troops, Frémont seized Cairo, and by various demonstrations checked the aggressive attitude of the Confederates on the Kentucky and Tennessee borders, and of the Southern sympathizers in Missouri. Before he was transferred out of the West in November, 1861, Frémont had raised an army of fifty-six thousand men, and was already advancing upon an expedition down the Mississippi.

Engagements of the Civil War

Losses: *Union* 4 wounded. *Confed.* 2 killed, 1 wounded.

—Norfolk and Portsmouth, Va., occupied by Union forces under Gen. Wool.

11.—Confederate Ram *Virginia* destroyed in Hampton Roads by her commander, to prevent capture.

15.—Fort Darling, James River, Va. *Union*, Gunboats *Galena, Port Royal, Naugatuck, Monitor,* and *Aroostook. Confed.* Garrison in Fort Darling. Losses: *Union* 12 killed, 14 wounded. *Confed.* 7 killed, 8 wounded.

—Chalk Bluffs, Mo. *Union*, 1st Wis. Cav. *Confed.*, Col. Jeffers' command. Losses: *Union* 2 killed, 5 wounded. *Confed.* 11 killed, 17 wounded.

15, 16, and 18.—Princeton, W. Va. *Union*, Gen. J. D. Cox's Division. *Confed.*, Gen. Humphrey Marshall's command. Losses: *Union* 33 killed, 69 wounded, 27 missing. *Confed.* 2 killed, 14 wounded.

17.—In front of Corinth, Miss. *Union*, Gen. M. L. Smith's Brigade. *Confed.*, Outposts of Gen. Beauregard's army. Losses: *Union* 10 killed, 31 wounded. *Confed.* 12 killed.

19.—Searcy Landing, Ark. *Union*, 17th Mo., 4th Mo. Cav., 2 cos. 4th Ia. Cav. *Confed.** Losses: *Union* 75 killed, 32 wounded. *Confed.* 150 killed, wounded, and missing.

23.—Lewisburg, Va. *Union*, 36th, 44th Ohio, 2d W. Va. Cav. *Confed.* 22d, 45th Va., 1 battalion 8th Va. Cav., Finney's Battalion. Losses: *Union* 14 killed, 60 wounded. *Confed.* 40 k i l l e d, 66 wounded, 100 captured.

—Front Royal, Va. *Union*, 1st Md., Detachments of 29th Pa., Capt. Mapes' Pioneers, 5th N. Y. Cav., and 1st Pa. Artil. *Confed.*, 1st Md., Wheat's La. Battalion, 6th, 7th, 8th La. Losses: *Union* 32 killed, 122 wounded, 750 missing. *Confed.**

23 and 24.—Ellerson's Mill, Mechanicsville, and New Bridge, Va. *Union*, 33d, 49th, 77th N. Y., 7th Me., 4th Mich., Tidball's Battery. *Confed.*, 8th, 9th, 10th Ga., part of 1st and 4th Va. Cav., 5th La., battery La. Art., squadron La. Cav. Losses: *Union* 7 killed, 30 wounded. *Confed.* 27 killed, 35 wounded, 43 captured.

24 to 31.—Retreat of Gen. N. P. Banks' command (*Union*) from Strasburg, Va., down the Shenandoah Valley, including Middletown and Newtown the 24th, Winchester the 25th, Charlestown the 28th, and Harper's Ferry the 24th to 30th. *Confed.*, Stonewall Jackson's command, including the troops engaged at Front Royal the 23d. Losses: *Union* 62 killed, 243 wounded, 174 missing. *Confed.* 68 killed, 329 wounded (includes losses at Front Royal the 23d).

27.—Hanover C. H., Va. *Union*, 12th, 13th, 14th, 17th, 25th, and 44th N. Y., 62d and 83d Pa., 16th Mich., 9th and 22d Mass., 5th Mass. Artil., 2d Maine Artil., Battery F 5th U. S. Artil., 1st U. S. Sharpshooters. *Confed.*, Gen. L. O'B. Branch's N. C. Brigade. Losses: *Union* 53 killed, 344 wounded. *Confed.* 200 killed and wounded, 730 prisoners.

30.—Booneville, Miss. *Union*, 2d Ia., 2d Mich. Cav. *Confed.** Losses: *Confed.* 2,000 prisoners.

—Corinth, Miss. Evacuation by Confederate army under Gen. Beauregard. Occupation by Union troops of Gen. Halleck's command. End of siege begun April 29. Losses: (No detailed report on file.)

—Front Royal, Va. *Union*, 4th, 8th Ohio, 14th Ind., detachment 1st R. I. Cav. *Confed.*, 8th La., 12th Ga., Ashby's Va. Cav. Losses: *Union* 8 killed, 7 wounded. *Confed.* 156 captured.

31 and June 1.—Seven Pines and Fair Oaks, Va. *Union*, 2d Corps, 3d Corps, and 4th Corps, Army of the Potomac. *Confed.*, Army commanded by Gen. Joseph E. Johnston, as follows: Gen. James Longstreet's Division; Gen. D. H. Hill's Division; Gen. Benjamin Huger's Division; Gen. G. W. Smith's Division. Losses: *Union* 790 killed, 3,627 wounded, 647 missing. *Confed.* 980 killed, 4,749 wounded, 405 missing. *Union* Brig.-Gen'ls O. O. Howard, Naglee, and Wessells wounded. *Confed.* Brig.-Gen. Hatton killed, Gen. J. E. Johnston and Brig.-Gen. Rodes wounded, Brig.-Gen. Pettigrew captured.

JUNE, 1862.

3.—Legare's Point, S. C. *Union*, 28th Mass., 8th Mich., 100th Pa. *Confed.*,

* No record found.

The Last Struggle for the River. The fall of Vicksburg was imminent in July, 1863, and seeing this the Confederates determined to make one last herculean effort to retain a hold upon the Mississippi and prevent the Confederacy from being divided. General Holmes collected a force of about nine thousand Confederates and advanced through Arkansas upon Fort Curtis, the principal defense of Helena. There General Prentiss opposed him with a garrison of but 4,129. In the early dawn of July 4, 1863, Holmes hurled his forces upon the battlements of Fort Curtis. He was met with a resistance entirely beyond his expectations. Not only were the Confederates mowed down by the fire from the fort, but the gunboat *Tyler* lying in the river enfiladed the columns pouring through the ravines to support the attack. It was impossible to withstand the deadly rain of shell and shrapnel, and the order was given to withdraw. On the field were left two thousand dead and wounded Confederates.

GENERAL SAMUEL RYAN CURTIS

Most of the dead were buried by the victorious Federals, and more than a thousand wounded were taken prisoners.

Fort Curtis was named for General Samuel Ryan Curtis, who assumed command of the Federal District of Southwest Missouri at the close of 1861. The battle at Pea Ridge, or Elkhorn, Arkansas, near the Missouri border, March, 1862, was a Confederate reverse and was followed by the transfer of the principal Confederate commands which fought there to other fields, leaving Curtis in control. After a stubbornly contested march across Arkansas he arrived on the Mississippi, July 13, 1862, and began to fortify Helena. From that time it was held by the Federals undisputed until the attack of General Holmes. The day of the repulse at Fort Curtis, Vicksburg surrendered to Grant; Port Hudson, Louisiana, on the east bank, yielded to Banks five days later, after a siege of six weeks, and the Mississippi passed forever from the control of the Confederacy.

From the Meserve Collection.

FORT CURTIS, HELENA, ARKANSAS

24th S. C., Charleston, S. C., Battalion. Losses: *Union* 5 wounded. *Confed.* 17 wounded.

3 to 5.—Fort Pillow, Tenn. Evacuation by Confederates and occupation by Union troops commanded by Col. G. A. Fitch.

5.—Tranter's Creek, N. C. *Union*, 24th Mass., Co. I 3d N. Y. Cav. Avery's Battery Marine Art. *Confed.** Losses: *Union* 7 killed, 11 wounded.

6.—Memphis, Tenn. *Union*, U. S. Gunboats *Benton, Louisville, Carondelet, Cairo,* and *St. Louis;* and Rams *Monarch* and *Queen of the West. Confed.*, River Defense fleet of 8 gunboats. Losses: *Confed.* 80 killed and wounded, 100 captured.

—Harrisonburg, Va. *Union*, 1st N. J. Cav., 1st Pa. Rifles, 60th Ohio, 8th W. Va. *Confed.*, 1st Md. and 58th Va. Losses: *Union* 63 missing. *Confed.* 17 killed, 50 wounded. *Confed.* Gen. Turner Ashby killed.

8.—Cross Keys or Union Church, Va. *Union*, 8th, 39th, 41st, 45th, 54th, and 58th N. Y., 2d, 3d, 5th, and 8th W. Va., 25th, 32d, 55th, 60th, 73d, 75th, and 82d Ohio, 1st and 27th Pa., 1st Ohio Battery. *Confed.*, Winder's, Trimble's, Campbell's, Taylor's brigades, 4 Va. batteries of " Stonewall " Jackson's command. Losses: *Union* 125 killed, 500 wounded. *Confed.* 42 killed, 230 wounded. *Confed.* Brig.-Gens. Stuart and Elzey wounded.

9.—Port Republic, Va. *Union*, 5th, 7th, 29th, and 66th Ohio, 84th and 110th Pa., 7th Ind., 1st W. Va., Batteries E 4th U. S. and A and L 1st Ohio Artil. *Confed.*, Winder's, Campbell's, Fulkerson's, Scott's, Elzey's, Taylor's brigades, 6 Va. batteries. Losses: *Union* 67 killed, 361 wounded, 574 missing. *Confed.* 88 killed, 535 wounded, 34 missing.

10.—James Island, S. C. *Union*, 97th Pa., 2 cos. 45th Pa., 2 cos. 47th N. Y., Battery E 3d U. S. Art. *Confed.*, 47th Ga. Losses: *Union* 3 killed, 19 wounded. *Confed.* 17 killed, 30 wounded.

14.—Tunstall's Station, Va. Stuart's Va. Cav. fire into railway train. Losses: *Union* 4 killed, 8 wounded.

16.—Secessionville or Fort Johnson, James Island, S. C. *Union*, 46th, 47th, and 79th N. Y., 3d R. I., 3d N. H., 45th, 97th, and 100th Pa., 6th and 7th Conn., 8th Mich., 28th Mass., 1st N. Y. Engineers, 1st Conn. Artil., Battery E 3d U. S. and I 3d R. I. Artil., Co. H 1st Mass. Cav. *Confed.*, Garrison troops commanded by Gen. N. G. Evans. Losses: *Union* 85 killed, 472 wounded, 138 missing. *Confed.* 51 killed, 144 wounded.

17.—St. Charles, White River, Ark. *Union*, 43d and 46th Ind., U. S. Gunboats *Lexington, Mound City, Conestoga,* and *St. Louis. Confed.*, Gunboats *Maurepas* and *Pontchartrain,* 114 soldiers and sailors commanded by Lieut. Joseph Fry. Losses: *Union* 105 killed, 30 wounded. *Confed.* 155 killed, wounded, and captured.

—**and 18.**—Evacuation of Cumberland Gap, Tenn., by Confederates of Gen. C. L. Stevenson's command, and occupation by Gen. G. W. Morgan's Federal division.

18.—Williamsburg Road, Va. *Union*, 16th Mass. *Confed.** Losses: *Union* 17 killed, 28 wounded, 14 captured. *Confed.* 5 killed, 9 wounded.

25.—Oak Grove, Va., also called Kings School House and The Orchards. *Union*, Hooker's and Kearney's Divisions of the Third Corps, Palmer's Brigade of the Fourth Corps, and part of Richardson's Division of the Second Corps. *Confed.*, Armistead's brigade. Losses: *Union* 51 killed, 401 wounded, 64 missing. *Confed.* 65 killed, 465 wounded, 11 missing.

26 to 29.—Vicksburg, Miss. U. S. Fleet, under command of Commodore Farragut, passed the Confederate land batteries, under the cover of bombardment by Commodore Porter's fleet of mortar boats.

26 to July 1.—The Seven Days' Battles, in front of Richmond, Va., including engagements known as Mechanicsville or Ellerson's Mills on the 26th, Gaines' Mills or Cold Harbor on the 27th, Garnett's and Golding's Farms on the 28th, Peach Orchard and Savage Station on the 29th, White Oak Swamp, also called Charles City Cross Roads, Glendale or Nelson's Farm or Frayser's Farm, New Market Road on the 30th, and Malvern Hill or Crew's Farm on July 1st. *Union*—Army of the Potomac, Maj.-Gen. Geo. B. McClellan commanding. Losses: First Corps, Brig.-Gen. Geo. A.

* No record found.

**BRIGADIER–GENERAL
NATHANIEL LYON**

These fearless leaders by their prompt and daring actions at the outbreak of the war kept Missouri within the Union. Captain Nathaniel Lyon, U. S. A., a veteran of the Mexican War, had been on duty in Kansas during the "free soil" riots and knew what it was to see a State torn by dissension. At the outbreak of the war he was in command of the United States arsenal at St. Louis. Franz Sigel, a Prussian refugee, had settled in St. Louis in 1858, and in May, 1861, raised the Union Third Missouri Infantry and became its colonel. Under Lyon he helped to capture Camp Jackson, St. Louis, where General Frost was drilling a small body of volunteer state militia. On June 1, 1861, the command of the Federal Department of the West was given to Lyon, who had been

**MAJOR–GENERAL
FRANZ SIGEL**

made brigadier-general, and Governor Jackson, calling for fifty thousand troops "to repel the invasion of the State" left the capital for Booneville, June 14th. Lyon followed, dispersed the militia on the 17th, and other Confederate troops, under McCulloch, at Dug Springs, on August 2d. Meanwhile he had sent Sigel with twelve hundred men into southwestern Missouri, and on July 5th that intrepid leader

**MAJOR–GENERAL
JOHN C. BRECKINRIDGE**

fought the battle of Carthage. Greatly outnumbered, he finally retreated to Springfield, where he arrived on July 13th, and was later joined by Lyon. McCulloch had been joined by General Price, and although their forces now outnumbered his own five to one, Lyon determined to risk a battle. He met and attacked the Confederates at Wilson's Creek, August 10, 1861, where he was killed.

While the Federals were striving to keep the territory west of the Mississippi in the Union, John Cabell Breckinridge, who had been the youngest Vice President of the United States, resigned from the national Senate in October, 1861, to join the Confederacy. He formed an encampment at Hazel Green, Kentucky, and his personality drew many recruits to the Southern army in that much-divided State. President Davis gave him a commission as brigadier-general in November, 1861, and he was appointed to the command of a brigade in the Second Kentucky division under General Buckner. At the battle of Shiloh Breckinridge commanded the reserve corps consisting of three brigades, two of which he led in the struggle on April 6, 1862. General Johnston placed him south of the Peach Orchard, and he became engaged about one o'clock in the afternoon. When the Confederate army retired Breckinridge formed the rear-guard. After Shiloh Breckinridge was made major-general and in the break-up of the vast Western army he went to Louisiana, where he attempted, but failed, to drive General Williams from Baton Rouge on August 5th. Breckinridge took prominent part also at Stone's River, Chickamauga, Chattanooga, in the Shenandoah campaign of 1864, and at Cold Harbor.

Engagements of the Civil War

McCall's Div. 253 killed, 1,240 wounded, 1,581 missing.

Second Corps, Maj.-Gen. E. V. Sumner, 187 killed, 1,076 wounded, 848 missing.

Third Corps, Maj.-Gen. S. P. Heintzelman, 189 killed, 1,051 wounded, 833 missing.

Fourth Corps, Maj.-Gen. E. D. Keyes, 69 killed, 507 wounded, 201 missing.

Fifth Corps, Maj.-Gen. Fitz-John Porter, 620 killed, 2,460 wounded, 1,198 missing.

Sixth Corps, Maj.-Gen. W. B. Franklin, 245 killed, 1,313 wounded, 1,179 missing.

Cavalry, Brig.-Gen. George Stoneman, 19 killed, 60 wounded, 97 missing.

Engineer Corps, 2 wounded, 21 missing.

Total, 1,734 killed, 8,062 wounded, 6,053 missing.

Confed.—Army of Northern Virginia, Gen. R. E. Lee commanding. Losses: Maj.-Gen. Huger's Division, 187 killed, 803 wounded, 360 missing.

Maj.-Gen. J. B. Magruder's command, 258 killed, 1,495 wounded, 30 missing.

Maj.-Gen. James Longstreet's Division, 763 killed, 3,929 wounded, 239 missing.

Maj.-Gen. A. P. Hill's Division, 619 killed, 3,251 wounded.

Maj.-Gen. T. J. Jackson's command, 966 killed, 4,417 wounded, 63 missing.

Maj.-Gen. T. H. Holmes' Division, 2 killed, 52 wounded.

Maj.-Gen. J. E. B. Stuart's Cavalry, 15 killed, 30 wounded, 60 missing.

Artillery, Brig.-Gen. W. N. Pendleton, 10 killed, 34 wounded.

Total, 2,820 killed, 14,011 wounded, 752 missing.

JULY, 1862.

1.—Booneville, Miss. *Union,* 2d Ia., 2d Mich. Cav. *Confed.,* Gen. Chalmers' Cav. Losses: *Union* 45 killed and wounded. *Confed.* 17 killed, 65 wounded.

4 to 28.—Gen. Morgan's raid in Kentucky.

6.—Grand Prairie, near Aberdeen, Ark. *Union,* detachment of the 24th Ind. *Confed.** Losses: *Union* 1 killed, 21 wounded. *Confed.* 84 killed, wounded, and missing (estimate).

7.—Bayou Cache, also called Cotton Plant, Round Hill, Hill's Plantation, and Bayou de View. *Union,* 11th Wis., 33d Ill., 8th Ind., 1st Mo. Light Artil., 1st Ind. Cav., 5th and 13th Ill. Cav. *Confed.,*

Gen. A. Rust's command. Losses: *Union* 7 killed, 57 wounded. *Confed.* 110 killed, 200 wounded.

9.—Tompkinsville, Ky. *Union,* 9th Pa. Cav. *Confed.,* Morgan's Cav. Losses: *Union* 4 killed, 6 wounded. *Confed.* 10 killed and wounded.

12.—Lebanon, Ky. *Union,* 28th Ky., Lebanon Home Guards. *Confed.,* Col. John H. Morgan's Kentucky Cav. Losses: *Union* 2 killed, 65 prisoners.

13.—Murfreesboro', Tenn. *Union,* 9th Mich., 3d Minn., 4th Ky. Cav., 7th Pa. Cav., 1st Ky. Battery. *Confed.,* Gen. N. B. Forrest's Cav. Losses: *Union* 33 killed, 62 wounded, 800 missing. *Confed.* 50 killed, 100 wounded.

15.—Near Vicksburg, Miss. *Union,* Gunboats *Carondelet, Queen of the West, Tyler,* and *Essex. Confed.,* Ram *Arkansas.* Losses: *Union* 13 killed, 36 wounded. *Confed.* 5 killed, 9 wounded.

—Fayetteville, Ark. *Union,* detachments of 2d Wis., 3d Mo., 10th Ill., and Davidson's Battery. *Confed.,* Gen. Rains' command. Losses: *Confed.* 150 captured.

17.—Cynthiana, Ky. *Union,* 18th Ky., 7th Ky. Cav., Cynthiana, Newport, Cincinnati, and Bracken Co. Home Guards (Morgan's Raid). *Confed.,* Morgan's Cav. Losses: *Union* 17 killed, 34 wounded. *Confed.* 8 killed, 29 wounded.

18.—Memphis, Mo. *Union,* 2d Mo., 11th Mo. Cav. *Opponents,* Porter's independent forces. Losses: *Union* 83 killed and wounded. Porter's loss, 23 killed.

21.—Hartsville Road, near Gallatin, Tenn. *Union,* detachments 2d Ind., 4th, 5th Ky., 7th Pa. Cav. *Confed.,* Morgan's Cav. Losses: *Union* 30 killed, 50 wounded, 75 captured. *Confed.**

—Nashville Bridge, Tenn. *Union,* 2d Ky. *Confed.,* Forrest's Cav. Losses: *Union* 3 killed, 97 captured. *Confed.**

25.—Courtland Bridge and Trinity, Ala. *Union,* 10th Ky., 10th Ind., 31st Ohio. *Confed.,* Armstrong's Cav. Losses: *Union* 2 killed, 16 wounded, 138 captured. *Confed.* 3 killed, 5 wounded.

28.—Moore's Mills, Mo. *Union,* 9th Mo., 3d Ia. Cav., 2d Mo. Cav., 3d Ind. Battery. *Opponents,* Porter's independent forces. Losses: *Union* 13 killed, 55 wounded. Porter's loss, 30 killed, 100 wounded.

* No record found.

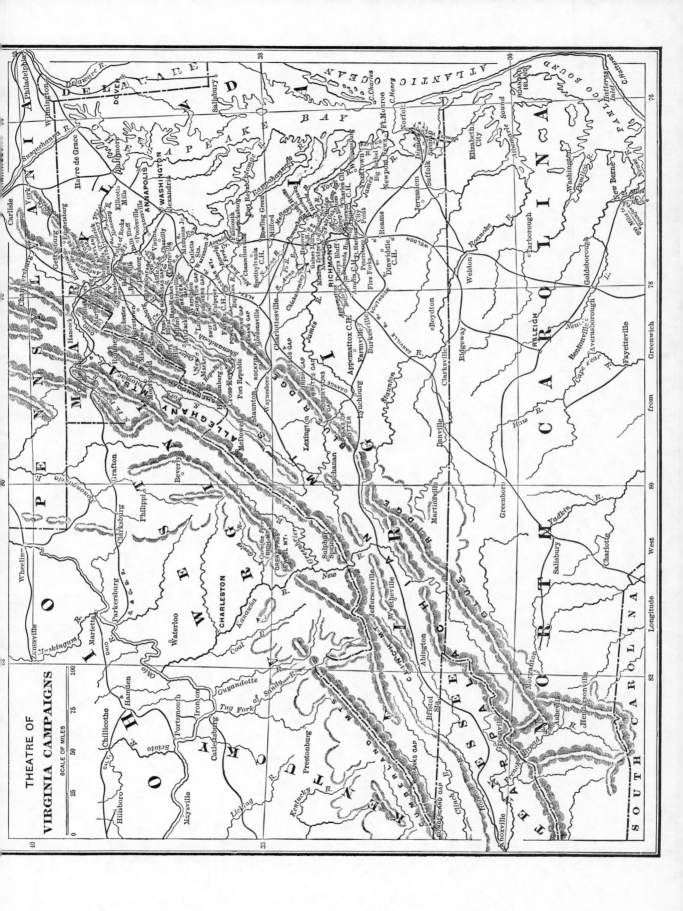

THEATRE OF
VIRGINIA CAMPAIGNS

SCALE OF MILES

0   25   50   75   100